Kant's
Little
Prussian
Head and
Other
Reasons
Why I
Write

The Burning Girl

The Woman Upstairs

The Emperor's Children

The Hunters

The Last Life

When the World Was Steady

Kant's Little Prussian Head and Other Reasons Why I Write

✽

AN AUTOBIOGRAPHY IN ESSAYS

CLAIRE MESSUD

W. W. NORTON & COMPANY
Independent Publishers Since 1923

FRONTISPIECE: My father, François-Michel Messud, looking out to sea from the balcony of the family apartment. Algiers, November 1942.

The names and identifying characteristics of certain characters in this book have been changed.

Excerpt from "October" from *Poems 1962–2012* by Louise Glück. Copyright © 2012 by Louise Glück. Reprinted by permission of Farrar, Straus and Giroux.

For information about permission to reproduce selections from this book, write to Permissions, W. W. Norton & Company, Inc., 500 Fifth Avenue, New York, NY 10110

For information about special discounts for bulk purchases, please contact W. W. Norton Special Sales at specialsales@wwnorton.com or 800-233-4830

Manufacturing by Lake Book Manufacturing
Book design by Chris Welch
Production manager: Lauren Abbate

Library of Congress Cataloging-in-Publication Data

Names: Messud, Claire, 1966– author.
Title: Kant's little Prussian head and other reasons why I write :
an autobiography in essays / Claire Messud.
Description: First edition. | New York, NY : W. W. Norton & Company, [2020]
Identifiers: LCCN 2020018802 | ISBN 9781324006756 (hardcover) |
ISBN 9781324006763 (epub)
Subjects: LCSH: Messud, Claire, 1966– | Novelists, American—20th century—
Biography. | Novelists, American—21st century—Biography.
Classification: LCC PS3563.E8134 Z46 2020 | DDC 813/.54 [B]—dc23
LC record available at https://lccn.loc.gov/2020018802

W. W. Norton & Company, Inc., 500 Fifth Avenue, New York, N.Y. 10110
www.wwnorton.com

W. W. Norton & Company Ltd., 15 Carlisle Street, London W1D 3BS

1 2 3 4 5 6 7 8 9 0

For FMM, MRM & DM, who've gone before;
for ECM; and, as ever, for JW

you are not alone,
the poem said
in the dark tunnel.

—LOUISE GLÜCK, "OCTOBER"

Contents

PART TWO

Criticism: Books

Three Essays on Camus and His Legacy

PART THREE

Criticism: Images

Introduction

As this collection goes to press, we are living through the COVID-19 pandemic, a period of intense suffering and loss for many, and for all a radical disruption of life as we have known it. In a few months' time, our situation will have evolved further; we can't yet know what our world will look like, nor in what ways it may have been irrevocably altered. What is certain is that the breathless hurtling of the past decade has been halted, at least temporarily, and that, as individuals and as a society, we are forced to reassess our priorities, our commitments, and our actions. Shocking disparities are laid bare that exacerbate the suffering of the most vulnerable. In the midst of trauma, there arises the possibility—by no means a likelihood, but wonderfully, the possibility—of positive change. We have the chance to rebalance not only our social but also our personal lives in hopeful ways, to work toward a more optimistic future.

What do I mean? The protagonist of Valeria Luiselli's recent novel *Lost Children Archive* observes that "something changed in the world. Not too long ago, it changed. . . . We feel time differently. . . . Perhaps it's just that we sense an absence of future, because the present has become too overwhelming, so the future has become unimaginable." On first reading this passage, early in 2019, I felt a bleak thrill of recognition; and then the question: Have we truly lost our future?

This overwhelmingness of which Luiselli writes has been a widespread experience of the last five or ten technologically dominated years. It is a terrible fate for human beings, distinguished from other animals precisely by our ability to conceive of the passage of time (as well as by a capacity for laughter, let's not forget): to lose our sense of a plausible future is to lose our humanity itself. It is to lose that "thing with feathers" called Hope, of course, released from Pandora's Box, and to be left instead only with the travails and misery that crowded around her. It is to lose our sense of purpose; to be enveloped in futility; to countenance defeat. In planetary terms, we live now, according to scientists, in the epoch of the Anthropocene, when man's folly has ensured the decline, if not the demise, of our beautiful Earth, and certainly of our way of life upon it. And yet: the COVID crisis has shown how dramatically pollution can be reduced overnight, by a change in human behavior.

In recent years, the dignity of small lives and small gestures has risked being lost: if not intended for an audience of thousands, or millions, communication has been routinely reduced to the abortive nubs of texts and emojis; and if it *is* for an audience of thousands or millions, communication tends to be visual or aural rather than verbal, because what millions can be bothered with profundity, sophistication, or subtlety? Who has the time to spare to read something that might require a little extra effort? And yet: the COVID crisis has revealed us to be capable of old-fashioned connection, and accounts abound of generous communication between neighbors and friends. Individuals and groups have found ingenious ways to stay connected in spite of social distancing; we have so swiftly remembered what it means to look out for one another.

We have lived in a nation—no, an era; because not only this nation but much of the world has suffered from these ills— crippled by our devotion to capitalism (I teach at an excellent university, from which 40 percent of the graduates go into finance: the shocking waste of fine minds on the pursuit of Mammon), beleaguered by hopelessness (what is the opioid epidemic if not the symptom of a people duped by false dreams, and wholly without faith in their personal futures?), and by rigorous utilitarianism (formed by a late capitalist mind-set, we ask always, What's in it for me? and eschew the ostensibly purposeless that is, in fact, our source of wisdom and of joy). We have inhabited a time and place in which falsehood and truth are fatally commingled (how many lies does our president utter in a day?); in which our ideals appear shattered and abandoned (leaders like priests and coaches are unmasked as predators, while our politicians prove corrupt and self-interested); and in which any sense of self is daily assaulted and abused by advertisers (whether corporate or individual, because what is an Instagram "influencer" if not a self-advertiser?). . . . In short, recent years have been, through a certain broad lens, a dark maelstrom, a hellscape from Hieronymus Bosch, in which, under the guise of the pursuit of pleasure, individuals are tortured, dehumanized, discarded, destroyed.

This ominous hurtling, the relentless ouroboros that is social media, the destruction of ourselves and our environs— we had come to see it as inevitable, and ourselves as the passive and ineluctable victims of forces beyond our control. Humanity has risked collective despair, than which there is no more certain doom for our planet and ourselves. But even in the

past two months, although at the mercy of a ravaging virus, we
have discovered that in other ways we aren't disempowered.
Crisis and extremity are by no means to be desired; and their
consequences—human and economic both—will be challenging
for the foreseeable future. But these extraordinary times have
also forced us to slow down, to think collectively, to seek hope, to
value the truth, and to celebrate resilience and faith in our fellow
human beings.

To find these resources, we may look to the past—to history
and to literature—to the vast compendium of recorded human
experience, from which we draw wisdom, solace, or, at the least,
a sense of recognition. In the matter of broad social movements
of recent years, we can look to the 1930s and shudder at the simi-
larity between our political and even intellectual patterns, and
those of that perilous period; we can read of it, strikingly, in a
1936 essay by Paul Valéry "Le bilan de l'intelligence," or in Timo-
thy Snyder's *On Tyranny* or *The Road to Unfreedom*. On a more personal level, when our abiding principles have seemed upended,
I've remembered an Enid Blyton story I loved as a child, about
a little girl who loves lying, until she gets trapped in the Land
of Lies, where untruths are praised and the truth disregarded.
On the matter of our foolish utilitarianism, I've channeled the
sardonic fury of Dostoyevsky's narrator of *Notes from the Underground*. Considering the opioid epidemic, I recall Odysseus and
his men in the land of the lotus eaters, or Tennyson's poem of the
same name: "What pleasure can we have / To war with evil? Is
there any peace / In ever climbing up the climbing wave?" When
it has seemed that we risk being the victims of our own race to
replace ourselves with technological advances, I remember that
Zeno foresaw this apocalyptic fate for humanity in the dark con-

clusion of Italo Svevo's 1923 novel *Zeno's Conscience*. Meanwhile, our political fiascos call to mind lines from *King Lear*: "Handy dandy, which is the justice, which is the thief?" or "A dog's obeyed in office."

It's all already happened, somewhere, in some way. It's all there to be retrieved. Each generation is unique, to be sure, as is each individual; and our concatenation of challenges is new in its particular configuration and in its intensity. But if we pause and listen to history and literature, we'll find, as Louise Glück puts it in "October", *"you are not alone, /* the poem said */ in the dark tunnel."*

Language makes this possible: language, and the written word. More astonishing an invention than the smartphone, than the internet, than computers: language, the filter that enables us to order our thoughts and experiences and to communicate them, albeit imperfectly. That enables us not only to ask for a glass of milk, or to say that we feel sick, but to speak of our sorrows and ecstasies, of our philosophical musings and our memories. I am daily amazed at this extraordinary medium—created by our distant ancestors out of nothing, still constantly evolving. A series of sounds came, at some point, to signify. A series of squiggles on papyrus, then parchment, then paper, came to signify across time and space. The written or printed word enables the transmission of thoughts and experiences across centuries and cultures. The English language, with its enormous and elastic vocabulary, enables precision and the deployment of connotation as well as denotation. Our human passion for storytelling—not simply for sharing information, but for giving meaning and shape to events—has motivated individuals and armies. From Homer onward, stories have held up a mirror and taught us who we are and what we believe. The dissemination of the written word, from the time of Gutenberg, has enabled us to tell stories of great depth and complexity, and to share our analyses of these stories. I don't just mean literature: history, too, is the analysis of human stories; as are psychology, anthropology, law, and even philosophy itself. The dramatic prevalence of the image over the written word in our present moment is akin to a return to the caves at Lascaux: immediacy has its advantages, but nuance isn't one of them.

As a writer, I have staked my life on the possibility of the original expression of authentic experience; which is to say, I firmly reject the idea that everything has already been said, that we are merely echoes or "samplers" of the cacophony around us. I have always agreed with Nabokov, in believing that part of the magic of the written is that the writer and the reader climb the mountain from opposite sides to meet at the top: the reader creates her own experience of each text, influenced by connotation and allusion, by her life and literary histories. Each individual reader's version of a text is unique; even as the experience is largely miraculously shared. Literary language is a kind of spell, a performative utterance: words conjure worlds out of air, and fictional characters from Oedipus to Huck Finn to Holden Caulfield can have more substantial and abiding reality than people of flesh and bone.

Philip Larkin raises an ironic smile—"Life is first boredom, then fear. Whether or not you use it, it goes"—but only the most melancholy and pessimistic take his wisdom for the whole truth. We retain agency; we need not be bored. Just as we are pressingly called to be active custodians of our planet, we must also be custodians of human knowledge and of our own minds. We need not be alone in our experiences, nor passive: the riches of all human thought and imagination are available to us. If we were to ensure, as a society, that people's basic needs were met, then we might recognize that a truly richer life doesn't require money, or access, or things: each of us can be nourished by the richer life of the mind. Frederick Douglass was born a slave, and yet when we read his writings, we encounter a mind profoundly free, a mind able to articulate itself in language both urgent and lucid, that serves as a reminder that power over language is power *tout court*.

We have seen around us and in ourselves, too, the dissatisfactions of a life based on a constant need for the new. Now more than ever, it's within our grasp to live differently, to remember that we're animals, embodied, sensual creatures, and that what we feed our minds will shape us as surely as what we feed our bodies.

When you read fiction, or encounter a work of art, you aren't directed like a sheep in a maze (even with an interactive video game, you're playing only with the options put into the computer by someone else); you are invited into an open-ended conversation. You're also engaged in an experience that is simultaneously wholly private and universal: your encounter with a work of fiction is yours alone. And yet in words, our encounters can be shared; our experiences thereby expanded and deepened. Even, or perhaps especially, reading opinions that differ from our own, we are challenged to articulate our own experience and its effects; and simply in the articulation, we live more deeply, more engagedly. The hurtling slows.

I advocate moreover for the actual, irreducible, and irreplaceable animal record—outside the age of mechanical reproduction, if you will. The movement of the hand that holds the pen; the imprint of the ink upon the paper; the dignity and intimacy of the individual letter, written for a particular addressee (and hence so different from a blog or post), without thought of other readers. The loss of what that represents philosophically is enormous: my grandparents, my parents, even my friends and I myself in youth, spent hours writing letters about what we were doing and thinking, where we were going and what we noticed, as a gesture of intimate communication. It signified that each of us mattered, that the person to whom I wrote mattered, and that our communication was important—often precisely because it wasn't widely shared. Privacy, intimacy, dignity, and with them, depth and richness of thought—all were a readily available part of daily life, for even the most modest among us.

The review and the essay remain a more public, yet ideally still intimate, version of the epistolary. Not a place to share one's private details, to be sure, but certainly to try to communicate, as precisely and with as much complexity as possible, one's experience of a work of art, or the evolution of one's thought. In the case of art reviews, it's a matter of translating one medium (visual) into another (linguistic); in the case of literary reviews, it's about distilling the greater experience of reading a book, endeavoring to render communicable something that in its totality will remain uncommunicated.

My paternal grandfather spent the better part of a decade in his retirement writing a fifteen-hundred-page family memoir for my sister and me. He did not expect anyone else to read it. He titled it "Everything That We Believed In." His undertaking was a gesture of faith in himself, in us, in language and the transmissibility of experience. The result is an extraordinary and life-changing document; nobody else need think so, but for me and for my sister, it is. My father, on the other hand, of more melancholic temperament, while a businessman during the day, spent his evenings, weekends, and holidays as a life-long scholar and thinker who, like Bernhard's account of Wittgenstein's nephew, remained a philosopher only in his head, and committed nothing to paper. My abiding memory of him in age is of a man in his library, in his leather chair, in a pool of light surrounded by darkness, wearing his half-moon glasses, with a book open on his lap and a scotch on the table beside him. He had nobody to talk to, with whom to share his considerable erudition; he lived in the splendid and terrible isolation of one who, while still retaining faith in the life of the mind and the power of books to speak to him, had renounced the possibility of being understood, the value of passing on his knowledge. Both figures have their Beckettian absurdity—my grandfather toiling at his desk (for what?), my father, reading voraciously alone (for what?)—but both also represent hope of a kind, and both inspire me to persist in my calling.

The literary and artistic works of the past twenty years, as much as those of the past several centuries, have shaped my understanding of the possible and of the world around me. From Italo Svevo and Albert Camus to Magda Szabó, Rachel Cusk, and Valeria Luiselli; from Alice Neel to Marlene Dumas—these are but a few of the artists whose voices resonate as I try to make sense of our human experience. Each is distinct in vision and approach; all share a rigor and intensity in their mission to illuminate what it means to be alive in their time. Memory and loss are recurring themes; honesty and precision also. Each of these artists galvanizes me differently, as do the examples of my father and grandfather.

The essays and reviews assembled here represent only a small portion of the literary, artistic, and intellectual conversations with which I've been preoccupied over the past twenty years. So many stories remain yet untold; so much that we have to learn, and to experience, is as yet largely hidden from the world. To attend to them is to slow the hurtling, to calm the chaos, to return to the essentials that make us human. It is to find the past and the present restored, and with them, the possibility of the future. We can't go on, we must go on: in this period of trial and transition, those of us for whom the power of the word is paramount must keep the flame alive, in the heartfelt conviction that nothing matters more.

—Cambridge, Massachusetts
April 14, 2020

Kant's
Little
Prussian
Head and
Other
Reasons
Why I
Write

PART ONE

Reflections

THEN

When we moved from the United States, where I was born, to Australia at the dawn of the 1970s, we had an immense tag sale, dispensing our more cumbersome toys to the neighborhood kids for pennies. I was four, my sister just six. A few treasures—the toy stove and its battery of dented pots— were stored against our future, to be opened, too late, in 1977 in Toronto, when we no longer had any use for them and disdained the very nicks and cracks that had made them truly ours. But for Australia, for life as it was to come, we could only take what would fit in our suitcases: Michka, my Russian bear, all of eight inches tall with a tiny red silk nose; white blanket, already holey and disheveled, crocheted by my French grandmother and indispensable; and a stuffed gray felt elephant with wobbly knees who ought to have stood up but couldn't, any longer, for which we loved him more rather than less.

But our beautiful finned vermilion car, last year's Christmas gift that we'd pedaled in furious jubilation around our cul-de-sac in Stamford, Connecticut, grudgingly shared by my sister and me, haughtily loaned to the neighborhood kids for a few minutes at a time—and never to the nasty Maguire boys next door— this car would not cross the ocean. It was the first toy sold at our tag sale—and, watching the Maguire boys take turns driving it, I ached. I ached enough to remember it, always.

We would not have a home again for months, and a car like that, never. Similarly, in my early childhood, my Canadian grandmother had, in her garage, an aged brown Jaguar, with a wood-paneled dashboard and elegant, luminous dials; and yet it, without explanation, while we were at the other end of the earth, ceased to be hers and was replaced by a sky-blue Toyota Corolla, later corroded by rust and therefore always, in my mind's eye, corroded by rust, a small and graceless conveyance with cold black vinyl seats. When, again, would she have a car like the Jaguar? Never. The Corolla would be my grandmother's last car altogether, as during those years she lost her sight, by agonizing degrees, to macular degeneration, and very soon, before we even returned from Australia, was unable to drive at all.

Before Australia, my parents had to prepare the way, so they left us for a month with our maternal grandmother in Toronto while they flew to Sydney—a long way, in 1970; a much longer way than it is today—and found a place to live, and a school for us to attend. On account of quarantine laws, they oversaw, too, the division of our two dachshunds, uncle and nephew, Big and Small: the former went to his native France to live with my paternal grandparents and dine on table scraps, while the latter, smaller, wilier, with more soulful eyes, stayed in Canada and became the bane of my grandmother's existence, ultimately tripping her and spraining her ankle on a winter's walk to nearby frozen Grenadier Pond (the same pond into which my mother in a much earlier winter, as a girl, had fallen through the ice, while walking one of a succession of family spaniels all named Nicky).

In Toronto, in my grandmother's house, my sister and I were

always happy. Which is not to say that we did not bicker, as bickering, from very early on, was our mode of interaction; but that
we adored my grandmother, and trusted her absolutely. She was
rightly sized for us, at little over five feet, and stout, with pillowy
white hair and a pillowy bosom (which we did not then know
to be made of foam and removed, nightly) and an array of silky
nylon dresses that seemed designed for hugging. She had small
but firm arthritic hands that held ours tightly and allowed us the
freedom to finger their odd bends and warts and calluses, and
the smooth, distinct ridges of her fingernails. In the mornings,
in a bed jacket with large buttons and her near-invisible hairnet (which we loved to pluck) upon her curls, she would invite
us, one on either side of her, into her high old marriage bed to
play games—"I Spy," or "I packed my bags to go to Boston"—and to
sing songs—". . . every little wave had its nightcap on, nightcap,
white cap, nightcap on . . ."; "Roll, those, roll those pretty eyes,
eyes, that, I just idolize . . ."—seemingly for hours. And how she
fed us: daily (in memory, at least), she granted us our favorite
meals: Campbell's tomato bisque soup and salami sandwiches,
or Chef Boyardee ravioli, eaten on the sunporch overlooking her
steeply tiered back garden, my sister and I vying for the privilege
of sitting on the stepping stool and so being able, with our feet, to
swing its folding steps in and out, in and out, with spooky creaks,
throughout the meal.

Even our grandmother's basement was a pleasure, its cement
painted oxblood, its warm air scented by laundry soap with, in
one corner, the basket into which miraculously issued the socks
and pajamas dropped through the chute two flights up. We had
a tricycle down there—no match, of course, for our lost car, but
still—upon which we whirled in circles on the red floor, avoid-

ing the dip in its center that was, most mysteriously, a drain. And on the half-landing between basement and kitchen, by the side door, the house's other secret and delicious feature: the hutch for the milkman, a box opened from both inside and outside the house, in which, still, in our early youth, milk, butter, eggs, and juice appeared magically before breakfast.

⁂

OUR RENTED HOUSE in Sydney was, and remains, the grandest place I have ever lived: Wolesley Road, Point Piper, a large mottled brick house with a circular drive and a high wall around the garden, a short walk from a little beach and a short drive from our school in Vaucluse.

The house was fronted by a portico, and before it, a small fountain, in which a bronze Pan piped eternally. A walled garden lay down an alley on the kitchen side, doubtless intended for vegetables but unplanted, and in it the owners had constructed a large chicken-wire aviary, left empty and forlorn. The lawn on the opposite side of the house, off the living room, broad and rolling and verdant, headed downhill toward the sea, and against its farthest edge nestled a row of fruit trees referred to, grandiosely, as "the orchard."

The rooms in the house were numerous and vast, the gloomy kitchen cavernous enough to echo, with two sinks and a great stretch of black-and-white linoleum and—or has an older child's imagination merely inserted it there, stolen from British children's books of yore?—a green baize door to separate it from the public rooms. The back staircase led up from this kitchen to the suite my sister and I shared, a bedroom and off it a large, windowed expanse dubbed "the nursery." Off the landing of that back staircase, the service flat waited, two rooms and a bathroom overlooking the empty aviary, with their own locking door. The house was full of the owners' furniture, while they, knighted by the Queen, had gone to live in London for a time. The surfaces throughout were dotted with knickknacks—Dresden shepherdesses, heavy cut-glass ashtrays—all valuable and at risk from our small and eager limbs, so that we were, from the first, discouraged from playing downstairs. I liked best the little cloakroom just to the right of the front door, which was small but high-ceilinged, so it felt like a tall, narrow box; and the enclosed porch off the dining room, which reminded me of my grandmother's little sunporch in Toronto, and overlooked the broad lawn. The furniture there was of dark green wicker, the chairs, befittingly, like thrones, their backs a peacock's fan.

My sister and I were enrolled at one of several girls' schools in the city. Ours, Kambala Church of England School for Girls, had (and still has) a magnificent property in Rose Bay next to the Sacred Heart Convent, looking back, from its green slope, upon the glistening bay, at the opera house and the harbor bridge and the winking white sailboats dotting the water. But in our first years, we traveled on, beyond the main campus and down the hill to Vaucluse, to the elementary school, Massie House, housed in a white stucco mansion among other grand houses in their enclave by the sea.

There, at first, I wore a yellow pinafore over my clothes and spent the afternoons pretending to nap, with a dozen other reluctant nappers, in rows of folding cots in a large, darkened room. I greatly envied my older sister her complicated uniform and its religious rules, and felt tremendous pride when I was sprung early from the confines of the nursery and kitted out for kindergarten.

We had uniforms for summer and for winter. The former was a gray-and-white-checked shirtdress, belted, worn with a straw boater banded in gray, with the school crest upon it. The latter was a gray tunic, beneath which we wore white shirts (with Peter Pan collars, while at Massie House) and gray-and-gold-striped ties (bow ties, with the Peter Pans), and topped by a gray felt hat, again banded with the crest. Gray socks; black oxfords; gray jumpers; gray blazers (with gold piping); gray knickers; gray ribbons (compulsory, if your hair touched your collar). We had gear, too: colored wooden rods with which to learn arithmetic, stored in gray plastic boxes with our names on them. We had color-coded booklets, a system called SRA, by which we learned to read, and they were kept in gray file cabinets in the classroom, to be shared by all. We had gym clothes, including regulation black sandshoes, and tasseled girdles to denote our sports house (mine was red, for Wentworth). We had plastic covers for all our textbooks, lined, sometimes, with wrapping paper, in order to make them more attractive. Later, we would have sewing baskets, wicker boxes with little handles and looped clasps, in which carded embroidery threads in riotous colors grew, inevitably, fatally entangled. Our book bags were of hard brown vinyl, square cases held in our tiny hands to thump against our legs, and tagged, like luggage, with our names and addresses.

Young ladies always stood when a teacher came into the room. Young ladies walked in crocodile file, two by two, when moving from one room to another, one building to another. Young ladies did not run. There was to be no eating in uniform in public. Hats must be worn at all times in the street. Young ladies did not yell. Young ladies strove, at all times, to be a credit to their school. The rules and rituals were endless, a language to be mastered and then—but stealthily, stealthily—trifled with. You learned the rules so that you might break them when the need arose.

From the first, I loved that school, everything about it, and granted my devotion to each demure and spinsterly schoolteacher with the same fervent passion: cross-eyed Miss Watt, whose myopia and bottle-bottom glasses gave her an underwater aspect, and whose tubular calves I still see swaddled in their thick tights bunched above black orthopedic shoes; smooth and quiet Miss Dixon, the headmistress of Massie House, universally adored, with her pale freckles and tidy golden bob; the brusque and spotty Miss Clarke, whose spiky hair was always a little greasy, and whose difficult affection I was particularly proud, by the end of the year, to have won. My sister traveled upward, of course, always a year ahead of me, and I took her lessons—her especial fondness for Miss Dixon, for example—to heart.

When we were at Massie House and living on Wolesley Road, my mother found a driver to take us to and from school. His name was Gary, and he could barely have been twenty, but to us he was a man, with his stubbled chin and blond fur along his arms. In his battered blue station wagon, he picked up more than half a dozen little girls each day. Whether this constituted his sole employment we never knew, but he was prompt and reliable in spite of his scruffiness. At first I didn't care for his car, or at least, not for the front seat: none of us did, because whoever sat next to him had to suffer his spidery hand upon her thigh, moving, often, up beneath her skirt almost to her knickers. We squabbled each afternoon for the safe seats in the back (in the mornings, the front fell to the hapless two who were picked up last), until I discovered that Gary would pay me two cents a day to massage his shoulders while he drove, and that this employment not only swelled impressively the belly of my piggy bank, but also spared me, in permanence, the loathed front seat.

It wasn't for some months, until I offered to massage my father's shoulders and he registered horrified surprise at my proficiency, at my even knowing what a massage might be, that Gary's oddities came to light at our house, and our subscription to his service was abruptly stopped. (I distinctly recall, however, the dwindling number of girls in the wagon over that time: each girl, then, must have confided to her parents the horrors of the front seat, and was quietly removed from harm's way. No parents phoned each other, though, or they did not, at least, call my parents; perhaps because we were foreign, or perhaps because each outraged adult assumed the others knew. Or indeed, in keeping with the tenor of the times, because nobody wanted to make a fuss about something so trivial.)

Gary was replaced by my frazzled mother in her brown Austin Mini, a more salubrious but altogether less prompt chauffeur, for whom we waited at the curb many times while torturing ourselves with the grisly possible causes for her tardiness: car crashes, conflagrations, a broken neck at the bottom of the long front stairs on Wolesley Road. Her chief advantage, when she arrived, lay in her willingness to drive us directly to the Milk Bar in Rose Bay for chocolate bars, or, better yet, to the neighboring bakery, from which we emerged with slabs of chocolate cake, or sticky buns, or hard-frosted confections named lamingtons, which we ate openly, cheerfully, in our uniforms with our hats off, protected from the rules, from the marauding prefects who might sentence detention, by our magical parent, whose own lips bore telltale traces of chocolate or sugar.

During this time, swiftly, we learned the rules of the lan-

guage, its codes as vital for survival as those of the school or of
Gary's blue car. We learned to speak with Australian accents,
broadening certain vowels and closing others, so that we would
sound the same as our friends; although at home, we spoke to our
parents like little Americans; and in the car, spoke one way in
the backseat and another when addressing the front. We learned
the slang ("Have a fab Chrissy!") and the popular songs (I'm not
sure I have ever heard a recording of "Seasons in the Sun," but
I know its lyrics perfectly from the playground), and the references, learning by heart the advertising jingles off the television,
which I can sing to this day ("Sun and surf, it's all so great, here in
Queensland, super state!"). We let fall the North American trap-
pings as efficiently as we had let go of our little red car, and we
learned not to look back, and not to look forward, but instead to
read the present, to parse its details as efficiently as possible, in
order—this was surely the hope; it remains, always, the hope—to
pass for a native. I do this in spite of myself wherever I am, even
now, including, and least successfully, in France, because I am
half French; but always with an awareness that it cannot wholly
succeed, that I will be found out, and with the question, in the
back of my mind, of how much of a freak, how far outside the
realm, I appear to the others to fall. By how far have I failed, in
my local masquerade?

TO RETURN, THEN, to our grandmother's that first Christmas was a
shock, our first introduction into the ongoing schizophrenia of
the unsettled life. From Sydney's incipient summer, its clammy
heat, we flew through days and nights to the snowy lawns of
western Toronto, to the hedges and porches festooned with

Christmas lights and the brown slush of the streets. We found my grandmother and her house and its beloved contents the same as we had left them, though frayed somewhat by the anxious teeth of the dachshund, Small, who, missing us, or most importantly, missing Big, with whom he had shared everything since birth, had taken to gnawing the edges of the broadloom and scraping at the doors with his claws. We rediscovered our little room, and, in the mornings, our grandmother's high bed, and her hairnet, and her particular powdery, perfumed smell, as if we'd never abandoned them; and the trike waited in the basement, and the stepping stool on the sunporch, its seat patched with silver duct tape, still creaked in its satisfying rhythm.

But the Jaguar was gone, the sky-blue Corolla in its place; and Joy, the girl next door who had been our playmate, had moved away to the West Coast; and most painfully for my mother, my grandmother had sold the family summer cottage without informing her, complete with all its contents, on the grounds that it was too much work to keep up, but actually in some sinisterly ruthless way to teach us all, her daughter most of all, that you cannot go away and come back to find things the same, that leaving has consequences, some of them bitter, that you cannot, indeed, ever come back at all. This, of course, was something that my father, *pied-noir* and son of a peripatetic family, child of the Second World War, had already long ago learned and would spend a lifetime imparting to his children; but it was new, then, to my mother, who wept at the loss of a place she had loved, and loved with her father in it, and he now long dead; and new, too, to my sister and me, who were young enough to accept that this was just the way of the world, and to turn on the television and memorize another set of advertising jingles and to try, for a few weeks, in the company of cousins and other Christmas visitors, to pretend—in our new furry hats with pom-poms, and our coats with velvet collars, of no use in Australia—that we were a legitimate part of this world, too, and not mere pretenders.

On the Sunday before Christmas, my grandmother took us all to her church downtown, the central United Cathedral surrounded by missions and a park in which the indigent slept. She was a fixture in that place, as old as the century, having paraded with her congregation and walked into it as a girl when the United Church of Canada was formed, sometime in the 1910s, belonging there as much as it is possible to belong. She thought, perhaps, that the force of her connection extended to the rest of us, that because she was at home we would be also; and in this spirit she dispatched my sister and me, unwilling, to the Sunday school in the basement.

There, bathed in hideous fluorescence, with the murky gray of the Toronto winter sifting balefully through the small, high windows, we perched at the front of the room by the Sunday school teacher, a buxom girl with crooked teeth and a surprising persistence in interrogation. With a circle of moon-faced, bug-eyed, pallid children around us, their gaze upon our unusually tanned skin (it was summer in Sydney, after all), their ears cocked for our antipodean syllables (perhaps we were not so adept at shifting from one English to another as we imagined?), we were introduced as two Australian visitors, there to tell the others what it was like "down there."

I remember the scarlet fury of my cheeks, the twitching misery of that hour, to which I responded with sullenness and a furrowing of the brow, while my sister gamely chatted and revealed snippets of our private, our secret, other life, as if it were less real, or of the same reality, as the dingy brick and gray linoleum and folding chairs around us, of the same reality as the brittle, bosomy instructor or the indistinguishable Christian children who were her charges. Like riding the red car: my sister just got on with it, which, in time, I would learn from her, to smile and smile and be a villain, and that our hold on this other life, like our memory of the red car, was not the less for that.

Because the truth is that the other life, the hidden one, or ones, is not the less real, nor as real, as the life before us. It is infinitely more real, blooming and billowing in the imagination in its fecundity and fullness, colored and enlivened by so many objects, so many sounds and smells, so many minute moments that can never, never be imparted. It is wrong to think of them as past: Sydney, then, was just beginning; and Toronto was, in our lives, a constant, and then, for a time, a home; just as Toulon, my father's family's chosen place, remained until just a few years ago my life's one unbroken link. They were concurrent presents, and presences, and somehow because of this, and magically, they have remained always present.

If I crossed the ocean today, would I not find my childhood friends dangling from the monkey bars, their ties flailing and their crested hats in a pile upon the grass? Would I not find my grandmother, at the end of another long journey, with Small upon her lap and her warped fingers reaching out to hold mine? And somewhere, even, if I could only travel that distance—a few short hours as the crow flies, but unimaginably far in truth—is the red car with its glimmering fins, and the house by the stream, the first bed and the first home, known to me only as a place where always, already, I didn't quite belong.

NOSTALGIA

Growing up, my sister and I went every year to stay with our French grandparents in Toulon. Their apartment was on the highest floor of a four-story building in a gated compound on top of a cliff on the outskirts of town, with a roof terrace and enormous windows looking out to sea. There we would run wild with a gang of summer kids, clambering down the cliff path to the beach, carving our initials in the aloes on the way; shouting, "Marco . . . Polo," for hours in the pool (irritating the matrons with their careful breaststroke) and sunning ourselves on its slatted deck. After dinner, we would gossip and flirt by the big tree on the stone plaza or race around in games of hide-and-seek along the leafy pathways, our sandals' slaps echoing on the concrete.

Our grandparents' world was one of immovable routines, into which we kids slipped easily. Meals fell at religiously allotted times—lunch at twelve-thirty sharp, supper at eight p.m., with an aperitif hour beforehand—and the rituals of their preparation were, like the postprandial *sieste*, sacrosanct. Over breakfast, our grandfather planned the day's menus for lunch and dinner, recorded in tiny, meticulous script in a spiral notebook (we could look up what had been eaten on a particular date years previously).

He departed for market by eight a.m., carrying his list. In childhood, we would accompany him: to the butcher, the baker, and finally the bar/tabac, to buy the day's newspapers, magazines for our grandmother, and cigarettes for our aunt. (He shunned the nearest grocer after she asked him to pay for parsley, which was not done, and ever after made a detour for vegetables and milk.)

Upon his return, Odet, the housekeeper, almost our second aunt, laid out the groceries and set about cooking lunch, the day's main meal, always three courses, while our grandfather retreated to his study upstairs to read and to write. Our grandmother, meanwhile, elegantly gaga from early on, was arranged— beautifully dressed, coiffed, and *maquillée* by Odet, like a precious doll—in an armchair by the dining room window, where she could gaze out at the infinite, always-changing sea, or look down at the electric-blue swimming pool, or put on her glasses and pretend to read the magazine placed in her lap. In the late morning, around eleven, Odet brought her a tray bearing a little crystal glass of Coca-Cola fortified with blood from a raw steak, to keep up her strength and hopefully to ward off what were mysteriously referred to as her malaises.

My sister and I were free to roam with our friends, morning and afternoon. We were not required to lie down after lunch the way the old people did, in sepulchral silence, the metal blinds lowered against the Mediterranean glare, though we were asked not to swim for an hour after eating, for fear that we might suffer an unspecified attack and drown. It was requested only that we appear for lunch properly dressed; that we help clear the table and do the dishes; and that we resurface just before cocktail hour, to help lay out the little bowls of pretzels and nuts and to set the table for supper. (Dinner dishes were tidily stacked in the sink and left for poor Odet to tackle in the morning, which she tried to do silently so as not to waken us. The dishwasher, although present, did not function for as long as our grandparents lived: they did not believe in it.)

After our grandfather's death, in 1998, my father hoped to sell the place: Expensive to maintain, it needed updating and was difficult to get to. Even within the compound, to reach the apartment required climbing seventy-two steep steps from the nearest garage; both of our grandparents had been housebound in their last years. Our aunt sold her interest in the property to my sister, and my sister and I begged our father not to sell.

My niece was just born then, and although my husband and I didn't yet have children, we planned to. My sister and I wanted passionately to retain this beautiful place we had always known and loved. Our father agreed to help defray the costs, and over the years that followed, we brought our kids to fall asleep to the sounds of the waves on the shore far below and the cicadas' saw, to play the games we'd played ourselves, to climb over the same rocks and swim in the Mediterranean, to sit in the same restaurants and eat the same meals. Our maiden aunt lived in another, smaller flat in the compound, and she bestowed upon the children, in a modest way, their French birthright: endearments and simple sentences in French, snippets of culture (when they were infants, she gave our daughter a *Bécassine* doll and our son a stuffed *Milou*, a.k.a. Snowy, the dog from *Tintin*), a sense of belonging.

But our aunt died in 2012, and the apartment felt as though it were dying also. It sat empty almost all of the year, tended only by a cleaner who stopped by twice a month, or said she did. We finally decided we had to sell the flat and went to visit it a final time, in the summer of 2015. We arrived late at night, having flown from London and driven from Nice. The hot-water heater was on the fritz, apparently irreparably, as it transpired, and we hadn't been there twenty-four hours when the entire antique fuse box blew. The Wi-Fi my brother-in-law had set up a few years before proved defunct, and at some point a phone bill had been overlooked, so we had only our American cell phones. Busy ants formed an unbroken convoy from the kitchen terrace to the pantry cupboard. The woman paid to clean the flat had been ill and had instead sent a friend: The wrong-size sheets barely covered some beds and dangled to the floor over others. Dust bunnies skittered eerily across the marble floors.

We strove to see it as an adventure—like camping!—heating water to bathe on the gas stove and dining on baguette and cheese by candlelight. But, in fact, much time in the subsequent days was spent trying to locate plumbers and electricians (trickier than you'd imagine, with no local phone or phone book, and no Wi-Fi) and awaiting their visits. Not only did the water run cold, it trickled lamely from the tap: the pressure, never good, was reduced almost to nil. The blinds upstairs in my grandfather's study hung in tatters, and somehow one of the large windowpanes there had cracked. In the terrace planters, the skeletal remains of shrubbery clattered in the wind. Dust billowed up from the bookshelves if you moved a single book.

In spite of the beautiful burning sunlight, the air redolent of lavender and rosemary, the delicious sticky salt water drying on our skins; in spite of the nightly winking lights of the ferry to Corsica crossing from the harbor to the inky horizon; in spite of the softness of the ancient worn sheets on which my grandmother had embroidered her initials as part of her trousseau—in spite of it all, we knew, on that last visit, that it was time to go. Without a fortune, we couldn't fix time's damage (the electrician, in his thirties, had never seen a fuse box as old); we couldn't even slow it down. Just like a person, the apartment needed to be loved, to be inhabited, to be filled with routines and with life—just as my grandparents, my aunt, and Odet had done for so many years. I didn't need to memorize the pathways or the vistas; I knew them as well as I know my own fingernails. For all of us, saying goodbye weighed, a great sadness; but it felt inevitable, even necessary, like burying an aged relative after a long illness.

I returned just once, the following January, with my sister, to sign the papers. Our neighbor opposite on the landing bought the flat for her daughter's family. It was winter, and we walked hurriedly through the emptied apartment on the eve of the sale, pausing to sweep the dust left by the movers and to fill a garbage bag with a pile of our grandfather's precious papers, somehow overlooked. Bare of its familiar objects and clutter, illuminated only by the wan overhead lights, the apartment looked forlorn. The metal blinds on the floor-to-ceiling windows, fully lowered against the blustery night, rattled slightly. My sister and I climbed to the roof terrace and stood leaning against the rail, looking out one last time upon the most glorious view I know: the vast, incessant sea, the enormous canopy of sky, mutable and immutable, eternity itself.

THE ROAD TO DAMASCUS

I.

I went to Beirut in June 2010 because my father was dying.
This sentence, palpably illogical—my father was not dying in
Beirut—is nonetheless true.

When my father was in the hospital in 2008, after nearly dying
from a perforated ulcer, then from MRSA, a super-bug, the doctors said to him, categorically, "You drink, you die." We all heard
them. We talked about it. And for almost two years, he did not
drink, and he didn't die.

And then, early in 2010, in remission from a cancer diagnosed a year before that, he started drinking again. I don't know
whether he died because he drank; or whether he drank because
he was sure he was going to die; or because he was afraid to die
and wanted to forget about it; or because he just wanted, by then,
to die. After all, my mother, who had Lewy body dementia, was
slipping quietly away. It is strange to understand that all of these
can be true at once. Suffice it to say: he drank; he died.

In late April 2010, my father had a stroke. They realized, once
he was in the hospital, that after a respite of ten months his esoph-
ageal cancer was back in force. His throat was fully dammed:
there was not even room in his gullet for his spit to slip down
to his stomach. The oncologist, a bluff fellow of the old school,

eminently clubbable, who prided himself on his frankness and resembled British generals in black-and-white war films, with his bow tie and his tidy white mustache—confided, oddly jauntily, in the hallway outside my father's room some days later, "Within six to eight weeks he'll be in trouble."

In between the oncologist's first prognosis in the corridor of the hospital and my father's last breath, there was a Bergsonian eternity, moment upon moment upon moment of Being. My father was always intolerant of small talk and banality: he very much wanted time to *mean*. In this sense, those last three months were very much his time. But inevitably, too, there was stupid time, interspersed between the significant time—time that wouldn't necessarily, in ordinary circumstances, have been considered stupid, but which, in the context of death, became strangely preposterous. Watching television of course becomes impossible in a crisis. But even the matter of living my own life became largely absurd to me: teaching classes, participating in panel discussions, attending readings—ridiculous. Perhaps ironically, the daily household tasks, when rarely I was at home with my family, seemed immensely precious: making breakfast, folding the children's clothes, the small connections to the ordinary, a place where we wanted the children at all costs to remain.

Some months before, I had committed to going to teach in Beirut for a fortnight in the second half of June. When the oncologist first gave my father six to eight weeks, it was the beginning of May. Six weeks would coincide almost exactly with my departure for Beirut; eight weeks with my return. I didn't know what to do, whether to cancel the trip straightaway. Two years before, when my father was so ill, I had canceled everything, stopped my life altogether. Afterward, I came closer to jumping off a bridge than ever before. This time, with this knowledge, it didn't seem a good idea simply to withdraw.

"Just wait and see," said my husband, my sister, the doctors. "Just wait and see."

For some weeks, my father seemed still to be getting better. He had physical rehab sessions and his walking improved. He ate well (they had put in a stent, a wire mesh, as I understood it, not unlike one you might use in gardening, to keep his esophagus open), although he complained of the soft food: pureed meat in gravy, mashed potatoes, pureed carrot. We brought him little things he liked to eat and could manage: chocolate truffles, olives, caviar.

He was on enormous doses of painkillers, and when they were not working well he complained of great pain. But in the time after they kicked in and before he slept, or after he slept, he was utterly himself. We talked about things we could never have discussed before—whether he believed in God and believed in an afterlife; whether he was afraid to die; whether he was happy with his life. We pushed his wheelchair around the lovely gardens of the nursing home, pausing by the stone Buddha, counting rabbits, keeping track of the blooming and wilting of flowers, watching the planes fly overhead. We kept an eye out for the jeweled hummingbirds that hovered over the roses and lilies; we monitored the slow disintegration of the fairy village my children had built out of sticks and leaves in a flower bed one drizzling Saturday. My mother spoke in an awed whisper of the horse-riders who passed at dusk at the edge of the field: it seemed, as crazed hallucinations go, most wonderful.

But as the weeks went by, and my time to leave approached, my father was clearly suffering more. By the end of May, they had stopped his rehabilitation. The stretches when he was awake and not in pain grew shorter; the pain, when it was present, grew more intense. One of the nurses explained that it was as if a digger were scooping away at his insides: an internal excavation. My mother, unable to articulate her terror, grew intensely anxious, a wraith flitting through the corridors of the nursing home whenever I was not there, or my sister was not there, always looking for us, for someone, driving my father crazy. So much fear.

And still I clung to the prospect of Beirut. I was to teach at the American University there, a trip organized by the International Writing Program at Iowa in conjunction with the American University of Beirut (AUB), and with assistance from the State Department. It was the pilot program for a possible regular summer teaching course: only two of us were going, a poet and myself, a fiction writer. In those weeks, as I waited for the details of the trip, I had in my mind the State Department–sponsored visit I'd made to Istanbul several years before—a week of classes and meetings with writers and university professors and students, a trip that offered me the promise of Turkish culture like a glorious flower unfolding, mysterious and immense and amazing. The teeming enormity that is Istanbul and the intensity of my encounters had imparted to that visit a particular aura of necessity. It had seemed important to go to Istanbul; it had seemed important for me to go to Istanbul; it had seemed important for me to go *at that time* to Istanbul.

Needless to say, Istanbul was also bound up with my father. Istanbul was the first city my father had consciously fallen in love with, as a boy of ten, arriving at its mouth by boat with his family in the middle of the Second World War. My grandfather, who was sentimental, described it as a *coup de foudre* for his child. My father, who was, if not less sentimental, considerably more reserved, conceded that he had wanted from the first to go back there.

My grandfather was a consular attaché in the French Navy, at that point under orders from Vichy, and so my young father and his younger sister were boarded outside the city at the residence of the Sisters of Our Lady of Sion in Therapia (now Tarabya), where they spent the forty days that their parents remained in Istanbul. My grandparents, briefly childless, inhabited a furnished flat overlooking the Bosporus and engaged in minor derring-do, befriending *sub rosa* the English envoy to Turkey, a man named Ellerington, who would resurface later in the war in Algiers when they were finally all officially on the same side. My father and aunt were photographed, meanwhile, tiny and lost in the overgrown gardens of the *pensionnat* in Therapia, where few children remained because it was summertime.

Over those weeks, my father and aunt learned to swim in the Bosporus. The children were tied under the armpits by ropes and dropped into the water by a near-nun (it would seem that the Sisters of Sion were complicatedly nunnish but not fully nuns) in a near-habit who then paraded up and down the jetty holding on to this lead. In this way the children, ostensibly undrownable, swam several lengths without being drawn out into the strait by the swift current to perish at sea. I am not sure whether the swimming mistress held the rope of one child at a time, or of several children at once, like a dog-walker in Central Park.

More than half a century later, my father remembered the beauty of the light on the Bosporus, the precise yet glaucous outlines of the buildings in Sultanahmet in the early day. He had held that beauty in his mind's eye, in palimpsest—the overlaid and changing memory of all his visits to the city. He returned to Istanbul as a teenager, for a summer, as soon as he was able to travel alone, and had his wallet and passport stolen before ever he arrived at the port—a vanishing which seemed somehow symbolic: to be searching, in the maze of a city, for something essential and irretrievable, for some impossible belonging.

Much later, he learned Turkish and embarked upon a Ph.D. at Harvard on Turkish political parties. He and my mother passed through Istanbul on their way to Ankara, where they lived for six months in the late 1950s in order for him to pursue his research. She, not yet thirty, fresh from Toronto, whose limited travel experience had been entirely in Western Europe, wrote home detailed and emotional letters to her parents, describing what it was like for a young Canadian woman in Ankara in 1959: her indignation when she witnessed a bus driver deliberately running over a dog; the thrill of collecting shards of ancient pottery at a friend's archaeological dig; her alternating frustration and amusement at the daily struggles to communicate with the housekeeper. She approved of the food, although not as much as my father, who would all his life love this cuisine best of any. He, meanwhile, filled a briefcase with notes in his spiky scrawl, in French and English and Turkish, a briefcase that moldered for many years in the basement of my parents' house in Canada and which, after his death, we finally threw away.

My father abandoned the Ph.D.—my mother did not ultimately care for life in Ankara; and besides, my father felt that if they wanted to have children, he would need to earn what he called a "proper" living. Instead, as a businessman, he amassed, over fifty years, a scholar's collection of books on Byzantium, the Ottoman Empire, the Armenians, the Turks, the Middle East more broadly.

Upon his death he left behind hundreds of volumes, although how many of them he had read I cannot say. He left, that is to say, substantial traces of the life unlived, of the internal life, which as we all know is both hard to discern and the only one that matters.

And so in this sense it had been a pilgrimage for him, my trip to Istanbul, a trip he was then still well enough to applaud and appreciate. It was my own trip, too, of course—the thrill of the invitation, the excitement of setting one foot in Europe and another in Asia, the little glasses of steaming tea served on the ferries from one side of the strait to another, the view of the passing boats from my hotel room, the joy of wandering the mosques and Topkapi Palace alone on my day off, of negotiating the subway system with my three words of Turkish, of slipping into the plush seats at the cinema alongside a wonderfully cantankerous old American acquaintance from Boston and his deferential Turkish student, to see, of all strange things, Marjane Satrapi's *Persepolis*—no, it was my own trip, too. But its ultimate raison d'être was my father.

So, too, with Beirut. My father, before ever he saw Istanbul, was a child in Beirut. Beirut was his Eden. My grandfather was first posted there as naval attaché to the French Consulate in 1936, before the war. My father was just five years old; my aunt three. They lived in a villa on an ascendance at what was then the edge of town and is now indiscernibly incorporated into the city, a place that has not only vanished but the very notion of which has vanished. It was my grandparents' first moment of relative prosperity: until then, they had been frankly poor, and only in Beirut did they have the luxury of a housekeeper. There, too, they bought their first furniture, which they would take with them to their next posting, only to have it evaporate a few years later, mid-war, when the ship carrying it belatedly back to Algeria was tor-pedoed in the Mediterranean.

From Beirut, in 1939, they were dispatched to Salonica (now Thessaloniki). There, they heard word of the French defeat and the armistice. My grandfather—who spent a decade of his retire-ment writing a fifteen-hundred-page handwritten memoir of his life for his granddaughters, for my sister and myself—records the shame and horror of this development; but he was also a follower of rules and of order, and so rather than rebel, he followed the command that then emanated from Vichy, taking him back to Beirut in 1940, and then on to Istanbul in 1941.

Their Beirut of before the war is recorded in family photo-graphs as a time of outings and parties: the children are captured in elaborate fancy-dress (my father as a court page, in red velve-teen bloomers with white and gold brocade, complete with feath-ered toque; my aunt as a tiny princess, in layers of frothy skirts) among others similarly attired, all staring dumbly off into the corners of the frame, as photographed children are wont to do. The grown-ups are pictured smiling in the streets or at the St. Georges Hotel on the waterfront. Their letters talk of the ease and beauty of it all, the fragrant flowers in the garden, and the warmth of the local welcome. There was food enough for everyone. At the weekends, there were outings to the mountains; throughout, an abundance of fresh oranges and sweet cakes and coffee. And always, the sunshine and their beloved Mediterranean extend-ing outside to the horizon.

The return to Beirut in 1940 was much darker. Food, while plentiful in comparison to other places, was considerably more difficult to procure than it had been. The children suffered from headaches and earaches and colds. Housekeepers were in short supply, as was money to pay for them. My father, now nine and stoical, lived with his family in an apartment on the Rue Achrafieh, at the summit of the hill in what is still today the Christian district. There was then a French air base across the road. The children attended the French elementary school only a few blocks away on the corner of the Rue de Damas—the Road to Damascus—where now there stands a large modern tower containing offices, luxury apartments, and shops.

My father and aunt did not know that times were worse: they knew only that they had returned to their beloved Beirut. All through the rest of the war that was their childhood (by the time it was over my father was almost fourteen, and no longer, strictly speaking, a child), after they were back in Algiers, keeping a chicken in a muck of straw on their tiny balcony for its eggs, until the afternoon it took alarm at the children's antics and fluttered dizzily down to the courtyard only to be slaughtered by a neighbor for supper; or queueing endlessly for rations to find that the meat—or the rice, or the butter—had run out; or hiding in the air raid shelters overnight in the unsettled stretch when school was canceled for weeks, and my grandmother, in hope of salvaging the year, dragged my father around to tutor after tutor—including, for Latin, an aged monk in grimy attire crammed with his parents into a small and filthy flat on the outskirts of town, with an entire flock of pigeons in cages on the porch; or being shipped out to ancient aunts in the countryside in the hope that there they would have calm and food—throughout all that time, the children spoke of Beirut as the answer. My father wrote more than once in his looped still-childish hand to his father, far away—first in Toulon, then in Dakar, then in Casablanca—that he wished they were back in Beirut. Beirut, where, for the children at least, everything had been good.

None of the complications of war featured in my father's Beirut—or if they did, they did so only decades later, in retrospect. My father's Beirut was his happy home, the place he could first clearly remember, where life was comfortable and Mummy and Daddy were happy and school was exciting and everything seemed to lie ahead, and to be possible. The city's perfection was always a myth, but a myth so perfectly imprinted that when, before I left for my own trip there, I sat next to him in the nursing home and asked him to draw a map of the city as he remembered it, he shifted in his wheelchair and closed his eyes for a moment, and then, having moved the pen back and forth above the page a few times in a hovering motion, drew a perfect outline of the city's coast and penned in the port, and the St. Georges, and the American University in Ras Beirut, and the Pigeon Rocks offshore, and the Rue de Damas heading inland and uphill—all exactly as they are in life, although, since leaving in 1941, he'd only been back in Beirut for forty-eight hours some thirty years later, just before the civil war, a stopover born of a somewhat garbled matter of lost luggage on the way back from Hong Kong. When I showed the map to my Lebanese architect friend, he marveled at its accuracy.

And then, too, my father put down in the same black ink and of course with the same certainty the souk where they shopped for food, and Tanios, the central department store to which his mother used to take him, and the air base across the road from his apartment building, all of these things gone now, or transformed beyond recognition, and certainly beyond caring, in a city which has suffered and survived so much in the intervening decades.

Yet for as long as he lived they existed, absolutely, in all their vividness, in my father's memory, and he could indicate them for me on a scrap of lined yellow paper and so insist upon their continued reality, their absolute importance, perfectly preserved in every detail—you do know, don't you, that in the moment in which he closed his eyes before he drew his map, he knew the quality of the light, the shadows cast by the buildings in the road, the clattering of the cars passing, and the mingling smells in the street of cooking fat and gasoline and dirt, and the ruts in the pavement beneath the thin soles of his shoes, and the fine layer of dust upon those shoes, and the weight of the department store door and the texture of its handle as it swung open, and the warmth, too, of his mother's hand, cold now for almost thirty years—in the precious box of his childhood mind for seven decades and finally, finally taken out unblemished, at the last, for me.

And now he is dead and these memories have dissolved into the ether and all that remains is the yellow slip of paper folded and already worn in the pocket of my diary, a mere desiccation, a sign stripped of its significance. Everybody thinks this, I know, but I think it now with great confusion: How can it be that all that is in us dies with us? How can it be that those memories, that Beirut—which had existed seventy years in its locked corner of his mind, but not the less real or immediate for that—have now simply ceased to be? I cannot understand it. That we cannot know something unless we are told it: this seems to me the greatest weakness of any supposed divine plan, the primary reason to doubt.

On the afternoon when he drew his map, I asked my father whether he would like me not to go. "All you have to do is say you'd like me to stay," I said. "And I will stay. I can cancel it." I had in my head that the trip was important, somehow important for my father and in order that I might bring him some gift—not an actual gift, of course, but an emotional gift—and that this would make his parting easier. I was aware even as I had this idea in my head that it was a silly, novelistic idea and not a true thing; but then, too, on some level, even when he was so sick, I really wanted to go. I had also been with them, my parents, almost all the time for six weeks, and it was hard; and he was in pain and often sour-tempered and she was growing increasingly anxious and I wasn't sure that I could do this indefinitely, this nursing thing.

My father may have read my mind. He closed his eyes again— the kind of closing that may have been thinking or may have been necessary to ride out a wave of pain, this latter a type of eye-closing I know only from childbirth—and then he said, "No. I think—I think it's . . . important that you go."

And so I went.

II.

What did I want from Beirut? Did I think I would encounter my father there, a child of six, or nine, walking purposefully through the streets in short trousers and long socks with a lock of dark hair falling over his right eye? Surely not, although . . . Did I think I would unearth a Francophone enclave for whom my father's distant childhood would also evoke something, whatever it might be, and prompt at least a ruminative conversation about the city of that period? Perhaps. And did I think I might walk on the same pavement and stand before his old apartment building and take a photograph to carry back with me to put upon his table in the nursing home in Rye Brook, New York, thereby returning to him both some scrap of his past life and some trace of its present continuation? Naïvely, yes. He was so certain in his mind that it all existed still somewhere that he almost made me believe. It was as if I believed I would be traveling not only across space but across time, into the very distant but perfectly preserved place he had laid out in his little map.

And at the same time: Did I envisage a trip like my visit to Istanbul, in which the city was opened to me in its various marvels, past and present, and its various atrocities, too, by the generosity of my influential and devoted hosts? Yes, that certainly. I certainly imagined that I would be introduced to writers, professors, journalists, and politicians, would be conducted through refugee camps and have explained to me by passionate interlocutors the history of the Naqba as it has affected Lebanon; and then the history of the civil war; and the history since the civil war; and so on. Only by imagining such a grand tour could I justify leaving him; without that, it was an abandonment.

I was, on my father's account but also simply for itself, passionately interested in Beirut. I wanted so much from it. Beirut, meanwhile, proved to be dispassionately uninterested in me. Our pilot program, it transpired, in spite of the fancy names attached to it, was merely that: a pilot program at the American University (a beautiful campus by the sea, and as close to a private American college as can be found outside the United States) for a two-week summer class in creative writing for undergraduates. My lovely and immensely patient poet colleague and I were furnished with a windowless classroom, a milling contingent of bright and, for the most part, motivated students (all of them impressively Anglophone and many unnervingly Americanized), a fluorescent hum, an ugly carpet. Like so many Rapunzels, we were then locked in for three hours each morning for two weeks. The curriculum was up to us. But for a few young women in hijabs, we might have been in Allegheny or Eugene.

As for my father's history, nobody cared. Why should they? The image of my father as a child—a colonial child, so long ago—did not capture their attention even for a second. I bored my poet colleague with my insistence on my mission; and I bored my architect friend. Our hostess, raised largely in the U.S., nodded vaguely when I asked her about it; her husband, raised in Beirut and barely younger than my father, shrugged and turned away. The night they invited us to supper, I plagued their other dinner guests, including a Belgian woman of about my own age who was compiling for the office of tourism a walking tour of the old sights of Beirut. She, at least, promised to look at old maps: Rue Achrafieh? It should be locatable.

In the meantime, I tried to inquire about that time; but everybody—including our hostess's husband—was too young to remember. Somehow, this had not occurred to me before I went: that if my father, at seventy-nine, was dying, so, too, was his generation, the people who might remember the time before Before. Besides, there had been too much pain since then; and I found that they did not want to talk about that, either. The people I met were happy to discuss the rebuilding of the downtown, and how they felt about it—too Disney, or just right? Was the influence of Solidere good or bad? What about the choice to restore certain examples of colonial architecture rather than those in the Ottoman style? And in moments of greater intimacy, what did they really think about Rafic Hariri, and his reconstruction plan, and his assassination? The residents, both young and old, were keen to show off the lively downtown, and to suggest beautiful hotel bars or stylish restaurants where we might spend an evening.

This was the strangeness of Beirut: it was to me like a city in a dream, a city wiped clean. With its lovely prospect overlooking the sea, its youthful and worldly population, its expensive shops and perfectly rebuilt arcades and plazas, its surface resembles very closely someone's ideal of Beirut. Unless you poke around for a while on foot, you will not see much evidence, beyond the relentless construction, of the total destruction of their civil war—with the notable exceptions of the hulk of the Hilton Hotel, a punctured and hollowed concrete misery purposefully retained as a reminder; and the smaller, squatter ruin of the St. Georges on the waterfront, maintained in its decrepitude by the owner who, I was told, despised Hariri and his tidy beautification of the downtown. While I was there, a new Four Seasons opened by the water, a shiny white tower with its balconies turned to the sea, outside of which pooled glossy black limousines. Repeatedly I saw these limousines—often SUVs with Saudi or Abu Dhabi plates—pull up suddenly and eject their passengers, smooth young men on cell phones, with white kaffiyehs, holding the hems of their pristine white djellabas above the dirt as they dashed into Dunkin' Donuts or Burger King for a snack.

When I observed to my architect friend how few Western tourists I glimpsed in Beirut, he laughed. "Nobody here cares about Western tourists," he said. "You come for a week, two at the most, on a tight budget. You buy nothing, and you go away again. We want tourists from the Gulf, or from elsewhere in the Middle East. We want people who will buy a villa or take a floor or two in a luxury hotel, stay for months, spend millions. That's what keeps the city booming."

Moreover, he added, "Beirut has always been the party center for the Middle East. You can find anything here—sex, drugs, gambling, all of it. Last year there was a Middle East bear convention in town—big, hairy gay guys from all over the Arab world."

The new Beirut is a fantasy city, the place where dreams come true. Its own history—and there is so much history there, in a place where ruins are revealed at almost every construction site: not just recent ruins, but Roman ruins, or Phoenician ruins—becomes no less unreal than its present. For obvious reasons, nobody from there wants to talk about the past, nor even, as long as things remain quiet, about the present—the students at the American University are asked to refrain from discussing politics—and nobody who is not from there really wants to know. Instead, you can marvel at the reconstruction, superficially lament the political instability just below the surface, and sip your cocktail while admiring the spectacular views.

While in Lebanon, I made the pilgrimage to Baalbek, to the Roman ruins of what was Heliopolis, Rome's capital in the Middle East. The city is located in the Bekaa Valley, about a hundred kilometers east of Beirut over the mountains, deep in Hezbollah territory. Baalbek features some of the best-preserved Roman architecture in the world. The scale of the site and the perfection of the Temple of Dionysius in particular defy description. But perhaps what was most extraordinary of all was our sense that the ruins were ours.

For at least the first hour, my poet colleague and I were all but alone. A guide or two hovered at the entrance, smoking cigarettes and kicking dust, hoping for a job. But we were able to amble among the giant pilasters and plinths, up and down the fractured steps, under the arches, and among the walls, in total silence, the sky enormous above us and the mountains, framed by the ruined arches, snow-tipped at the horizon. We slipped into history without any human interruption whatsoever. At one point we perched upon a carved boulder in the shade of a massive stone wall, and, like children, ate our snack brought from home, of soggy butter biscuits and slightly salty lukewarm water. I think I even swung my feet. Looking around at the empty permanence of all these discarded stones, blocks for giants tumbled as far as the eye could see, I experienced a moment of genuine wonder: it was as if we'd discovered the ruins ourselves, as if, since the gods had abandoned their playground, no one else had seen it.

And yet, of course, this fantasy was rife with irony. Why were there, even later in that long morning, so few visitors wandering the temples at Baalbek? Could it be because for so many years, until recently indeed, it was a physically dangerous place for tourists to venture, and they did so at their peril? The ruins lie deep in Hezbollah-controlled territory, a fact brought home along the route by exuberant Hezbollah posters and statues, and chiefly by the immense murals at the site's entrance, one of them depicting Hassan Nasrallah, the leader of Hezbollah, wielding a rocket launcher beside photographs of Jerusalem, Tel Aviv, Haifa, and Ben Gurion Airport under crosshairs.

The effect was of simultaneous kitsch and horror. And then there was the inevitable strange realization that this, too, was just life, no more nor less, and that for the guide awaiting his customers or for the crooked-toothed woman selling pita with *za'atar* in the street outside, the mural of Nasrallah was no stranger than, to me, a billboard advertising McDonald's on the Massachusetts Turnpike.

Unexpectedly, this very experience of dislocation—to be a benign tourist floating along the surface above a subterranean political nightmare—was perhaps the closest that I came on this strange Lebanese journey to homage to my father, and to an inadvertent reliving of my youth. There was a reason why my long drift through Baalbek felt so known, from the stones against the big empty sky to the painfully eager salesboys outside the few trinket-shop-cum-cafés on the periphery, and the disagreeable huckster with his scraggly, fly-infested camel, offering rides: these familiars were the extras of my childhood.

Throughout the 1970s, our curious and surely not oblivious father carted his wife and small children to vacation not at beachside resorts but in impending global hot spots, usually before the shit had officially hit the fan: I remember my mother painfully yanking my hair into braids in a Lima hotel room before dawn, before we set out to catch an early plane to Quito, and shouting at my father, "This is not my idea of a holiday!" Among other junkets, we visited Ethiopia in 1971 (we stopped also in Kenya, but the projected Ugandan portion of that trip sadly had to be canceled due to some trouble with a dictator), Guatemala in 1973 (my sister and I wondered aloud why we were the only tourists around), Sri Lanka in 1975, and so on. These are not journeys one would undertake lightly now, when we have a fuller awareness of "dark tourism" and its complexities: but I see it, in my family, as my father's compulsive reenactment of and attempt to resolve his own childhood traumas.

My memories of these childhood travels are, in one regard at least, not unlike my father's childhood memories of Beirut: blissful to me, they represent an isolate gem of privileged innocence in the midst of unacknowledged oncoming darkness. Whether that gem was a falsehood or a strange little truth I cannot quite say. But I can see why he would have wanted, however unconsciously, to re-create that strange and precious state. It was, in *his* youth, the happiest state; to be protected and only faintly aware, in the middle of *someone else's horror*. Surely this is not a false question: Is the quiet banality of a place less real than its incipient evil? Isn't life, most strangely, and even in evil, always made more real by its banalities?

What do I remember about Ethiopia? Not unrest or famine. Not global Cold War politics played out on an African stage— although my parents would for years tell the story of the TASS reporter who dandled me on his knee on a bus upcountry. No, I, who was five and half years old, remember our propeller plane spitting fire from its engine ("Look, Mummy, there are flames out the window!"), landing in a field on the way to Lalibela, and a squealing gaggle of children in rags running up, begging smilingly for pencils and touching my sister's blond hair.

What do I remember of Guatemala, when I was seven? The market ladies in their vivid ponchos and mannish hats, their eyes downcast and their wares laid out, most orderly, upon blankets, in the street running down from the pristine white church in Chichicastenango.

Of Sri Lanka when I was nine, I recall the murky green swimming pool at the Holiday Inn (we could not see the bottom, which disturbed my mother, but not sufficiently to forbid us from swimming in it) and the vastness of our glorious family room at the Galle Face Hotel, the biggest and most old-fashioned hotel room I'd ever seen, with its crisp linens, its dark wood, and its lazy ceiling fan. I remember my sister turning cartwheels along the green sward abutting the seafront, and being given a garnet ring by our parents for her birthday.

Any possibility of bloodshed and horror is excised from my

memories of these places; or rather, more accurately my father gave us these places without horror. He gave them to us as sites of innocent joy.

This is an impossibility, of course. The very attempt is perverse, a denial of reality. But I can see now that this is what he attempted: we didn't take off to Majorca or the Bahamas or Hawaii for our childhood holidays; and it now seems a wonder that we didn't vacation in Belfast or Santiago. What it meant to him—atonement, escapism, folly—I cannot say, nor can I now ask. But when in Beirut I leaned over my dorm room balcony and saw a lone European mother walking her two small, fair daughters, in matching dresses, along the street, I held them in my mind until I spoke to my husband that night: "I saw my sister and me today," I told him. Not my father as a child, but myself.

I cannot say what drove my father, but what his lessons taught me, I realize belatedly, is to be a novelist. To understand that most of *what is* you can only imagine, and can imagine only through the often contradictory traces of what you can see. To understand that always, at the heart of things—whatever the ideas and ideologies, the violations and violence, the strangenesses of culture—always at the heart are the ordinary people, and there is just life, being lived: tables and bread and toilets and scissors and cigarettes and kisses and illness and death; just life.

III.

I'd been living in my American University dorm room for a week when my sister said on the telephone that my father was asking for me. I was on the balcony, speaking on the local cell phone that I'd acquired from a dusty little shop opposite the university, peering over the balustrade at the passersby. It was nighttime, but my street in Ras Beirut did not go quiet in the evenings. The World Cup was everywhere. Every possible screen was illuminated—the green of the soccer pitch glowed in apartments and outside cafés—and cars drove honking at all hours through the neighborhood.

Back at the nursing home, the days had a different rhythm. My aunt, terrified of flying, a lifelong smoker who suffered to go without nicotine for the duration of a transatlantic flight, had traveled from France to hold her older brother's hand, in spite of the pain of her three half-healed ribs following a fall early in the spring. My sister had taken a leave of absence from her demanding corporate job in Paris to be in Connecticut for a month, and was conducting business over her BlackBerry from well before dawn until after noon each day, before heading over to the nursing home to stay with our parents until after supper. My mother would barely leave the room for fear that something might happen to my father, even though there were times when she did not exactly know who he was. (I rang once and, after speaking to her, asked her to pass me to him. "Your father isn't here right now," she said. "Are you alone?" "No . . ." "Is there a man in a wheelchair in the room?" "Yes." "Let me speak to him, then.")

Our immediate family is small; everyone was there but me. My sister said that my father was in pain for longer stretches each day—even though they'd added a new type of painkiller, these did not seem to help very much—but that there were still good moments. He knew this would not continue for long—he'd said to my aunt that what he feared was not death but the pain—and he wanted me to be with them, for us all to be together, before the pain was too much. Before he had to go into the land of morphine, and away.

Our trip to Baalbek took place over the weekend, when I already knew I would be leaving. On the Sunday morning, I went to a local swimming club, a collection of vivid pools by the seafront near the Luna Park, a place suggested by my architect friend. Not surprisingly, I found that I could not in good conscience lounge by the chemical-blue water and enjoy the hot sun and the children splashing. I was obsessively reading Rabih Alameddine's novel *The Hakawati*, about Lebanon and a father's death, about a young man traveling from America to Beirut to stand at his father's bedside, and to try to defer his father's death by telling all the stories in the world. *Of course* that was what I was reading: a book about my father, about my calling, about Beirut. But I couldn't read it on the deck chair by the swimming pool by the sea near the Pigeon Rocks.

I experienced the spiritual equivalent of not knowing where to put your hands: I could not ignore what I knew was taking place without me. I could not fully be where I was; and even as I did not want to be in the King Street Nursing Home in Rye Brook, New York, I'd reached a point where I couldn't be anywhere else. My father could not protect me from death any longer, not even by sending me away: the time had come for us to join together and meet Death at last, not (as for Alameddine) in Beirut but in, as it would happen, a residential hospice in Stamford, Connecticut.

Just before I left Beirut, my kindly hostess took me to find the Rue Achrafieh. Her younger Belgian friend had located it on an old map; and we could see, in fact, that all along it had been right there on the current map as well, its trajectory largely unchanged. That said, for a week I'd looked and hadn't been able to find it—why not? it was not a small or remote street—and nor had anybody else. It was as if it had been hidden by sorcery and only belatedly revealed.

Rue Achrafieh was a road of apartment buildings, most of them new; of one or two small villas, bearing the smallpox pockmarks of the civil war; of an unobtrusive mosque on the side where the French air base must have been; and of large tracts of waste ground, hidden behind hoardings, from which sprouted saplings and giant bushes could be seen to wave their green, fronded arms. Much had been destroyed and subsequently razed. At one point, you could see through to the next street, where there stood—as in London after the Blitz—half a house, sheared down the middle like a doll's house, revealing half a floor, and half a wall, and the flocked wallpaper at the back of the living room, and the tatters of curtains fluttering at the gaping windows. This although the war had been over for twenty years. Here, at last, just a few blocks off the tourist route, stood evidence of the time Before. Not, alas for my father, evidence of the time before Before: his era was too long gone for that. But at least, here, I could discern the city that might have arisen after his city.

My hostess approached a group of old men playing backgammon, perched in a circle on the ubiquitous white plastic chairs in a smaller vacant lot near the top of the street. Silver-haired, they were elegant in their dress shirts and pressed trousers, idling away the afternoon; but close inspection—and an inquiry in Arabic by my hostess—revealed that while old, they weren't old enough. The eldest was perhaps in his early seventies, barely born in 1940. Their inspection of me was patient, neutral—looking me over from head to toe, accepting that I take a photograph of them, they weren't hostile, but they weren't interested, either. So much water under the bridge. They shook their heads, blew cigarette smoke out in satisfied whorls over the scrubby ground, and returned to their game: my search dismissed with the flick of a hand.

On Wednesday, I flew to Paris, and thence to New York. I arrived in time to celebrate my aunt's birthday, a day after my father's. I spent the next three days with my family; on the Thursday night, my husband and our children and my sister's children arrived from Boston. That Saturday, we assembled tasty delicacies from the local traiteurs, and held a family picnic on the patio of the nursing home, my father in his wheelchair, all of us in the sunshine, the children shouting and playing tag and soccer and cartwheeling across the crispy midsummer lawn. We told jokes; we laughed. My father was happy, and for perhaps an hour was unaware of his pain.

Of course, when I gave them to him, he didn't care about the posters of old Beirut, or even about the photographs of Rue Achrafieh (in a quick glance, nothing looked familiar, to him or to my aunt). He sampled only the tiniest crumb of his beloved halvah. By then, he'd traveled already too far along his road—as it were, to Damascus. But he was smiling, for all of us, over those few days, making us see only the beauty in this dangerous place, just as he had as a child been made to feel safe in danger, and had also made us, as children, feel safe. He showed us what was beautiful as though the danger did not exist, as though he might surmount the pain, as though we would be able to hold his hand always.

So began the end of the end of the end. One day soon thereafter, he insisted on getting up to sit by the window, for what would be the last time. "Why, Daddy?" I asked. "If it hurts, stay in bed."

"Because I don't want to miss—" He gestured at the wide world through the plate glass, "All this."

But the pain, by then, was too great; and the call for relief too intense. He was transferred to the hospital the next day; and a day later to the hospice; and when next I saw him, he was asleep, in the blissful release, the terminal sleep, of morphine. He opened his eyes to smile and wave at the children—his particular fluttering of his stubby fingers, with his hand held up to his cheek. Later again, he opened his eyes to speak once more to his wife. He whispered, without opening his eyes, of my sister.

And on the last morning, as he slept so sweetly, as placid as a child at last, after a day of thrashing and fretting and rattling, I held tightly to his safe, warm hand—although it felt, as it always had, as though he held mine—and wished him Godspeed on his journey: not to my Beirut, but inshallah, perhaps to his, to the pellucid safety and hope of before Before, a place for which I have, in my diary, his neatly folded map, but to which I can never go.

TWO WOMEN

When my father was first dying—that's to say, in the time we thought he would die but he did not; the time when he made a belated and miraculous recovery and was returned to us, like a character in a fairy tale, for two years, three months, and five days—my aunt, his younger sister, tried to insist upon a visit from the priest. My mother, although diminished (as yet undiagnosed, she was already undermined by the Lewy body dementia that would fell her), resisted valiantly, because my father (at that time off with the fairies, as the expression has it; apt, for the fairy-tale-like nature of that time) could not; and the priest was kept at bay.

But two years later, when he was actually dying, fully and utterly presently himself, my father—my obdurate and fierce father, whose will we feared and admired in equal measure—could not resist his sister in her zeal. Which is how he came, in the nursing home, reluctantly to take Communion from Father Bob, the once-a-week visiting pastor in a baby-blue open-collared short-sleeved summer shirt, who, with short plump fingers, unwrapped the host from a rolled hankie in his breast pocket like a wee snack saved from lunch.

"Isn't there someone," my father asked me pleadingly, "who could do this in French?"

Alas, I shook my head, I did not think so.

Being a man of his word, having promised his sister, my father opened his mouth for the host with all the enthusiasm he might have shown for a cyanide tablet. It was, of course, in addition to a display of religiosity from one who abhorred falsity and religion both, the first moment in which he had performatively to acknowledge that he accepted his imminent death. There were many reasons to balk at the preposterous scene of which he was unwillingly a part, carefully shaven and combed though his skin was a blotched mess, his Brooks Brothers button-down tidily ironed, his torso pinned awkwardly in his wheelchair, in the antiseptic white-tiled room overlooking verdant gardens in Rye Brook, New York, where the nursing aides, all as Catholic as my aunt, were visibly relieved to see my father saved from damnation at the last. One woman in fuchsia scrubs, standing out in the hallway, clasped her hands and gave thanks to God. The morning of this encounter was almost the last time my father forced himself from bed, his pain by then too great. A few days later he would be transferred to the hospital, and thence to the strange, liminal calm of hospice, to be granted the benison of morphine, and, soon thereafter, of eternal rest.

But he accepted all this—the muttered prayers of Father Bob, who drew the sign of the cross upon my father's inviolable forehead, and the aides' hallelujahs—only when my mother was not in the room. Even half-witted—by then she'd lost many of her wits, though she'd struggled so valiantly and for so long not to let it show that I feel a traitor even now to acknowledge it—she would not have permitted my aunt's meddlesome Catholic hand. After the fact, she fumed; and remembered that betrayal longer than, by then, most things.

.   .   .

THEY HAD VOWED when they married to keep religion out of it: she was a mild Anglican, and he a lapsed Catholic, child of passionately devout parents. (My French grandparents, their unconventional union blessed by papal dispensation, slept all their married lives beneath a crucifix draped with a rosary from the Vatican.) For each of my parents, the other's religion carried swaths of meaning—or, in the case of my mother's for my father, of meaninglessness. My father had rebelled against the swaddling quotidian faith in which he had been raised, but considered my mother's watery Christianity to be no faith at all. My mother, meanwhile, raised petit-bourgeois and socially aspirant in mid-century Toronto, fully of her place and time, considered Catholicism sentimental and vulgar—by which she meant "working-class." We had at home a framed professional portrait of my French grandparents, black-and-white, both in profile: "It's very Latin," my mother would whisper, with evident distaste. "Very Catholic." She would have turned it to face the wall if she could.

This meant, in practice, that the pact against religion had been against Catholicism, first and foremost. I don't know whether my father knew, when he and my mother married, how the edict might shape their lives and ours. I don't know whether he ever wanted, before his deathbed, to return to the church of his childhood; but in that moment it was to his childhood that he returned: he longed for the prayers in French because only in French did they have meaning for him; it was only to his French self that they could speak.

His sister, my aunt, our Tante Denise, never left the Church.

She, like her parents, slept beneath her crucifix, and indeed ultimately died beneath it, watched over by nuns paid to pray at her
bedside, rather than by us, her faithless North American nieces.
Years before, contemplating retirement, she often wondered
aloud whether to join a convent; in fact, when she stopped working, she gave herself—her time, her love, what little money she
had—to the church, and more specifically to a particular priest,
the fantastically named Père Casanova, with whom she more or
less fell in love. Always meticulous, she undertook for years, pro
bono, the accounts for his parish; but more indulgently, she fed
him—gorged him, even, upon luxuries: filet mignon, truffles,
expensive cognac—and lavished him with gifts; an expensive
Aubusson carpet was, we came to know, among her donations.
She blushed and grew giddy when he waved his carved ivory cane
or swirled his embroidered raiment in her direction and praised
her piety, or when, in mufti, he stopped by her apartment for an
aperitif or two. She spoke so earnestly of leaving her property
and worldly goods to the Church that we assumed she'd written
it into her will.

This was late in life, of course, when my sister and I had
spouses and children of our own. We made fun of my aunt behind
her back for being so perfectly like an aging spinster from a
Trollope novel—by "we" I mean my mother, of course, and my sister and me. Our father remained silent, his face darkening when
we joked about his sister: her lifelong defender as well as ours,
he was, in such moments, rudely torn. With distance, I have to
acknowledge that he was thus torn throughout his life, possibly
almost all the time. After they'd all died—first our father; then,
two years later, within months, my mother and my aunt—my sister observed that it was as if he'd been married to both of them, as

if he'd shuttled all his life between two competing women. Need-less to say—and it was never said—they hated each other.

AS THE STORY went, my mother met my father on a bus in the rain at Oxford, where they both attended summer school in 1955. Their first date was a picnic with an intimidatingly sophisticated American woman also on my mother's program named Gloria Steinem, and a Texan chap she brought along. My Canadian mother, tall and slender, resembled Ingrid Bergman; my father, who then had (albeit briefly) a full head of hair, was Latinly handsome. Both were shy. Their romance blossomed not only in Oxford but over the subsequent months in Paris, my mother's European foray prolonged on my father's account. By letter, she threw over her Canadian boyfriend—a young solicitor of the society to which she had been elevated, in adolescence, by her family's improved fortunes; my sister and I knew his name because our Canadian grandmother, when cross with our father, would mutter darkly that Margaret should have married Armstrong instead—and did not return home until she and my father were engaged.

Margaret's parents were far from entranced by the match: for starters, François-Michel was French, not to mention Catholic—in their small world the French were reputedly philanderers. He was only a student (and would remain one, for some years), his prospects unclear. Apparently his parents—then en route to Buenos Aires, a city the very existence of which may have seemed doubtful to the Canadians—had no money.

Margaret's parents, amusingly surnamed Riches, had only lately risen from scrimping modesty to modest grandeur (my grandfather, a patent attorney, wrote the insulin patent for Banting and Best): a mink, a sheared beaver, and a belated diamond engagement ring for Marjorie; a Jaguar and a convertible both, for Harold; a lakeside summer cottage for all three to enjoy, though they remained in their same little house in their then-dowdy neighborhood in Toronto's West End (their expansion had its limits). My Canadian grandparents promptly wrote a letter to their future in-laws inquiring about their son's future plans, about how he proposed to keep their only daughter in the style to which she was accustomed. I've seen the letter; they actually used that phrase.

My parents were in touch only by correspondence for over a year, until my father arrived in Toronto a few days before their wedding, in late July 1957. Algeria, the land of his forebears going back over a century and the complicated home of his later childhood, was at that time in violent turmoil; his parents, recently resettled in Argentina, could not afford the journey to Canada. They sent instead my father's younger sister, Denise, my only aunt, to represent the family.

In the photos, she smiles gamely. She'd had a horrendous crossing from Paris by plane, with severe turbulence and a long layover in Gander (this, her first air travel, instilled in her a permanent aerophobia); and once she'd arrived, with only minimal English, she had to put on a dumb-show of eager jollity. Still plump then—her obsessive thinness came later, a lifelong near-anorexia made possible by chain-smoking—she was pale and rather horsey-looking, but you can see the courage and willing with which she stands alongside her brother, among these strapping alien Canadians: my grandfather Harold, who died before I was born, looks like a bona fide giant. And yet it's strange, surely, that in so many photos my father is flanked on one side by my tall mother—in her pristine cream peau de soie faux-Dior dress that accentuates her fine waist, her elegant calf, her swan-like neck—and on the other by my plain and solid aunt (whose physique I unfortunately inherited), in floral chintz.

From the beginning, my father had two women to take care of: in his old-school, patriarchal worldview, that was how he understood it. At the time of their wedding, he and my mother surely didn't know that my aunt would never marry; they did not anticipate her imminent nervous breakdown, nor her subsequent lifelong fragility—she was never not on lithium, after that; even when, toward the end, she drank so heavily that she'd collapse naked in her own vomit in the front hall of her apartment, even then she was on lithium—nor her inability to be alone. Although even as a child, nicknamed Poupette, little doll, she'd been timorous and highly strung, asthmatic and sickly, and had been billeted for months to an aged relative in the Algerian countryside because she was so traumatized by the bombardments in Algiers. And she was, except as a young girl, plain, and as I say, at that point in her young womanhood, plump, with thick ankles—the sort of thing that my grandfather surely pointed out to her (he told me, when I was a teenager, that I'd be good-looking were my legs not so heavy; and wondered whether there existed an operation whereby my ankles might be slimmed). She would have been clear in her own mind that she wasn't readily marriageable.

IMMEDIATELY AFTER MY parents' wedding, they boarded a ship for Le Havre. I can only imagine their bafflement: having known one another intensely for just a few months, they then hadn't seen each other for many more; had met again in the flurry of festivity and wedding preparation; had married; and were suddenly cast into greatest intimacy, in a tiny cabin on a rolling ship upon the high seas. My aunt doesn't feature in the shipboard photographs; I assume she had a return ticket by airplane, though there's nobody left to confirm this. I think of my prudish mother, my extremely private father, embarked not only upon a newly sexual life in their tiny cabin, but sharing seasickness, too—vomit? diarrhea?—at a stage of uncertainty when they may still have eyed one another warily, thinking, *You don't look quite as I remembered. Your left eye is smaller. Your skin is a bit bumpy. Your laugh sounds strange.* And at the same time: *Here we are, joined for life, till death do us part.* Of these early months, my mother confessed that she'd have turned tail and fled for home, were it not for her mother's voice in her ear muttering, *I told you so.*

Their first months together were spent in a small town in northern France, where my father completed his military service, and my mother—her French still a work in progress—spent such lonely days that she welcomed the pair of black-clad Mormon missionaries when they rang the bell, and chatted with them for an hour. They then moved for a time to my grandparents' apartment in Paris, where my father had a job—though they would soon decamp again, for Boston, where he enrolled in graduate school at Harvard, in Middle Eastern studies.

THE SALIENT FACT about their Paris sojourn is that they shared the small flat with my aunt. She'd been living in Paris for some months by then. There, working in an office, she fell in love with her married boss. This love, like all the romantic loves in her life that we know about—including her passion for the Père Casanova—proved unrequited. Denise spiraled into depression. It was 1958, and as she told it, the hostility toward her *pied-noir* background was everywhere palpable, sometimes even malicious. The Algerian War raged. The famous Pontecorvo film *The Battle of Algiers* describes events of 1956–57, culminating in the arrest of the FLN leaders in September of '57; the following months saw the rise of the OAS, a right-wing colonial terrorist organization fighting against the FLN, with the support of certain military factions. The attempted coup in Algeria of May 13, 1958, led to the collapse of the Fourth Republic in France—Algeria's troubles brought France to the brink of civil war—and precipitated the return of an aging Charles de Gaulle to the French presidency. A new constitution was drafted; the Fifth Republic was launched. But the Algerian War would not end for another four bitter years.

A lyrical or mythic narrative of what resulted, for lonely young Denise, might glancingly propose that the violence and distress of the nation—France's inability to maintain power over its colony, Algeria, while at the same time being unable to liberate it—manifested as a crisis in my aunt's psyche, she a young woman who could neither be free from her abandoned homeland (whence her parents also had departed, of course, first for Morocco and then Argentina) nor at home in metropolitan France. Whether her collapse was precipitated by the unattainable love of a man, a family, or a country, her Algeria; or whether by the political unrest around her, and the ways in which she saw herself as implicated in that unrest, as a young *pied-noir* woman in Paris passionately committed to a French Algeria, surrounded by peers who largely felt otherwise and considered her, a colonial in the metropole, an interloper—it's impossible now to know; and was perhaps impossible to know even then. She fell, through no fault of her own, on the wrong side of history. She fell through the cracks of history, perhaps. And she fell alone, while around her, for better or worse, her family was coupled: woebegone, she slid between her parents (their union legendarily happy), and mine (theirs ultimately not).

Which is to say: when my aunt's breakdown began, on the cusp of twenty-five (she was four months older than my mother; in 2010, she would die just two months after her), she was alone in Paris: her parents on another continent, in another hemisphere; her brother and his new wife some distance away. But then they moved into the flat on the Avenue Franco-Russe along with her: Denise, François-Michel, and Margaret. My still-newlywed parents—less than a year married, I think: they hardly knew each other! They tried to make room for themselves—my mother tried to make room for herself, I should say—among my grandparents' furniture and the matter of Denise's troubled life. Denise quit her job; she stayed in, sitting, when not sleeping, on the sofa; she wept; she smoked; she did not eat the meals that my mother prepared (because my mother understood preparing meals to be her wifely role); she shed the extra weight that had so discomfited her; she stared into space; she wept some more.

This, too, I try to imagine, from my mother's point of view, or even from my father's. Many years later, my mother would say to my sister and me, apropos apparently of nothing, "Always remember that when you marry someone, you marry their family, too." Those months in that small flat: a month is comprised of weeks, a week of days, a day of many hours, each hour of many minutes. My father out between breakfast and supper; my mother and my aunt at home, together, bridging the language gap as best they could, harboring and hiding their mutual dislike. My aunt histrionic; my mother cool to the point of unresponsiveness; my father, in the evenings, the go-between, himself tempestuous and hardly intuitive, nightly mixing cocktails, his sole domestic talent, in an effort to keep the peace.

Eventually my aunt was dispatched to Buenos Aires, to the care of her parents. There she spent an exhilarating decade, made great friends, became fluent in Spanish, and again fell fruitlessly, impossibly, in love, once more with a married man, always with lithium as her guardrail. She never again left her parents: they traveled the world as a trio, and when the old couple retired to Toulon, she went with them, and found employment nearby. They signed their letters "Pamande"—Papa, Maman, Denise.

THESE TWO WOMEN, Denise and Margaret, so profoundly different, were yet not wholly unalike. Each lived by a set of unspoken rules, complex webs of necessity inferred by my sister and me, internalized and absorbed without explanation. Figuring out the world, in childhood—figuring out how to be a girl, how to be a person—meant learning these women's signals and, in time, attempting to parse their meaning. (Our father loomed large in our lives, but, during those years, in the way of a Greek god: he was rather frightening, and usually not at home. Many fathers then weren't: a business suit, a sort of passport, liberated them to travel.) We were issued occasional Delphic pronouncements— such as our mother's about marrying families; or another of her infamous comments, about my aunt: "Getting the idea she was a good person is the worst thing that ever happened to her." Sometimes, we encountered instead inexplicable actions, as when my aunt, the night after my wedding, in a crowded hotel elevator in London, attempted to press into my hand a wad of French francs—a gift? Why, in that moment? Why at all, when she and my grandfather had already presented us with an expensive set of luggage? When I declined to accept it, she flew into a rage, the quelling of which required our best diplomatic efforts—not only mine and my husband's but also those of my sister and my father and my grandfather too. My mother, needless to say, did not get involved, and later simply rolled her eyes. After threatening to return to her room, Tante Denise was eventually persuaded to join us for supper, and in the photos at the Greek restaurant she smiles as if nothing had happened. Years later she said, out of the blue, "If I'd known you were going to keep your name, I would never have come to your wedding."

THE RULES THAT shaped my aunt's world were those of devout Catholicism above all; but also those of petit-bourgeois *pied-noir* society in the first half of the twentieth century, influenced too by the rigid French naval order of my grandfather's profession. Denise was profoundly devout; she collected religious artifacts, rosaries and holy water, and believed in signs and wonders. She kept secrets only, as she saw it, to make others' lives better: she hid the worst, which is why, in the end, we heard about her terminal diagnosis only from her doctor—she never mentioned it. We were always told that her terrible (solo) car accident occurred because she fell asleep at the wheel; though the timing suggests, in retrospect, greater volition. Still, she maintained a sunny face for as long as she possibly could. She had a terrible temper—what could she say? God had given it to her—but she was loyal. Deference to the patriarch, and to all elders, was absolute. The role of women in her world was clear, and fixed: we were on earth to marry and bear children. My aunt, a spinster with a successful career—a lawyer, which was the profession that my mother longed to practice, Denise worked also as an accountant—was referred to by her parents as *"pauvre Denise"*—in part because of the breakdown, the lifelong lithium, but chiefly because she'd failed to fulfill her role. They were sad that she was childless; sadder still that she remained unmarried. Theirs was not a secret pity, but overt, accepted. It was understood that in her single, childless state, Denise would stay close to home: caring for aging parents had been, for centuries, the lot of unmarried daughters. They had resigned themselves to this as far back as Buenos Aires—Pamande!—and took care of her at least as much as she did them.

After my grandmother died, my aunt guarded my grandfather like a wolf: when, at a restaurant with a close friend, he tripped and fell while my aunt was parking the car, she banished that friend from their lives. Ensuring his welfare and longevity became her focus, and she did her job well: at ninety-four, my grandfather died in his sleep, after a short illness, with all his wits—and his family—about him. After which, my aunt turned her attention to her older brother: thereafter, she rang François-Michel daily. They discussed the weather, their ordinary activities, her parish, her neighbors. She did not complain, not to him, not ever, no matter how desperate she felt. Theirs was *"la famille du sourire"* and her job was to bring him happiness. From across the Atlantic, Denise would care for him, in spite of my mother (who clearly didn't know properly how to do so). She would do so in a spirit of religious and relentless self-abnegation and self-sacrifice.

Meanwhile, her own existence grew ever more monastic and spartan: having saved very little, she embraced poverty almost like a child playing at being poor. She accepted gifts from my parents—from my father, really—as her birthright: an emerald ring, an amber necklace, a Burberry raincoat, her apartment—

but for herself, she ate little, bought nothing, wore clothes and shoes until they fell apart, dried her husk of a body with rough and threadbare ancient towels. She did keep up always her Clarins foundation, her expensive lipstick—a deep dried-blood color, from Yves Saint Laurent: my mother loathed it, called it ghoulish—and her weekly *mise-en-plie*; these appearances were a matter of Catholic dignity, of French patriotism almost, a sunk cost. Beyond that, with the exception of cigarettes, she could forgo almost anything. She could, and she would, want less, use less, need less, demand less than anyone else: in this, at least, in being last, she would be first.

Even as she whittled down ever further her person and her material desires, she grew desperately needy and enraged. She became a hurricane of fury. This was when and why she took to drink, the drink that would ultimately, along with the cigarettes, kill her; but which proved the only means by which she could allow herself to be unfettered. She drank Johnny Walker when my parents bought it for her, but otherwise Label 5, a lowly brand of scotch sold in chunky embossed bottles some of which she saved to refrigerate tap water—not for herself, who preferred all drinks tepid, but for her visitors.

Drunk, Denise became greedy, garrulous, avid. When we were away, she kept count of how long since we'd visited, and a few drinks in would throw out the exact tally in astringent reproach. She quarreled with lifelong friends, taking issue with their inconstancy, their insufficient attention. When we were there, she'd force our arms around her neck, pull us close, plant loud, soggy kisses on our cheeks, rumbling in our ears in her raspy Louis Armstrong fag-end of a voice, in a fug of tobacco smoke—French Marignys had, with time, turned to Marlboro reds. Scrawny in age, and haggard, she developed particular tics when drunk, a way of tucking her hands into her waistband and rocking back and forth in unseemly pelvic thrusts; a way of thoughtlessly licking her forefinger, then pawing with the saliva at a raw, red patch on her face; a way of grinding her loose lips, ruminating almost, so that you couldn't ignore the prominent teeth behind them. Her pale blue eyes, always watery behind their thick glasses, grew filmy and red-rimmed—and frightened, and sad.

Repelled by her, we were also guilty, even loving, in our repulsion: Tante Denise became a doppelgänger, a part of me that I feared, abhorred, accepted, and defended in equal measure. God forbid we should end up like Tante Denise—*pauvre Denise.* She was our Christian test, or one of them—mad, pathetic, noble, generous, oppressive, funny, deluded, brave, so lonely, and trying, always trying, until she couldn't try anymore. In her ignominious last years, of her naked drunken self, I was reminded always of Jane Bowles's character Mrs. Copperfield, who wants to drink gin until she can roll around on the floor like a baby. Being a woman was too difficult; in the end, maybe all along, Denise wanted only to renounce.

MY MOTHER'S SET of life rules, on the other hand, was that of a Protestant Anglophile with social aspirations in the Toronto of her youth. Effortless superiority and keen wit were *de rigueur:* you were supposed to be beautiful (or not, if you weren't) without making a fuss about it, wear practical sturdy shoes, get straight A's without being seen to work, you were to be always polite and, when necessary or even amusing, cutting in your politesse. Gentle and considerate, even passive by nature, Margaret had nevertheless developed the sharp tongue her adolescent milieu (a private girls' school) had required, and often spoke like a character out of Anthony Powell or Muriel Spark. Of a college friend of mine she memorably said, after the girl's one visit, "I've never met such a nonentity. I kept forgetting she was in the car." Insecurity could make her mean; matters superficial got under her skin: she envied her friends their mink coats, their Caribbean vacations, their husbands' deaths. She enlisted us, her daughters, as her defenders in arguments with our father; and raised us to understand that her life had been ruined by marriage to a man who didn't support her liberation, or believe in her capabilities. "Never, never be financially dependent on a man," she would hiss, or, because she felt our father dismissed her intellect, "Never, ever marry anyone who isn't as smart as you are." "I've wasted my life on his dirty socks," she said. "Don't ever get stuck like me."

But the messages confused, because she never left him—she never so much as went overnight to a friend's house or a motel. She railed against François-Michel, but when we criticized our father, she'd defend him; when we told her our secrets, she'd pass them on to him. We came to know that her allegiances were more complicated than she wanted to let on. Moreover, for someone who bitterly described being a wife and mother as "the waste of a life," she mastered the housewife's tasks with stellar preeminence: a magnificent cook, she prepared three-course meals even on weeknights (my favorite dessert was zabaglione, an egg yolk and marsala confection whipped over heat into a fiery, airy froth: it took twenty minutes over the stovetop at the last minute, but she'd make it sometimes just for the four of us, for fun); she kept house impeccably; everything was ironed, from shirts and dresses to sheets and pillowcases, nightgowns, underpants, my father's linen handkerchiefs. She could remove any spot from any fabric; darn socks; invisibly repair moth holes. She saved left-overs in tiny dishes in the fridge, and old twist-ties, and washed out plastic bags and hung them up to dry.

She taught us that good stewardship was a moral strength; so, too, was thrift. This was not incommensurate with her sense of superiority and her sharp judgments of others—for a child of the Depression, greater continence was an expression of superiority, indeed. She came from, aspired to, a Canadian society of hardy, broad-shouldered women, capable and resilient. She eschewed makeup, and fine clothes: when my father bought her beautiful things, she stuffed them, tags on, in the back of her closet. She used Eucerin as her face cream, and in my entire life, possessed one ancient blue eye shadow; her waxy lipsticks came from the drugstore. She never paid more than thirty dollars for a haircut, and seemed almost to take pride in having great bone structure (Ingrid Bergman!) but looking shabby—the perfect counter-point to Tante Denise, who, although homely, always made the most of herself. (My sister and I thought of it—think of it still—as Protestant vs. Catholic, and Canadian vs. French.) She knit-ted elaborate sweaters; she created and tended beautiful gardens; she trained beloved dogs, and walked them miles, and played ball with them and talked to them: she adored dogs. She read thou-sands of books, developed unexpected areas of erudition (e.g., nineteenth-century women travelers in Asia and Africa; histo-ries of fonts and presses; all facts about the Bloomsbury Group). And she wrote letters, amazing letters, many of which I am for-tunate still to possess.

BOTH WOMEN FORMED me, even as they shaped my father's life. Albeit differently, they taught my sister and me that we should ask for, and expect, less, even as they encouraged us to strive for more, lessons that seem quaintly old-fashioned now. In the parking lot of the nursing home where Father Bob delivered the last rites to my father, my mother, mildly demented, remarked, with sadness in her voice, but also with considerable calm, "There's still so much of life to get through, once you realize that your dreams won't come true." She'd never taken up much space, but in those last years she took up less and less, ever polite, obliterated but gracious to her ten-month-bedridden end. Tante Denise, meanwhile, erased herself little by little in a different, uglier way, with the help of Label 5. She called the Atlantic "that accursed ocean," but managed nevertheless to cross it to be with her brother when he was dying. She largely ignored her sister-in-law at that point, and picked fights instead with my sister. Once François-Michel was gone, Denise saw no reason to hold on, and her alcoholic suicide began in earnest.

MY FATHER HAD, all his life, two women to take care of (four, if you count my sister and me). He was devoted to his sister, and he adored his wife; though they irked him, each in her way. He, who had no time for gossip, said nothing behind their backs; in fact, I never heard him criticize my aunt at all; though he and my mother quarreled a great deal over the years.

Denise knew what she was supposed to be (married, a mother, sweet, submissive), approved wholeheartedly, even judgmentally, of those traditional ideals, but couldn't for the life of her fulfill them. We've often wondered whether her unrequited heterosexual loves were for show, and whether, in our era, or without the pressures of her Catholic faith, her intimate life might have unfolded differently. Margaret, in contrast, despised what she was supposed to be (married, a mother, sweet, submissive) and yet was most successfully all of these things. What she wanted instead she was too submissive to attain. From the two of them I learned that to hope for happiness, or peace, even, I should strive to be everything, but also that I was probably doomed: there's still so much of life to get through when you realize that your dreams won't come true.

PAINFULLY, BOTH MY mother's and my aunt's identities involved profound self-loathing: they believed, as so many women have been brought up to believe, that they were inadequate as they were. I have struggled, with uncertain success, to divest myself of that legacy. Yet much that I internalized from these two women I still uphold: the joy and dignity of small pleasures, the gift of requiring less in order to find contentment, the Christian ethics that teach us to put others before ourselves, to be humble, to be kind. Curiosity, openness, fearlessness, generosity of spirit, above all love—these things I also learned from them. To live with an open heart and an open mind, and to live with kindness— truisms, perhaps, but not less admirable goals for that. If there's an afterlife, I don't believe access to it lies in the hands of Father Bob, with his hankie-wrapped host; nor do I believe there's particular merit in my mother's urge to banish potentially assuaging rituals of faith. If I'd only found the priest between Stamford and White Plains who could deliver the last rites in French, my father might have been consoled. Even without believing, he might have been consoled.

HERE'S HOW I like to remember them, my aunt and my mother. When I was small, perhaps six or so, I knocked over my water glass on the table in the Vietnamese restaurant in Le Pradet, near my grandparents' home in the south of France. My father, who couldn't tolerate mess and still less embarrassment (he, too, carried a lot of anxiety), roared at me, and I broke into tears.

"Don't be sad," said Tante Denise, putting an arm around my shoulder. "Accidents happen. They can happen to anyone—even to grown-ups." (She spoke in French, of course, and so the words she used were deliciously literal to my childhood self: *grandes personnes*, big people.) She grasped her full wineglass by the stem and turned it over on the table, so that the red wine mixed with my water on the textured white paper cloth in an expanding red swirly sea. "See?" She laughed. "It doesn't matter!"

And my mother, Margaret Riches Messud: her gentle soul, even to the end, before and after the bitterness and disappointment. She stood, or rather teetered slightly, in our kitchen, in the last year of her life, beatific, while I, in my turn, fumed: I'd taken her three times within an hour to the bathroom because she kept forgetting she'd already been ("Are you sure, Mama?" "Yes, I'm sure"). Each trip was a lengthy ordeal on account of the Parkinson's; she couldn't manage any of the practicalities herself.

"Isn't it wonderful?" she whispered, eyes alight, apropos of nothing. I was aware that she spoke in all sincerity and yet, at the same time, that she perhaps didn't know entirely that she lived with us, nor perhaps quite who I was, that I was her daughter. "I just love being here," she said, "and I just wish I could spend all my time with you." And she smiled at me, at the world, like a blessing, and she reached out to hold my hand.

MOTHER'S KNEE

Each of us is made up of our lived experiences, of course; but also, both consciously and unconsciously, of all the stories that we have heard, read, or watched. Without realizing it, we come to understand what a story is and how it means by the accretion of narratives in our heads.

We know without being told that an hour spent watching the Kardashians is quite different from an hour spent reading Kant; by extension, an hour spent reading Harry Potter is different from an hour reading the works of Primo Levi. I say this with no disrespect to Harry Potter, an enormously compelling and influential series of books enjoyed by millions; but simply to point out that one set of books is a fantasy about the struggle between "good" and "evil"; whereas the second is, well, *for real*, not because it's nonfiction but because it is the complex, contradictory, scrupulous, and self-knowing account of one man's experiences during the very real Second World War. (In this internet age, in which fantasy seems bafflingly to have attained the status of a new reality, let it be reiterated: actual reality is intractably, awfully, and profoundly real; and actual facts are the record of that intractable reality. Not to grasp this is to succumb to a potentially fatal ethical corruption of the soul.)

As kids, we devour the stories that fall beneath our hands (or eyes). As a child in Australia and Canada, I read Enid Blyton, Eleanor Farjeon, Ivan Southall, and Farley Mowat, along with Judy Blume, E. L. Konigsburg, and Ursula Le Guin. The narratives each of us happens upon are of course culturally specific, and change over time; although some seminal stories persist. What my kids, now teenagers, have read at school is more contemporary and diverse in authorship than what my schools offered when I was young, which is an excellent thing; but in middle and high school they still read the *Iliad*, the *Odyssey*, and Shakespeare, which is just as important. What they read for pleasure is also quite different from what I read: thirty-five years ago, YA didn't exist as a genre (with the exception of S. E. Hinton's *The Outsiders*), and so, from the age of twelve or thirteen, I plundered my parents' bookshelves for reading material.

More specifically, I turned to my mother's library. Both my parents were avid readers, the sort of people (more common then?) whose ideal weekend outing was a long drive to an excellent secondhand bookstore, where they'd spend an hour or two browsing in church-like silence and emerge each bearing a stack of unexpected discoveries. Plus, wherever we lived, my mother was among the most devoted patrons of our local library, supplementing her reading material with stacks of plastic-covered hardbacks, of which she kept a meticulous list in a notebook in her handbag so as not to run up fines.

My father read almost exclusively nonfiction: history, biography, philosophy, cultural criticism. He had a particular interest in the history of Christianity in the Middle East, and collected a vast number of books about Mediterranean history and Byzantium; but he could also surprise us. I remember going to summon him to supper and finding him in his leather chair, wearing his half-moon glasses, deeply ensconced in Greil Marcus's *Lipstick Traces*. My mother, on the other hand, read chiefly novels and literary biographies, and as I was myself from the first a lover of fiction, it was in her footsteps that I eagerly, unthinkingly followed.

As a child, you take your experiences for granted and imagine that they're normal. For many years I thought that every family subscribed to more magazines than they could possibly read (the prized *New Yorker* in the loo, my mother's only truly private space; the *New York Review* in piles upon the sideboard; the *Atlantic* and *Harper's* on the floor by the living room sofa, usually open to the middle of a long article, left unfinished), and stacked their books in double rows on the shelves so as to fit more in, before starting to pile them behind armchairs and under beds.

By the same token, for a long time I believed that the books I read were more or less universally known. It didn't occur to me that by borrowing and devouring books selected by my mother, I was being shaped by her predilections, thoughts, and desires. If I hadn't loved what I read, I might have balked and explored a different canon—which, in time, I did, of course. By my late teens, I'd become a devotee of Faulkner and Dostoyevsky—"Why such sinister books?" my mother would ask with a sigh. "So depressing! Isn't life difficult enough?"—but that was later. What I took in at my mother's knee—the first adult novels and stories that I read—formed my literary tastes and gave me a particular sense of what made a novel enticing. Only later would I discover that apparently fewer people were attracted by these books than were keen to read Faulkner or Dostoyevsky, let alone Hemingway or Fitzgerald: it was as if my mother had shown me the pleasures of the 11th arrondissement without first taking me to see the Louvre or the Eiffel Tower.

I don't know why I read Mary Wollstonecraft's *A Vindication of the Rights of Women* in seventh grade, other than that my mother had a copy in the guest bathroom. It can't properly count as a formative book for me, because at the age of eleven I didn't really understand it (even the syntax was difficult). But I knew from conversations with my mother that it was important. I do remember reading Antonia White's *Frost in May* at about the same time, a wonderful novel published in 1978 by Virago as one of its first reissued classics. (Thank God for Carmen Callil and her amazing publishing enterprise!) Many my age and older will recall the novel's army-green glossy spine, its cover image of a little girl, in three-quarter view, in Victorian clothes, with her hair up. After reading the book, I longed to be Catholic—but, importantly, I knew that longing was hopeless, because to attain the desirable, insouciant sort of Catholicism, you couldn't be a convert. I want to say that my mother had a subscription to Virago's early publications, as we seemed to collect them all at our house; but it's entirely possible that she was careful to purchase them from her beloved bookstore, Britnell's (a Toronto staple until its closing in 1999; and now, I believe, a Starbucks: say no more). I eagerly consumed, in those early teenage years, the novels of Daphne du Maurier, Elizabeth Taylor, and Molly Keane, women whose fictions are stored in the same part of my brain as the names and interests of the kids in my eighth-grade class.

My mother had a great love of the Bloomsbury group, on account of which Virginia Woolf's glorious diaries fell into my young hands (upside down if you will: Volume 5 first), and not long after, Vita Sackville-West's *No Signposts in the Sea*, along with a romp—highly inappropriate for my tender age—by the name of *Ermyntrude and Esmeralda*, subtitled "a naughty novella," written by Lytton Strachey with illustrations by Erté. (It was the beautiful drawings that first attracted me, and sparked my early adolescent passion for Erté's fashion illustrations. At around the same time I was obsessed with Edith Piaf, and would listen over and over again to my parents' records. Weirdly, I also loved The Who, and was particularly proud of my red vinyl of *Who Are You*. This was in the era of *Grease* and *Saturday Night Fever*. I did not think any of my interests odd.)

On the heels of Antonia White and Elizabeth Taylor came my mother's beloved Barbara Pym, along with Elizabeth Bowen, Muriel Spark, and Ivy Compton-Burnett, whose dialogue I sometimes found hard to follow. Soon thereafter, she introduced me to the stories of Katherine Mansfield, and then the works of Edith Wharton (whose former house in Hyères, now the botanical gardens, was in my youth a restaurant where we went with my French grandparents for Sunday lunch—idyllic for children, as we could run free after the meal), and a Canadian canon—from Emily Carr's *Klee Wyck* to Margaret Atwood, Mavis Gallant, and the *grande dame*, Alice Munro—all of them I have held dear ever since. But perhaps most influential for me in those teenage years was my mother's love of Jean Rhys: without asking, because she did, I read all the novels, darker and darker, from *After Leaving Mr. Mackenzie* to *The Wide Sargasso Sea*.

My father was French; we had cousins in Paris; and from earliest childhood I loved that city best. We used to stay in a hotel off the Champs-Élysées called the Windsor, owned by the company my father worked for. It had an old cage elevator, a grand piano in the lobby, and the wonderfully elegant old lady who lived there permanently was, to me, the Old Lady from Babar. The Windsor was much grander than the hotels inhabited by Jean Rhys's protagonists; but reading her novels reminded me of our family's visits to the city, of arriving near dawn on a winter's morning and walking the wet pavements of the Champs-Élysées in the chill and lowering gloom, waiting for the first café to open so we could have breakfast. (Years later, studying in Paris for a semester during college, I daily walked the streets around Montparnasse, peering into the hotels that Jean Rhys actually lived in, with their narrow entrances, worn carpet, and red flocked wallpaper: a far cry from the Windsor of my childhood, they were to me equally romantic.) Jean Rhys gave voice to a plethora of dark emotions, neuroses, and disappointments that I barely knew I anticipated, when I read about them; but I was entranced.

From there to the women of the Left Bank was but a few books and a couple of years: Djuna Barnes, H. D. and Bryher, Gertrude Stein and Alice B. Toklas, Janet Flanner . . . And then beyond: Christina Stead, Sybille Bedford, Shirley Hazzard—the list of the twentieth century's remarkable women writers goes on, and on. By the time I reached university, I thought of these women as all but extended family. I haven't read many of them in years, but still consider them my literary aunts and cousins.

Each of these writers was for me an exhilarating discovery; and the ways in which they overlapped or were connected in life, along with their curious, uprooted trajectories (my own young life involved much displacement)—their work and biographies helped me believe that a literary future might be possible for me. I didn't really know then about the glamorous derring-do of Ernest Hemingway, or Fitzgerald's drunken decline in Hollywood: I learned that writers lived in poverty in bedsits in North

London, eating baked beans out of tin, like Christina Stead; or retired, forgotten, to Cornwall, where they heard their obituaries read on the radio while still alive, like Jean Rhys. If they were very lucky, they lived near where they'd grown up, and had friends, and possibly even occasionally, if only briefly, found love. I knew these women writers had had difficult lives, but I thought, at least, that they'd attained some kind of immortality: I didn't understand then that they were literarily underrated or even sometimes forgotten. Surely if these books were all over my house, and if my mother and her friends discussed them so eagerly, it was because everyone read them?

There were plenty of more widely acclaimed classics (by men) I didn't get to for years, because I spent my time instead reading the women. Because of these writers and their books, I've known all my adult life that women's stories compel and fascinate, that the gamut of literary possibility is open to everyone. Yes, many of these women writers led challenging, sometimes crushing lives: penury, isolation, lack of recognition, illness. But the paths they forged showed me that it was possible to pursue my passion, and to tell the stories—true, complicated, often dark, often funny (often dark and funny at the same time)—that matter to me.

My mother, who curtailed her own creative and professional dreams in order to take care of us, her family, nevertheless granted her daughters a legacy she could not readily claim for herself: the voices of all the women she admired and whose work she so loved became, from early on, the voices in my head also, many of the voices that shaped me as a reader, and that have surely shaped me as a writer, too.

KANT'S LITTLE PRUSSIAN HEAD
AND OTHER REASONS WHY I WRITE

Several years ago, we sat down with our children to watch a television series about the cosmos. It proved essentially unwatchable for me, in part because what the presenter was saying gives me vertigo.

All he had to do was to lay out for his viewers the earth's cosmic address: Earth, the Solar System, the Milky Way Galaxy, the Local Group, the Virgo Supercluster, the Observable Universe. To remind those of you who may have forgotten, the Milky Way is one of about a dozen galaxies in the Local Group, which in turn is but one of thousands of clusters of galaxies in the Virgo Supercluster. The Observable Universe involves a very large number of superclusters of clusters of galaxies, and extends more than ten billion light-years in all directions. More than that, the presenter explains, "Many of us suspect that all of this—all the worlds, stars, galaxies, and clusters in our observable universe—is but one tiny bubble in an infinite ocean of other universes."

This news evokes the feeling I had several times in youth, when lying in a field staring up at the night sky, that I might fall into the infinite void. For people like me, the idea mostly provokes anxiety. Oh, there's wonder, too, to be sure—how can one not marvel at our unlikely existence?—but this reawakening to humanity's insignificance reawakens in me also my nine-year-old self, a child whose response to the magnitude of the universe might have been, "Then I guess there's no point going to school today. And maybe not much point getting out of bed, either."

Fortunately, age, experience, and general busy-ness make it largely possible to repress our knowledge about the cosmos. Once we'd turned off the television, I could let go fairly quickly of my vertigo. There were dishes to be done, dogs to be walked, children to be bustled to their beds—the stuff of life, as we call it, when we don't deem it the impedimenta to the life we might have lived, that life of the mind that, for all except the hermits among us, is ever more reduced and pushed to the margins by the contemporary world's demands, by family and students and homework and emails, and so on.

As Thomas Bernhard's scathing narrator recalls, in his brilliant novel *The Loser*, while reflecting upon his friendship with the pianist Glenn Gould (who is, needless to say, the narrator's figment, a version of the genius that only partially resembles the man himself—but that's another story)—anyway, the narrator recalls Glenn saying:

> Fundamentally we are capable of everything, equally fundamentally we fail at everything, he said, I thought. Our great philosophers, our greatest poets, shrivel down to a single successful sentence, he said, I thought, that's the truth, often we remember only a so-called philosophical hue, he said, I thought. We study a monumental work, for example Kant's work, and in time it shrivels down to Kant's little East Prussian head and to a thoroughly amorphous

world of night and fog, which winds up in the same state of helplessness as all the others, he said, I thought.

A good friend of mine, a philosopher and a Kant scholar, has devoted the past twenty years to interpreting passages of Kant's *Critique of Judgment*. It is but one of the briefer texts in Kant's monumental work; and yet, in order properly and thoroughly to understand it, she has committed all of her adult life thus far, and considers her labor far from complete.

For almost all of us, such serious focus on Kant's thought is impossible. For most of us, if we apprehend even "a so-called philosophical hue," we consider ourselves in pretty good shape. It's like the dizzying enormousness of the cosmos in reverse: if, in order properly to understand a paragraph of Kant, one would need to engage in a lifetime of study, what are we to make of the entire breadth of his oeuvre—the Observable Universe of his oeuvre, if you will? And what, beyond that, are we to make of the fact that Kant's published writings represent already a careful ordering and editing and articulation into intelligible language of his philosophy, of his conscious thought? And beyond that, given that his thought arose in part from his experience, experience all but entirely lost to us—made up of countless minutes and hours and days and years of life upon this planet, of Kant's individual and particular life—how are we to conceive of the unknowable vastness that was Kant?

And further: If Kant is just one philosopher among thousands, just one German among millions, just one man among billions—how can we conceive of the entirety of uncommunicated and incommunicable human experience? What infinite invisible universe of Bernhardian "night and fog" is this, in which we must drift—the great genius Kant, according to Bernhard, "in the same state of helplessness as all the others"?

Thomas Bernhard was a writer who took the dark view. The shrinking of Kant's mind, the breadth of his interests and wisdom, down to his little East Prussian head does seem like a loss; but maybe, too, it's like the freeze-dried vegetables in packet soup: merely awaiting water for reconstitution.

In contradiction of Bernhard's darkness, I'll offer a quotation from a 1980s British film, *The Long Good Friday*, in which the gangster Harold Shand (brilliantly played by the late Bob Hoskins) gives a speech at a party on his yacht in the Thames, welcoming the American Mafia to London to collaborate on some white-collar crime in the East End: "Hands across the ocean," he says in his Cockney growl, bullish and optimistic. "Hands across the ocean."

Because, of course, Bernhard is absolutely right—of so much of our lives we retain but "a so-called hue," philosophical or not; but to convey what Bernhard laments as "a single successful" sentence—that, I firmly believe, is cause for celebration. Even a single successful sentence can be transformative; and a single poem or novel can alter someone's life forever. *That* is "hands across the ocean," and it's a meeting that happens if not only, then most fully, through language. With words, we can travel across nations and through time; we can inhabit lives far from our own.

Here's the first paragraph of Tolstoy's *Childhood*, his first-published novel (1852):

> On the 12th of August, 18— (just three days after my tenth birthday, when I had been given such wonderful presents), I was awakened at seven o'clock in the morning by Karl Ivanitch slapping the wall close to my head with a fly-flap

made of sugar paper and a stick. He did this so roughly that he hit the image of my patron saint suspended to the oaken back of my bed, and the dead fly fell down on my curls. I peeped out from under the coverlet, steadied the still shaking image with my hand, flicked the dead fly onto the floor, and gazed at Karl Ivanitch with sleepy, wrathful eyes. He, in a parti-coloured wadded dressing-gown fastened about the waist with a wide belt of the same material, a red knitted cap adorned with a tassel, and soft slippers of goat skin, went on walking round the walls and taking aim at, and slapping, flies.

So swiftly, intimately, Tolstoy draws us into the experience of young Nikolai, his semiautobiographical protagonist. Specificity is essential—from the first, we know it's the twelfth of August, the late summer—and if we pause there, we can feel the light of a late summer morning, the sleepy air before the day's full heat, and what it is to waken into it. We can hear the intermittent buzzing of the flies, now swooping, now crazy against a windowpane. We know, too, that our narrator has just turned ten, and his "wonderful presents" are still in his mind: he evokes, in passing, the particular delight of that birthday, of reaching the double digits, of the pure joy of one's birthday presents, if they're the right ones, when you're ten—and this simple Tolstoyan specificity renders Nikolai's world both present and vivid to us. We, too, have been ten years old; we, too, have been wakened, unwilling, at seven in the morning; we, too, have felt the laziness of late summer, as we have been irritated by the buzzing of its flies; and although we may never have seen one made of "sugar paper and a stick," we have surely wielded, or at least seen, a fly-swatter.

Each of us, then, can imagine the particular displeasure of opening an eye—on what should be such a glorious morning—to the sound of the swatter's slap, to the faint but unmistakable sensation of a fly's corpse falling in our hair. The particular image of Nikolai's patron saint may be unfamiliar, but we can sense its frame trembling on the bedstead above our head, and can imagine, too, raising a hand to steady it. In a matter of sentences, we are fully in this room, with this boy, seeing, hearing, and feeling as he sees, hears, and feels. This Tolstoy gives us in a shared language, in familiar words, if you will. His simple, lucid descriptions insist upon the transparency and commonality of his words.

But key to this particular August morning is the zeal of Karl Ivanitch. Now, Karl Ivanitch is thus far, to the reader, merely a name, a void. But we understand, simply by the way that name is evoked, that for Nikolai, the words "Karl Ivanitch" imply much more. The physical description Tolstoy offers us will evoke him as clearly as any photograph, in his gown, cap, and slippers; but it's his restless fly-baiting wander that gestures toward the tutor's personality that we will come to know: fierce, even obsessive, crucial in young Nikolai's life, but also petty, and somehow absurd. All this is here, from the outset.

What Tolstoy achieves—and what any fiction writer hopes to achieve—is, in fact, magic. I use this term not sentimentally, but literally. Tolstoy conjures for us a world familiar enough that we can place ourselves in it; and then, more profoundly, he conjures its inhabitants. Nikolai *knows* Karl Ivanitch; and the promise, if we read on, is that we shall know him, too, that Karl Ivanitch will enter our private imagined world and live there along with the jostling population of characters, real and fictional, who fill our consciousness and shape our lives.

Because naming is magic. Spells are essentially a private language; and the magic that they work is very particular. If, for example, I say to you the name "Marjorie Riches," you may have some idea about how the name sounds English, and old-fashioned; or about the literary potential—either ironic or symbolic—of a character with the surname "Riches."

But if I say "Marjorie Riches" to my sister, I am performing an act of magic: I am conjuring a person. Marjorie Riches was our maternal grandmother, and simply in saying her name I am recalling an entire life, in my childhood, in Toronto: the heavy front door of her gray stucco house; the cul-de-sac above High Park on which she'd known all the other residents forever. I am raising her before us, and in us: the tiny ridges of her fingernails and the wart-like callus on her left index finger; the shiny, papery quality of the skin on her hands; the slithery sound of her synthetic floral dresses against her slip when she pressed us to her chest; the difference in the size of her blue eyes behind their glasses (where they looked enormous) and without them (where they looked quite small); the slightly duck-like flare of her nose; the flossiness of her granny's perm, upon which she wore a hairnet at bedtime.

I am conjuring, too, our child's delights in her house, with its laundry chute and the hatch next to the side door for the milkman, where foil-topped bottles and pounds of butter would appear before breakfast; the oxblood-colored concrete floor in the basement with a drain in the middle, around which we rode a tricycle in circles, at speed, even when we were too big really to do so and our knees were pulled up to our chins. I'm bringing back the bowl of pastel-colored nonpareils on the side table in the living room, our lunches of tinned ravioli in wintertime, eaten on a creaky stool in the sunroom overlooking the snowy garden. I am conjuring, simultaneously, the apartment of her old age, and the high firm ship of her long-widowed marriage bed, and her glossy crimson Underwood typewriter that she kept on a little table near the window. There is her jewel box full of sparkly clip-on earrings, and the powder-puff music box with its filigree silver-work. Here, now, we picture the particularity of her handwriting, the slight downward slope of her signature—whether she wrote "Marjorie Riches" or, on all our cards, "Grandma." And here, too, the warm, flowery smell of her neck, which lived in her scarves long after she died, and which, having taken a few of them home to my apartment (I was an adult by then), I would inhale greed-ily every so often just to bring her back, until one day the scent was finally gone. I can hear her persistent habit of clearing her throat, that so irritated our mother; and know again the intent way she had of listening as she grew blind, with her eyes looking off slightly to one side of your face, focused but unfocused.

To tell you these things is to give you but a tiny fraction of what her name means to me, of the magic that her name carries now, since my parents' deaths, for just two of us on this planet, for my sister and for me. It is to make of Marjorie Riches a little Cana-dian head to stand upon its stake next to Kant's little East Prus-sian one: but I would insist, again, that this, even in its near-total failure, is cause for celebration. With various proper nouns I can, in this way, bring to life, for different constituencies, so many different moments in my life, a few words carrying great weight, in the way of a private, or magical, language: I can bring back my life as a child in Sydney, Australia; or summers spent with my French grandparents in Toulon, France; or, more recently, the year I spent with my family in Berlin.

How does this relate to fiction, to why I tell stories? In part, because to the outside, in my summarized self, I have only a "little American head." I am chiefly "an American writer." But, like many of us, I'm a mongrel, a hybrid, made up of many things. My childhood was itinerant, my identity complicated. My father was French, my mother Canadian. I grew up in Sydney, Australia; in Toronto, Canada; and then at boarding school in the United States. I went to graduate school at Cambridge University, where I met my British husband. I didn't live in the United States, outside of school, until I was in my late twenties. Like every single one of us, I can echo Walt Whitman in asserting that "I contain multitudes." I am who I am because I was *where* I was, *when* I was; and almost all of it is invisible to the world. This is true, of course, for each of us.

I'm not at all ungrateful for all my life's disruption, but I know what Salman Rushdie meant when he wrote his important essay "Imaginary Homelands": "home" for me, such as it is, is in my mind. Rushdie wrote: "It may be argued that the past is a country from which we have all emigrated, that its loss is part of our common humanity." I, for my heart, couldn't afford to lose these things. I could, instead, tell stories: I could become a writer. As Flannery O'Connor once said, "Anybody who has survived his childhood has enough information about life to last him the rest of his days." Albert Camus's character Meursault puts it slightly differently in *L'Étranger*: "a man who had only lived for a single day could easily live a hundred years in prison. He would have enough memories to keep him from getting bored." I couldn't save them all—just as one can't fully capture a single day, just as Kant is reduced to "a single successful sentence," or to his little East Prussian head. But I could save fragments, I could convey a "so-called . . . hue." Knowing that I must necessarily fail, I could only try, with the particular gift of the English language at my disposal, its opportunistic magnitude, its extraordinary and elastic vocabulary: more than that, I could not *not try*.

And I could go further: I realized that in *making up* stories, as in reading stories, I could create a contained world in which an experience is shared in its entirety. I could invent characters, name them, evoke them, and around them a society, or a landscape, born of my experiences but as free as my imagination. Weaving together the known and the unknown, the public and the private, I could cast a spell.

After reading Tolstoy's *Childhood*, and then its companion pieces *Boyhood* and the unfinished *Youth*, there is much we don't know and will never know about Nikolai's upbringing. But how much we *do* know, and how much we have *experienced ourselves*, and internalized. Karl Ivanitch, first seen in his wadded dressing gown, will be forever familiar to us, buffoonish, poignant, passionate, and uniquely himself. He will join the ranks of our relatives, his name a magical evocation, along with Effi Briest, or Leopold Bloom, or Mrs. Dalloway or Anna Wulf or Okonkwo or Portnoy or José Arcadio Buendía . . . If I say to you "Marjorie Riches," it may not carry much meaning for you—yet. But if I say any of these names, or Hamlet indeed, or Humbert Humbert or Raskolnikov—then we're talking, with the thrill of a shared secret knowledge, the evocation of so many formerly private relations and experiences we have had with our books.

Fiction, as Picasso said of art, is a means of "seizing power, of imposing form." It's a way of navigating between a shared conventional language—to return again to Tolstoy, we all know what the twelfth of August is; we've all been ten years old—and a private, magical language—Nikolai knows exactly who Karl Ivanitch is, while we do not; but through Nikolai, *we, too, will know him.*

If I tell you a story about an elderly woman in Toronto who may or may not be called "Marjorie Riches," I am "seizing power" of a kind. I'm sharing my magical language, and casting a spell. My magic will always be partial, always a failure, a shrunken head next to life itself. But as my friend has given her life to understanding and explaining a small portion of Kant, I give mine to describing—that is, to attempting and failing to understand and explain—some small portion of life itself.

If all language were already shared, then ours would be a dull and limited world. That would be the world of functional discourse—almost of internet English, if you like—in which we live much of our lives. And of course, if language were entirely private, no communication would be possible. The terrain of a fully private language is madness or dementia. It's the situation where "hands across the ocean" can't quite bridge the gap, where we the recipients, the readers, are left without access to experience, where it remains veiled, not shared.

When my mother, in old age, began to lose her memory and her lucidity, she sometimes spoke in poetry, in an oracular language. In the last two years of her life, she was often quiet—she who had been so vitally social—and once, as she sat in silence, I asked her what she was thinking. With a wry and wistful smile, she answered, "Shards of memory, and new worlds discovered."

This beautiful postcard from across the abyss, from the incommunicable private island of her later experience, stays with me in each day. What is our hope for the experience of literature, if not to share this: shards of memory and new worlds discovered? What, indeed, if not this, is the best truth of our experience of life?

I have my own collection of little literary and philosophical heads, my own stock of single successful sentences. Each of us is constructed, like a magpie's nest, from these as much as from our childhood experiences and our temperament and our loves and losses. We are as much the sum of our lived literary experiences as of our literally lived experiences. This, of course, is what T. S. Eliot expressed in *The Waste Land*, and his is one of the essential sentences I carry with me everywhere. I've slipped it into several of my books. "These are the fragments I have shored against my ruins." That's all. It's why I write, really. Fail again, fail better—to cite another from my collection. A single successful sentence, a so-called philosophical hue. Each an invocation; each a hand across the ocean; each a seizing of power away from fear and desire; each a small magic.

OUR DOGS

People react differently to our canine situation. From what they say, I glean information about their natures. Of course, one way or another, they judge us—our dogs provide a morality play all their own.

We're a family of four, or of six: two adults and two kids (ages fourteen and eleven at the time of writing), with two dogs. They're relatively small dogs, although not (we like to believe) obscenely so. Myshkin is a standard-sized, red, short-haired dachshund whose antiquity is in some dispute: she came to us as a puppy in the fall either of 1998 or of 1999, so long ago we can't remember. Her junior consort, Bear, a rescue mutt, joined the family back in 2009, at which point he was said to be about eighteen months old. Part terrier and part min-pin, he's toffee-colored, scruffy, and professorial in aspect, with wiry legs and, once upon a time, amazing speed and agility. (Myshkin, incidentally, means "little mouse" in Russian, so we have, in name at least, two non-canine creatures; though only the first was named after the protagonist of *The Idiot*.)

At this point, Myshkin the matriarch, still silky and fine-featured, is deaf, blind, intermittently incontinent, and increasingly weak on her pins. Her sturdy front legs splay and slide with the effort of standing, and her back legs have a way of collapsing. She ends up reclining—like the Queen of Sheba or a beached whale, depending on your perspective—in unlikely places, occasionally almost in her own excrement, which makes constant vigilance imperative. She's so demented that half the time when you take her outside, she remains immobile but for her wagging tail, apparently unclear why she's there.

Oh, and did I mention that she reeks? Not just a bit of dog-breath, or even the comparatively pleasant scent of wet dog. It's a holistic foulness, emanating not just from her mouth, which smells like the garbage can behind the fishmonger's (hence her nickname: Fishbin), but at this point from her entire body, which, in spite of frequent bathing, carries about it the odor of a dung heap in hot weather. Her stench precedes her, and lingers in a room after she's left. It's hard to sit next to her, let alone take her on your lap, without gasping at the fecal, fishy gusts.

The worst of it, though, is her constant state of existential crisis, which has her either moaning or, more unnervingly, barking, for hours at a stretch. Dachshunds, though small dogs, have big dog barks: they bark loudly, deeply, and resonantly, in a way that can't be ignored. Our house isn't big, so we're never far from her barking. She's barking right now, in fact. If the phone rings, you can't hear what the caller says. If the radio or television is on, you won't catch that, either. But you can't stop the barking: lift her onto the sofa; take her off again; check her water dish; take her outside; through it all, with but a few minutes' respite, she will bark, and bark, and bark. And bark. Like a metronome. Sometimes, when we have dinner guests, we stash her, barking, in the car.

She was super-cute as a puppy. We chose her from the litter because she was the first to run to us and nuzzle our ankles;

though we quickly came to understand that food is her first and abiding passion, and she may simply have thought we had some to offer. Scent is the one sense really left to her, and she can still sniff out a candy bar in a closed handbag, or a cookie crumb underneath the fridge. It pleases her enormously to do so—the thrill of the hunt! And she can still thump her tail magnificently when caressed. We have adored her, and made much of her, lo these many years, and have overlooked some significant disadvantages (e.g., a lamentable penchant for coprophagy). Before we had kids, she slept on our bed; and latterly, in her great age, as she has taken up existential barking in the dead of night, she sleeps on our bed all over again, although now on a special (smelly) blanket at its foot, with a towel over her head.

Myshkin rules the roost; but Bear, too, has his ways. He was, when first he came to us, runty but beautiful, and restless. He could run like a gazelle, and, in the early months, skittish, took any chance to do so: he chomped through leashes and harnesses, he opened doors with his snout, he darted and feinted and fled. Half a dozen times we had to enlist bands of strangers—at the reservoir; on our block; in the parking lot at Target—to help catch him. You felt you got him in the end only because he let you. He could jump, too: one leap up onto the kitchen table, if you weren't looking, to eat a stick of butter. A single bound onto a wall, or down again. He was fearless.

I loved to walk him. I'll confess: I was vain about it. He was so dapper and elegant, so handsome and swift. After years of plodding along beside the plump-breasted dowager Myshkin, whose little legs and long body have dignity and power but not much élan (I've always maintained that dachshunds really do understand the absurdity of life), I was delighted to dash around the block in minutes, witness to Bear's graceful sashays. And I loved the compliments—he got so many compliments! A certain type of person loves a dachshund ("My grandmother used to have one of those; his name was Fritzie"); but anyone who tolerates dogs was taken by Bear. He had something about him, a star quality.

One late January evening in 2009, when my husband was out of town and a cousin was visiting, when I was in charge of the kids (then eight and five), the dinner, the dogs, and life, I took Bear for his twilight round. (It should be said that we've never been able to walk both dogs simultaneously, because their ideas of "a walk" differ so vastly.) Regrettably, I was multitasking: I had the dog, the bag of poo, and some letters to mail, and I was on the phone to my parents, who were then alive but ailing, and to whom I spoke every evening without fail. I'd almost finished the round of the block, was up on the main road at the mailbox, when, while trying to manipulate the leash, the poo, the phone, the letters, and the handle to the mailbox, I dropped the leash. It was the stretchy kind, its handle a large slab of red plastic; it made a noisy thud on the icy pavement.

Bear panicked, and bolted. I slammed my foot down on the leash. I was wearing clogs with ridged soles; the icy ground was uneven; and the leash, being the stretchy kind, was thin as a wire. I didn't catch it with my shoe. I stomped again, and again: too late. Bear dashed out into the rush-hour traffic. All my parents could hear down the dropped cell phone line was my long wail.

Being small, he was treated by Fate like a tumbleweed: having made it halfway across unscathed, he banged headlong into the bumper of a moving car on the far side of traffic, then rolled beneath it and out the other side. I recall only the headlights, made blurry by my tears, and the noise, in the encroaching dark; and seeing him, then, against the far curb, and hearing him howl.

I took him in my arms; his left eye protruded from his head as if on a stalk, or a spring—I thought, *How do cartoonists know this?*— and I cradled his little bloody head against my chest. I carried him down to our front porch, and sat with him on the step.

A woman, a stranger, whose car had been behind the one that hit Bear, had driven down my street. She had her two kids and her own dog in the car. She pulled over, and offered to help: she knew the way to the nearest veterinary hospital, whereas the one we'd used for Myshkin's gold-plated back operation several years before was forty-five minutes away, on the other side of town. She'd lead me there; I could follow in my car. I gestured at poor Bear—how could I simply put him on the seat beside me? He was shaking, almost convulsing. She, nameless Samaritan, offered me the company of her son.

That amazing child—a boy of perhaps eleven or so—sat in my car (a stranger's car) with Bear upon his lap (a pulpy, bloody thing, with an eye upon a stalk), and stroked the dog and whispered quietly to him as we crawled up the highway behind his mother in the rush-hour darkness to the hospital. (I had to leave my young cousin in charge of the kids. Thank goodness he was there. He was very amiable and unfussed about it, but I think supper was a bowl of cereal that night.)

The eye that had burst out couldn't be saved. The other they retained, though purely for cosmetic purposes: Bear can't see a thing. In the early days, he'd try to leap onto a piece of furniture that wasn't there—a wonderful sight in its way, to see him bounce high into the air and plop right back down—or he'd sit patiently facing a wall, his head slightly cocked, as if gazing upon a beautiful vista. Now he navigates the house as if he could see it all perfectly; unless we drop a suitcase in the hall, or move a chair.

The vet assured us that for a dog, sight is like taste or smell for humans, a secondary sense; and that Bear could lead a full and happy life without his eyes. Asked about the possibility of brain damage, she gave a wry smile: "Even if there is some, you won't be able to tell. It's not like he won't be able to do algebra anymore."

Tiresias-like, Bear is an inspiration, a teacher of how to make the best of things, how to enjoy what you have and not lament what you've lost. He has an aura of patient wisdom. No longer skittish, he no longer leaps; most painfully, he no longer runs. He tried, in the beginning, but a few sharp knocks subdued the urge. He's biddable, patient, and very sweet, largely content to let Myshkin order him about. (The only time they cuddle together is at the cageless kennel: we've seen photos, so we know it's true. At home, if he approaches her sofa, she'll growl at him.) I suffered grief and guilt after the accident; some part of me felt, too, that I was being punished for my vanity, for having been so proud of Bear's superficial charms.

I didn't mention earlier that the handsome Bear came to us with a fatal flaw. We suspect it may be why he ended up in that kill shelter in Georgia in the first place, when someone had clearly bothered to teach him to sit, to stay, even to stand on his hind legs. Bear is a widdler. When the postman comes—or the UPS guy, or the FedEx truck; and because we're book people, they, too, come almost daily—Bear erupts: he dashes to the door, hopping up and down in a fury; the hair on the back of his neck stands up; he roars for all he's worth and bares his tiny fangs. Unlike Myshkin, who has a grown-up bark, Bear has an awful, little-dog shriek, an indignity. And then, when he's danced around in his rage for a while, he all too often lifts his leg against a chair or sofa leg and sprinkles a few rebellious drops, just to make a point, sort of like flipping the finger at the guy at the door.

He did this from the first. We were working on training him out of it—a passionate young man came to the house to teach us how to think like a dog: re: the stick of butter: "Correction! He knows he's not supposed to do it *when you're in the room*. That's all"—but the training went down the tubes after the accident, apparently along with any memory of it. A bit of brain damage after all. We put a plastic sheet under the sofa nearest the front door, and that's been an improvement. Dismayingly, the vet has no other suggestions, though she shakes her head in sympathy. So in addition to the walking room-desanitizer that is Myshkin, we live, and our children are growing up, in a faint but persistent ammoniac fug.

So, to recap: we have the obstreperous, incessantly barking, stinky old deaf and blind dog who can't really stand up; and the completely blind pisser. Whenever we travel anywhere, they stay in a wonderful (spectacularly smelly) old house in Reading, where dogs are free to roam and a bevy of loving young women tend to their needs. It's like paying for a spa vacation for two extra kids. But we couldn't ask anyone else to take care of them: one animal virtually can't walk, the other ambles at his own sniffy pace (where once he looked always ahead and darted onward, Bear can now take half an hour to circle the block). One risks incontinence at unforeseen moments; the other, highly predictable in his incontinence, is virtually unstoppable. Myshkin needs to sleep with humans at night; Bear needs to go outside every three hours in the daytime. Who, we say, *who* could possibly put up with them?

As you can tell, we complain about our dogs. We berate the barking, perorate about the pissing, lament our enslavement, and throw up our hands at the bad smells. We curse when on our knees cleaning carpets; we curse when trying to quell the crazed barking at four in the morning; we curse when one or other of the dogs vomits yet again. My husband always jokes that a true vacation is when the dogs are in the kennel and we're at home without them. But we also stroke them and kiss them and hug them and worry about them. (My husband is always concerned that they're bored. Bear has grown quite stout from the snacks provided to alleviate his boredom, a beneficence I can't condone.) When we're in the house without them, we're baffled by the silence, and amazed by the free space and time (separate walks amount to seven or eight outings a day). We have, it's fair to say, a love-hate relationship with the animals.

This is where people have opinions. When you tell people about our canine situation, many can't believe it. They see it as our moral failing that the dogs are still alive. "Get rid of them," they urge scornfully. "What are you thinking?" We've been told that the dogs' behavior is a reflection upon our characters, that were we better alpha dogs ourselves, our pack wouldn't misbehave as they do. We've been told that we are weak, and that we owe it to our children to have these dogs put down. One friend even suggested that we're heartless to keep Myshkin going when she's lost so many of her faculties; although the vet, whom we visit repeatedly in hopes that she'll tell us when it's time, will give us divine dispensation, assures us that Myshkin is doing just great.

Then there are those on the other side. They don't just forgive us, they pat us gently on the back, offer quiet encouragement— "Good for you" or "It must be tough." Or they see it as hilarious, part of life's wondrous absurdity. Sometimes people even see it as an act of Christian charity. Or as a case of do-as-you-would-be-done-by. Or just plain old love. We prefer this, needless to say, to contempt and derision.

Really, of course, the difference is between those who believe that each of us controls our destiny and has a right to freedom; and those who don't. The former contend that we have the right, even the responsibility, to exert our wills, certainly over dumb animals, in order to maintain order and keep healthy boundaries. It's the only path to sanity, righteousness, and good action; and keeping these dogs in our lives is just sentimental claptrap. On the other hand are those who feel that life is a mucky muddle, in which unforeseen situations arise, and possibly endure; and that we must care as best we can for those around us, whatever befalls them, with faith that a similar mercy may be shown us in due course.

Before Myshkin was lame and foul and intolerable, she gave us years of affection and happiness. Even in her dotage, she's shown her love by inching ever closer, or by pushing her damp nose under our hands for a caress. For God's sake, she's shown it even by her barking. She waits up for her master to come home; she wakens us at dawn to start the day. And Bear: he's sweetness itself, except with the deliverymen and the sofa leg. If he can't prance or dart the way he did once; if he's no longer the most handsome dog in town; how, knowing what he suffered—and having caused that suffering, indeed—can I not love him the more?

We're torn, hoping for a deus ex machina that might liberate us from the discomforts they inflict upon us—my parents' dogs never barked obsessively, or peed in the house, which would give credence to those who say it's about our failure properly to lead the pack—but all the while we love their loyalty and generosity and, well, love. The dogs, after all, are the only people who are *always* glad to see us. Who are we to be anything but grateful for their affection and trust? Who are we to play God over them? And yet, what have we done all along but play God?

Or again: How does our strife with the dogs differ from our general strife? Could it not be said that our canine situation is simply our life situation? From deep in the doghouse, that's what it looks like to me.

HOW TO BE A BETTER WOMAN IN
THE TWENTY-FIRST CENTURY

Every Day, in Every Way, I'm Getting Better and Better . . .

—from a hypnosis self-esteem tape of the 1940s, as
reported by my mother

1. **Be Happy:** Count your blessings; meditate upon them; do not compare yourself to others (unless they are less fortunate than you); always look on the bright side; do not indulge in dark thoughts (if necessary, do not indulge in thought at all). You will feel better about yourself.

2. **Be Cool:** If you don't have something nice to say, don't say anything; be compassionate; be patient; listen to others, but don't talk too much; avoid being boring; avoid being funny (this may make some uncomfortable); avoid being odd (ditto); avoid honesty if necessary (ditto); don't lose your temper; ideally, don't have a temper. People will like you more, and you will feel better about yourself.

3. **Be Healthy:** Don't drink; don't smoke; don't take drugs (except antidepressants, which don't count); don't overeat; consume primarily green vegetables and pulses; avoid dairy; avoid carbohydrates; avoid red meat; avoid sugar (like the plague); avoid gluten; avoid mercury-tainted fish; avoid all but organic chicken; avoid pesticides; take regular exercise and enjoy it (it will work better if you enjoy it); don't carry any extra weight; don't stress; always wear sunscreen; always moisturize; always sleep seven hours and thirteen minutes every night; avoid ingesting chemicals; avoid getting wrinkles; avoid going gray; avoid getting saggy; avoid yellowing teeth; avoid all potential unattractiveness. You will not get sick, you will not age, and you might never die; people will admire you more; and you will feel better about yourself.

4. **Be Environmentally Aware:** Recycle; bicycle; walk; run (carry small children on your back or front; or place them in a small cart or contraption that will enable you to bicycle, walk, or run; try not to be afraid that they will be crushed by other vehicles); avoid driving (unless you have an electric car); avoid flying; avoid plastics; avoid genetic modifications; compost; grow your own vegetables (but not tomatoes, which waste water); install solar panels; use fluorescent bulbs (even though their light is ugly); avoid excess; avoid waste; avoid clutter; avoid paper; avoid. You will not save the planet (this is alas impossible at this late stage) but you may infinitesimally slow its destruction. You will feel righteous; people will admire you more; and you will feel better about yourself.

5. **Be Efficient:** Do not waste time; do not waste space; do not waste energy; do not talk to strangers; do not take naps; do not sleep in; do not stay up late; do not go shopping; do not take rambling strolls; do not have long conversations, on the phone or

in person; do not write letters; do not read books that have no clear purpose; do not major in English (or in any other humanities subject) in college; do not write by hand; do not make pointlessly elaborate meals; do not iron; do not procrastinate; do not daydream (if possible, do not dream); do not eat pointless foods (e.g., ice cream, radishes); do not pursue random tangents; do not read newspapers; do not read long magazine articles; do keep up with Facebook, Instagram, and Twitter, as they will give you all the information necessary for any brief social interactions you may have. Your efficiency will liberate you to take more exercise and meditate more. You will be seen to be efficient, and people will be impressed by you. You will feel better about yourself.

6. **Be Rich:** Invent an app; be a venture capitalist; be a Hollywood executive; be a movie star; be a pop star; start a clothing line; be a lifestyle guru; be a celebrity dermatologist; be a celebrity plastic surgeon; be a celebrity chef; be a celebrity professor; be a real housewife celebrity; be a member of a royal family; be a celebrity. If possible, be a green energy mogul; be a health and diet expert; be a politically engaged movie star or pop star; be rich while doing good. Avoid janitorial work; avoid manual labor; avoid manufacturing; avoid teaching; avoid caring professions; avoid medical work in unglamorous or dangerous places (e.g., inner cities; Liberia); avoid service industries; avoid literary or journalistic production; avoid research projects the outcomes of which are uncertain; avoid anything that pays little or seems ordinary. If you are rich, people will know you are successful. You will feel better about yourself.

7. **Be Good:** Don't have bad thoughts; don't do bad things; don't doubt; don't question; don't make trouble; don't be emotionally demanding; don't be socially awkward; don't be sharp-tongued and shrewish; don't be judgmental; don't be rude; don't be weird; don't be silly; don't be awful; don't "be yourself"; don't pretend to be someone you're not; don't be pretentious; don't be falsely humble; don't be lonely; don't be sad; don't be pessimistic; don't be grumpy; don't be alienated; don't be uncomfortable; don't be weary; don't be garrulous; don't be intolerant; don't be radical; don't be conservative; don't be greedy. Just don't. Ideally, you will meditate away the illusion of a self and then will both be very good and feel best about yourself.

TEENAGE GIRLS

When I was growing up, my family moved across cities and continents: By the time I was twelve, I'd had eight different homes in three countries and had attended five different schools. In each new situation, I aimed to keep my head down, learn the ropes, and fit in as best I could, though my cheeks still grow hot at the recollection of awkward interactions now thirty-five years behind me. My daughter Livia's childhood, by contrast, has been pretty stable: We've lived within the same five-mile radius of Cambridge, Massachusetts, since she was two, and she attended a single school for most of her childhood. Her classmates became like extended family: She had her close gang, but she knew and got along with everyone. They all bumbled through childhood side by side.

Then we left to spend her fourth-grade year in Berlin, where my husband and I had fellowships. There Livia and her younger brother attended an enormous bilingual public school, a long bus ride from our apartment. The adventure posed some challenges (the children spoke no German to begin with, nor did we know a soul when we arrived), but ultimately, the kids loved their time there, reveling in their independence and their friendships.

Coming home proved the hard part—not least because none of

us imagined it would be. Unusually for their Cambridge school, no new girls entered Livia's fifth-grade class. As her teacher eventually suggested, this may have been why the others treated Livia as if she were one. Certain early-teenage dynamics had to play out somehow, as the teacher saw it; the pack needed an outsider, a scapegoat, and Livia was the closest thing they could find.

While we were away, change had come over the girls like a spreading virus. For some—though not for many—proportions and features had altered: breasts budded and hips curved, or legs grew coltishly long. All the kids touched by puberty were self-conscious: some dressed coquettishly, their faces made-up, sizing up the boys with sneers and titters—while others hid in extra-large sweatshirts, postured like question marks to hide their new shapes. Then there were those still waiting (with dread or eagerness, depending) for their transformation. With these physical changes came tacit classification, a poisonous hierarchy of cool: a few months into fifth grade, Livia could have written out the class pecking order without pausing to think.

We had no intimation that this was coming. Over Labor Day weekend, I took Livia and her close lifelong friend, whom I'll call Jennifer, to an amusement park, where they tore around for hours. On the car ride home, they laughed, joked, and sang along to the radio, and chatted about what school would be like.

A couple of days later, when I dropped Livia in the playground and walked her brother into his classroom (he was still small enough then not just to permit but to enjoy this), I watched her approach a giggling circle of girls that included Jennifer. Walking back a few minutes later, I saw to my surprise that Livia still hovered awkwardly outside the circle: Nobody, including her best friend since nursery school, had widened the group to let her in.

My impulse, hard to overcome, was to go over and say something—after all, I'd known Jennifer all her life. But I remembered with a sick feeling the codes of youth and knew that I could only make things worse.

Thus began a season of torment for our beloved daughter. She began to question everything about herself. Why did Jennifer shun her? Jennifer tauntingly wouldn't say, and nobody else would explain. What had Livia done wrong? Was she not interesting enough? Not cool enough? Not pretty enough? Not thin enough? Not grown-up enough? Did she have the wrong clothes? Did she make the wrong jokes? Did she talk too much, too little, at the wrong times? Why, she kept wondering, why was this happening?

On the sidelines, I suffered my impotence, furious at rosy-cheeked Jennifer—with her glossy brown hair in its high pony, her second-skin leggings, and her insolent smirks. Furious, too, at her gaggle of friends, who took their cue from Jennifer and pretended not to know Livia. I'd seen friends' children, at other schools, wilt and shrivel under the pressure of their peers' unkindness. I'd read books about what today's teenage girls go through—struggles familiar from my own youth, such as eating disorders and depression, but also self-harm, in various upsetting forms. Then there were new and terrifying things. With the advent of cyberbullying, too often there are stories of this kind of behavior being taken to extremes, even leading to children taking their own lives. I couldn't barge into Livia's newly developing private life—I remembered the moms who read my friends' diaries, and I'd always been grateful that my own mother didn't—but I wanted her to know that I was at the ready, should she want me. I pointed out the advantages of some of Livia's other friends, straightforward, kind girls who cared more about swimming or science than lululemon and lip gloss, and I urged her to carry a book to school in the mornings so that she'd never be alone on the playground.

In my heart, I recalled with dread an experience from my own adolescence that has always haunted me. Jane, as I'll call her, was a childhood friend: we'd been at school together in Sydney from our earliest days until my family left for Canada after fourth grade. Well into my teenage years, I kept in touch with my Sydney friends by writing letters—this was many years ago, in the era of pen pals—and through letters from several of them I learned about what had happened to Jane.

Fierce, fair, small-boned, with enormous blue eyes, she'd never been one of my closest friends; but our all-girl school was small, and we all went to one another's birthday parties with the general bonhomie of family relations. In my last year at the school, I wrote a little play about kids who find treasure in a cave at the beach (strongly influenced by Enid Blyton's Famous Five series), and we performed it one afternoon for the whole elementary school. Jane had a big part—she was the star—and a lot of lines to memorize. During the performance, she jumbled them up and jumped from a moment well before the climax to almost the end. As a result, the play made little sense to the audience (it probably didn't make much sense anyway, but I didn't see that at the time), and the teachers, who'd canceled the last class of the day for it, were annoyed that my supposedly fifteen-minute play had lasted only half that time.

I, in turn, embarrassed in front of the teachers, spoke sharply to Jane (along the lines of, "How could you?"), and I remember my amazement at her confidence: She wasn't remotely flustered or ashamed to have messed up. She told me my play was stupid anyhow, and that she hadn't made it any more stupid by leaving some of it out. Imagine being so strong, I remember marveling, and so sure of oneself.

Jane's home life was always a bit mysterious: Her mother was, as I recall, younger than most of the other mothers, and she wasn't friendly with them. I never saw her father (though in those days, fathers were often invisible). Jane didn't have kids to her house to play, and I assumed it was because she lived somewhere small or because her mother worked, which was rare then. I remember that her birthday parties didn't include the whole class; I don't believe I ever went to one.

What my classmates, my pen pals, told me was this: By the time she was fourteen, Jane's relationship with her parents— her mother specifically—had grown particularly difficult. They fought all the time, one girl wrote to me, though she didn't say what they fought about. As one friend told it, Jane learned that her father wasn't her biological father, and somehow found out who this other man was and where he lived. Then she ran away to Queensland, about six hundred miles from her home in Sydney, to meet him. She showed up on his doorstep only for him to say that he didn't want to know her. She hitchhiked home, quarreled with her parents, and ran away all over again. For days nobody knew where she had gone.

Eventually, this same friend told me, her body was found in a cave along the shore in Sydney's Eastern Suburbs, not far from our school. Like something out of Enid Blyton but sinister rather than exciting, the cave filled with seawater at high tide. Jane had hidden inside, taken sleeping pills, and eventually drowned.

Far away in Canada, I assembled only fragments of fragments of the story, the shards narrated in my friends' letters, their own knowledge partial. What did their parents hear and not repeat to them? What did nobody know? The full truth of what occurred remained known only to Jane herself, who could never tell. (Recent research suggests that many of these details may have been embroidered, or at least that they were not public knowledge.) I made things up, inventing fictions to satisfy my own doubt and curiosity, my own desire to understand her unimaginable, nonsensical fate.

By the time I read our friends' letters, Jane had already for weeks, maybe more than a month, ceased to be. She no longer breathed or laughed or slept. But I remembered her so vividly—the timbre of her voice, the exquisite fineness of her shiny blond hair, the near-translucence of her elfin hands. We'd spent most of each day together from the age of four onward. I knew what she had for lunch (often what we called "fairy sandwiches," white bread filled with margarine and sprinkles). I knew she wasn't especially good at classes and didn't like to read aloud and that doing sports made her turn alarmingly red. I knew her gestures and her humors and how to make her laugh.

In fourth grade, this was what it meant to know someone; but in the space of a few years, she'd turned into someone—a teenager—that I not only didn't know but couldn't connect to the girl I'd thought I'd known. That stranger, not the Jane I knew, had thought her own life not worth saving.

We don't have easy ways to articulate the confusion and dismay that can accompany the great upheaval of childhood when the faith that we know ourselves and one another evaporates. Three decades after I'd thought I'd known Jane, I watched Livia traverse the thorny ground where we realize that how others see us doesn't necessarily correspond to who we think we are. We come to accept that other people may not experience what we do, and that, most painfully, we will never truly know what they experience. I could see so much from the vantage of age, but I couldn't fix a thing for her. As a mother, you want above all to shoulder the burden of your child's suffering, but all you can do is reassure her that the best is yet to be.

As things turned out, Jennifer eventually moved away. Livia ended up being friendly for a time with a couple of the girls who'd been part of the forbidding circle that September morning, but I could never trust them and kept a wary eye until Livia moved on again. She passed through a rootless period, flitting from group to group, the social configurations ever changing, like a restless cat trying and failing to find a comfortable place to rest. In ninth grade, Livia changed schools and found affirmation and ease with her new friends.

Years later, Livia still doesn't understand why her friend Jennifer turned on her, and honestly, nor do I. We can invent explanations, but they're just that—inventions. As the teacher suggested, it probably had little to do with Livia herself, and more to do with what happened in Jennifer's life during Livia's absence. Similarly, none of us from my class in Sydney will ever understand why Jane committed suicide, although we've all created explanatory narratives that enable us to sleep at night, to separate ourselves from the particular dread and isolation that drove so fierce a girl to such a desperate act.

I never did say to Livia, "If losing Jennifer is your hardest middle school experience, you'll be lucky," but I couldn't help but think it, recalling Jane's fate, and the troubled fates—not fatal, but so painful and so permanently damaging—of many girls I've known, whose crossing from childhood to womanhood has cost them dearly. I could only whisper from my distant maternal perch, "You're not alone," and hope that in the midst of it all, she could hear me.

THE TIME FOR ART IS NOW

In these relentlessly dark and riven times, I find myself beset by a near-ravenous hunger for beauty. My spirit lurches at a line of Shakespeare or Louise Glück—"All fear gives way: the light / Looks after you . . ." My eyes linger on the photographs of Nadav Kander, the paintings of Marlene Dumas, the sculptures of Sarah Sze. I reassure myself of the possibility of serenity by recalling Willa Cather's masterpiece, *Death Comes for the Archbishop*, or by listening to the extraordinary voice of Hannah Reid, the vocalist of London Grammar. I long for that expansion of my soul.

We have so much to learn. The ideals that have shaped my entire life thus far have been called into question by the election of this so-called president. They are ideals worth fighting for: a faith, as Martin Luther King assured us, that the long arc of history bends toward justice; that societies have the desire and capacity for improvement; that reflection and communication will foster greater compassion; and a belief that one of the most powerful paths to progress is through art and literature. I have believed in the value of knowledge and of truth. And I have believed that the quality of a life is not measured by money, celebrity, or material goods but by richness of mind, generosity of spirit, and by meaningful human relationships.

Along with these beliefs comes an endlessly renewed (and renewable) joy in the superfluous. By which I mean the things which thrill and enchant, delight and inspire, move and hold us rarely fall into the category of the necessary. I'm not making light of the necessary—food, water, shelter, health, employment, companionship—without which we manifestly can't survive. But what makes us human is our capacity for memory, for laughter, for passion, for grief, and for joy.

Ours is a bleakly utilitarian era. Every act, it seems, must be overtly purposeful, its value measurable, or else we deem it dispensable, a waste of time. Between the demands of social media (and our constant sense of inadequacy in the face of the thousands, nay millions, whose lives appear—often falsely—more orderly, productive, and impressive than our own) and the lessons disseminated by our culture and its so-called leaders (for example, that monetary wealth is the ultimate goal), we risk losing sight of what makes existence meaningful. None of us needs a mansion or a fat bank account. None of us is made fundamentally happier by a private jet, a drawer full of diamonds, a television show, or a YouTube channel. Nor does watching others accumulate these things enhance our own lives. Capitalism hoodwinks us daily. The stuff we buy, thinking it will improve our lot, proves to be bullshit—as is made evident from overflowing donation boxes at the Goodwill. These are the products of a culture of greed and self-interest. They dull us to our society's injustices and distract us from fighting against them.

But where might we find joy? Joy lies in immaterial superfluity. I find it in the long hours spent reading a book. I make this suggestion advisedly: to watch a film or a video is not the same satisfaction; when reading a book you create, for yourself, from marks upon a page, an entire, vivid interior world. You are spurred, of course, by the author, but the text is, in its particulars, uniquely and fully your own. Or you might find it in communing with a painting, sculpture, or installation until you feel you're part of it, or it is part of you. Or in lying in a summer field looking up at the dusk sky unfolding from palest pink to indigo, the awakening of the stars. Or in what Christopher Hitchens used to call "the ruined table"—the afternoon or evening lost in eager conversation long after the meal is finished, best enjoyed surrounded by empty bottles, dirty plates, and crumbs. Or in an afternoon ramble without direction or a timepiece, or in an evening spent listening to music—any music, anywhere.

There's no clear point to any of these things: they don't make money or burn calories or help you network or make you famous. They make you human. No robot will ever replicate the twinge behind my sternum or the filling of my throat when I hear particular phrases of Chopin or the Beatles; nor the lifting of my heart at a line from Keats or Elizabeth Bishop; nor the delicious emotional recognition of a scene in Proust or a Frederick Wiseman film. The moments that matter most often occur in our minds or imaginations. They may remain unarticulated, never breaking the surface of our lives, and yet they prove communicable nonetheless. That's what art can do; it's why art matters.

We must struggle to change our institutions, but our resistance to the depravity and depletion of these times must go beyond that. It must also occur in our souls. We are animals, and we must not forget that we live in our bodies; but we are animals blessed with memory and language. Each of us can create unprecedented beauty. We can transmit, even if imperfectly, the contents of our imaginations. We can learn from what has come before, and from what surrounds us. We are not doomed. As Shakespeare has it in *King Lear*, "the worst is not / So long as we can say 'This is the worst.'"

There is glory in each day, for each of us. It is waiting to be illuminated and observed. Auden wrote that poetry makes nothing happen, but in our hearts and in our lives, we know that is not true. Art has the power to alter our interior selves, and in so doing to inspire, exhilarate, provoke, connect, and rouse us. As we are changed, our souls are awakened to possibility—immeasurable, yes, and potentially infinite. If ever there was a time for art, it's now.

PART TWO

Criticism: Books

Three Essays on Camus and His Legacy

⚘

CAMUS AND ALGERIA:
THE MORAL QUESTION

"What a misfortune is the one of a man without a
city." "Oh make it so that I will not be without a city,"
the choir said [in *Medea*]. I am without a city.
—Albert Camus, *Notebooks, 1951–1959*

O ne Christmas when I was in my early twenties, my mother,
my sister, and I returned home from midnight services
to find my deeply private and resolutely lapsed father watching
John Paul II's mass at St. Peter's on television, his face wet with
tears. Distressed to see him thus, we asked why he was crying.
"Because when I last heard the mass in Latin," he replied, "I
thought I had a religion, and I thought I had a country." My father,
like Albert Camus, was a *pied-noir*, a French Algerian. Eighteen
years Camus's junior, he grew up in Bab el Oued, a working-class
neighborhood of Algiers not unlike Camus's Belcourt. There was
no money, but my grandfather was an officer in the navy. Camus's
father was killed early in World War I when his son was a year old,
and he and his brother were raised by their mother, who was illiterate and almost deaf, their fierce grandmother, and their largely
mute barrel-maker uncle.

My father, like Camus, attended the Lycée Bugeaud, where

Jacques Derrida was his classmate ("I always did better than him in philosophy," my father said), and the *faculté*, where he studied law. In 1952, he departed for the United States on a Fulbright scholarship—the list of French recipients that year shows him to be the lone student from Algeria—and thereafter he would always live in exile, in France, Australia, or North America. But surely he left home without appreciating that it would prove impossible to return.

My grandfather, just eight years older than Camus, hailed from still more modest origins in Blida, southwest of Algiers. His mother, an elementary school teacher and the daughter of an illiterate *garçon de café*, raised four children alone. The youngest, my grandfather, was, like Camus, a beneficiary of the meritocratic French education system of the period, and made his way from remote poverty to the prestigious École Polytechnique in Paris, after which he entered the navy as a career officer. A devout Catholic and passionate French patriot, he also adored his native Algeria: letters between my grandparents wax as lyrical about their beloved landscapes as they do about each other.

Nobody in my family ever spoke about the Algerian War. They told many stories about the 1930s and 1940s, when my father and aunt were children; but of what happened later, they were silent. In 1955, my grandfather took a position in Rabat, Morocco, and my grandparents did not live in Algeria again. In the late 1950s, when the war in Algeria was at its most fevered and vicious, my father was doing graduate work on Turkey at the Center for Middle Eastern Studies at Harvard: after his death, among his papers from that period, I found files of clippings on political upheavals in Egypt, Lebanon, Syria, Pakistan, India, Morocco, Libya, in addition to Turkey—but not one word about his homeland. My father's lonely tears twenty-five years ago were, as far as I know, his only expression of emotion about what happened.

On July 5, 2012, Algeria celebrated fifty years of independence from France. When Albert Camus perished in a car accident near Sens on January 4, 1960, at the age of forty-six, two and a half years before the Évian Accords that ended the war, he had become a figure of contempt and scorn for both the left and the right, seen as simultaneously naïve and dogmatic in his persistent hope for a moderate Algerian solution. As late as 1958, Camus wrote that his aim was to "achieve the only acceptable future: a future in which France, wholeheartedly embracing its tradition of liberty, does justice to all the communities of Algeria without discrimination in favor of one or another."

November 7, 2013, marked Camus's centenary. The artist and essayist—the author of *L'Étranger* (1942) and *L'Homme révolté* (1951)—has consistently held the reading public's admiration and imagination. But his attitudes on the Algerian question—excoriated by his contemporaries on all sides, and subsequently by critics as diverse as Conor Cruise O'Brien and Edward Said—remain controversial.

The publication in 2013, for the first time in English, of Camus's *Algerian Chronicles*, edited and introduced by Alice Kaplan and beautifully translated by Arthur Goldhammer, affords Camus the belated opportunity to make his own case to the Anglophone public. This book, in slightly different form, proved his final public word on the Algerian question when it was originally published in June 1958. Ending two and a half years of public silence that followed his failed call for a civilian truce in Algiers in January 1956—a silence that became, according to Kaplan, "a metonymy for cowardice" but that my relatives would have recognized as agony—*Algerian Chronicles* was published in France in 1958 to "widespread critical silence."

The lack of interest that greeted the book can be attributed in part to its publication fast upon the heels of Henri Alleg's *The Question*, the vivid and disturbing autobiographical account of the author's torture in the Barberousse prison in Algiers, an immediate best seller subsequently suppressed by the French authorities. This book, and the debates that arose from it, greatly affected French public opinion on the war; and it was, thereafter, impossible to ignore the facts about the French military's use of torture.

The Question was followed, a year later, by *The Gangrene*, an anthology comprised of the accounts of seven young Algerian intellectuals and students tortured by French authorities in Paris. This book, like Alleg's, was rapidly suppressed in France, and was translated into English by Robert Silvers, the founding and longtime editor of the *New York Review of Books*. As the American publisher Lyle Stuart wrote in his introduction to the U.S. edition:

> The tortures described in this book didn't take place on a lonely country road three miles from a primitive village. . . . They happened in the heart of Paris, France. They happened eight months after General Charles de Gaulle assumed power . . . less than three hundred yards from the Elysée Palace.

Camus had ceased to seem a relevant spokesman on the subject: he had been, in his youth, at the vanguard in his attempts to bring to public attention the plight of native Algerians, but it seemed to many that he had, throughout the 1950s, fallen out of touch with the realities of his homeland. This was not a matter of inattention or lack of commitment; it resulted, rather, from a worldview that could not conceive of an Algeria that was not French. When, in the midst of the atrocities—both by the French and the Algerians—as many around Camus came to accept the inevitability of an independent Algeria, and his beloved lycée teacher and mentor Jean Grenier pondered Algeria's fate were France to abandon it, Camus fiercely insisted: "She cannot, because she could never agree to throw one million, two hundred thousand Frenchmen into the sea."

Algerian Chronicles assembles twenty years of Camus's writings on Algeria, from his reporting on poverty in Kabylia for the *Alger républicain* in June 1939 to his call in 1956 for a civilian truce, first mooted in his column in *L'Express* and subsequently presented to the people of Algiers in a rowdy and poignantly disastrous town meeting on January 22 of that year. The selection is rounded out by his 1958 preface to the collection itself, and includes various illuminating appendices.

To witness the progression of his responses is to recognize above all the remarkable consistency of Camus's moral conviction, the dogged optimism of his outlook, and his unfailing ability, even in the complex turmoil of emotional involvement with the issue, to cleave to his own principles of justice. The positions that he took on Algeria in the 1950s can be anticipated not simply in his reporting from Kabylia, but in philosophical positions and notebook entries from very early on—as, for example, in his early pacifist tendencies when working on the *Alger républicain* in 1939; or in his open letter of 1948 to Emmanuel d'Astier de la Vigerie: "I merely say that we must refuse all legitimacy to violence, whether it comes from *raison d'état* or totalitarian philosophy. *Violence is both unavoidable and unjustifiable*."

There is little distance from this to his 1958 preface, in which he reminds the French that "we must refuse to justify these methods [reprisals and torture] on any grounds whatsoever, including effectiveness. Once one begins to justify them, even indirectly, no rules or values remain." And by the same token, he addresses the Front de Libération Nationale (FLN), the movement for Algerian independence: "No matter what cause one defends, it will suffer permanent disgrace if one resorts to blind attacks on crowds of innocent people." If criticism is to be effective, he continues, "both camps must be condemned."

Along with them, he chastises armchair intellectuals (implicitly pointing a finger at Jean-Paul Sartre) who endorse terrorist violence from afar:

> Each side thus justifies its own actions by pointing to the crimes of its adversaries. This is a casuistry of blood with which intellectuals should, I think, have nothing to do, unless they are prepared to take up arms themselves.

It was this moral lucidity that had provoked Camus's disenchantment with communism and underpinned his ardent opposition to the death penalty, a stance that prompted him to speak out, at different times, to save the lives of Nazi collaborators and FLN terrorists alike.

What changed, of course, was not Camus but the situation in Algeria. His 1939 visit to Kabylia—a mountainous region in northern Algeria populated by Berbers—exposed him to conditions of famine and destitution previously unimagined. Like

Chekhov visiting Sakhalin, he was profoundly affected by the suffering he witnessed. His impassioned articles are full of facts ("a family of eight needs approximately 120 kilos of wheat for just one month's worth of bread. I was told that the indigents I saw had to make their 10 kilos last the entire month") and radical proposals: "They will have more schools on the day that the artificial barrier between European and indigenous schools is removed."

In the event, this series did not contribute to any change in government policy. Rather, along with his other articles, it resulted in the shuttering of the *Alger républicain* and the effective expulsion of Camus from Algeria to Paris after March 1940.

When Camus again turned his journalist's eye to the subject of his homeland, it was in *Combat*, his Resistance newspaper in Paris, following the uprising that began in Sétif on May 8, 1945—the incident that essentially marked the beginning of the Algerian War (although there was no further violence until 1954). According to Alistair Horne in *A Savage War of Peace*, over five days in and around Sétif, 103 Europeans were murdered and 100 wounded; "many of the corpses were appallingly mutilated: women with their breasts slashed off, men with their severed sexual organs stuffed into their mouths."

The repression and reprisals by the French military claimed a far greater number of casualties: estimates varied from around thirteen hundred to an astounding forty-five thousand. As the poet Kateb Yacine recalled: "I was sixteen years old. The shock which I felt at the pitiless butchery that caused the deaths of thousands of Muslims, I have never forgotten. From that moment my nationalism took definite form."

While the details of these events were little reported in

France, Camus nevertheless devoted a series of articles to the "Crisis in Algeria." He once again laid out the distressing economic conditions, alarming statistics, and history of famine that underpinned the Algerians' call for freedom, pointing out, furthermore, that many Algerians had only recently fought for France. He denounced France's failure to make good on its long-standing official goal of assimilation and citizenship for all Arabs in Algeria, and warned that "if you are unwilling to change quickly enough, you lose control of the situation."

Camus concluded by endorsing the moderate Algerian leader Ferhat Abbas and his Party of the Manifesto, who called for an Algerian constitution and assembly; and, typically, by emphasizing the demands of justice: "We must convince ourselves that in North Africa as elsewhere, we will preserve nothing that is French unless we preserve justice as well."

Between 1945 and 1954, when the FLN was established (the name of the party, incidentally, that has ruled Algeria to this day), the Muslim population of Algeria became more and more radical in its demands, and moved inexorably toward revolution and a call for independence. Tellingly, perhaps, it was during this time that Camus, disillusioned by Stalinism, wrote *L'Homme révolté* (*The Rebel*), in which he questioned accepted accounts of revolution (including France's), and argued that all modern revolutions have ended up reinforcing the state's authority.

By the time of Camus's "Letter to an Algerian Militant" in October 1955, addressed to Aziz Kessous, an Algerian socialist and former member of the Party of the Manifesto (i.e., a radicalized former moderate), all sides were reeling from the horrors of the Philippeville massacre, a terrorist ambush on August 20,

1955, in which seventy-one Europeans and fifty-two Muslims died. It was followed by brutal French reprisals (according to the French, 1,273 Muslims were killed; according to the FLN, the number was 12,000). The Philippeville events prompted the conversion to the cause of French domination of the formerly liberal governor-general of Algeria, Jacques Soustelle; he wrote that for the Algerians of both races it was a terrible Rubicon over which there was to be no return.

Camus, in his letter to Kessous, lamented that "Algeria is where I hurt at this moment, as others feel pain in their lungs," a telling analogy from one who suffered from tuberculosis. He argued, still, for the peace that Soustelle could no longer envisage. "Bloodshed may sometimes lead to progress, but more often it brings only greater barbarity and misery," he warned, and in spite of the violence, held out his hand to Kessous: "I will be told, as you will be told, that the time for compromise is over and that the goal now must be to wage war and win. But you and I both know that there will be no real winners in this war. . . ."

By this relatively early juncture in 1955, Camus, in his beautiful, obdurate optimism, had parted company with reality. While he continued to believe that "the dream that the French will suddenly disappear is childish" and that there "will be no real winners in this war," the FLN was determined to attain independence by all necessary means. By September 1956, it was official FLN policy to attack civilians. One of its leaders, Ramdane Abane, said that "one corpse in a jacket is always worth more than twenty in uniform." Urban bombings became widespread.

At the same time, after Philippeville, the *pieds-noirs* were given permission to bear arms, thereby escalating levels of fear and violence; by late 1956, the right-wing terrorism sponsored by the French officers and activists who later formed the Organisation de l'armée secrète (OAS) was under way; and by January 1957, General Massu had been granted unlimited military control over the city of Algiers. Torture of Algerians and of European dissidents—such as Alleg, author of *The Question*—became commonplace; the FLN engaged in torture as well.

By the time of Camus's final public effort, his simple and heartfelt call for a civilian truce, in late January 1956, the situation in Algeria was irredeemably bitter:

> What do we want? We want the Arab movement and the French authorities, without entering into contact with each other or making any other commitment, to declare simultaneously that as long as the troubles continue, civilian populations will at all times be respected and protected.

This plea was met with resounding indifference on both sides; and following this failure any public position at all became, for Camus, untenable. As the Tunisian Jewish writer Albert Memmi wrote in late 1957:

> Camus has been forced to become silent because everything about North Africa paralyzes him. . . . It must be understood that his situation is by no means easy; it is not intellectually or emotionally easy to have all of one's family on a side that is morally condemned.

And from his contemporary perspective, Camus's biographer Robert Zaretsky eloquently observes:

> Camus' silence over the war ravaging his native Algeria, the source of nearly all his images of worldly beauty, did not transcend ethics. Instead, it flowed from his recognition that the humiliated were on both sides in this conflict: the great majority of *pieds-noirs* as well as Arabs.

Camus's honesty and consistency retain, in retrospect, a moral purity that few others could claim. He saw that "the era of colonialism is over," but felt that "the only problem now is to draw the appropriate consequences"—in this case, a moderate solution that would provide rights for all members of the society, including his own community.

Next to Camus, his peers seem cynical at best: Sartre and Simone de Beauvoir celebrated the FLN—as they had celebrated Stalin—from the comfortable remove of their Paris cafés. Raymond Aron's approach to the crisis was to produce a cost-benefit analysis proving that the colony was no longer a financially workable proposition for France and hence should be abandoned. The French military and government were responsible for acts of torture and violence that would irreparably compromise France's honor. And when Camus approached the great De Gaulle to propose the simple solution of French citizenship for all Algerians—this in March 1958, two months before the general retook power having used, among others, the slogan "We are all Frenchmen, from Dunkirk to Tamanrasset!"—De Gaulle report·dly scoffed, "Right, and we'll have fifty *bougnoules* [a racial slur] in the Chamber of Deputies."

In fact, Camus's plea for a truce was not entirely ignored. Germaine Tillion was a French anthropologist and writer who, like Camus, had spent time among the indigenous Algerians in the 1930s, in her case researching a doctorate on the tribes of the Aurès Mountains. Sent back to Algeria in 1954 by François Mitterrand (then minister of the interior), she produced a report on the conditions of Muslim life that was in harmony with Camus's perspective (*Algeria: The Realities*, published in English in 1958). Tillion was called, in June 1957, eighteen months after Camus's appeal, to a clandestine meeting with the FLN's leader, Saadi Yacef. As a result of their intense, four-hour discussion, she was charged with proposing to the French government (briefly, in that unstable moment, the Bourgès-Maunoury administration) a bilateral civilian truce.

As proof of his goodwill, Yacef agreed that the FLN would avoid all civilian casualties for a month—which, in spite of bombings by the FLN during that time, it did. Tillion, who approached De Gaulle as well as the government, returned empty-handed, and met again fruitlessly with Yacef in early August. He wrote to her: "We are totally responsible for what we do. But, alas, in your family, what is its line of conduct? One never knows. When we believe that at last reason is going to prevail, we are, alas, destined for a disappointment."

The French journalist Jean Daniel, himself of *pied-noir* origin, broke with Camus in the late 1950s over their differing views on Algeria's fate. Daniel had come to accept the need to negotiate with the FLN and the call for independence, whereas Camus could not. When Daniel told Camus that Algerian independence was "ineluctable," the latter replied:

What can that possibly mean for a journalist, even an engaged one, or for an intellectual? By what right do you decide the direction of history? The term "ineluctable" is reserved for the spectators who resign themselves to their own impotence to prevent the advent of what, at bottom, they hope for and to which they are already resigned.[*]

Daniel attributes Camus's intractability on the Algerian question to two fundamental issues: "On the one hand, poverty, and on the other, terror." Camus's profound rejection of terrorist violence is obvious in all that he said and wrote on Algeria, not least in his famous (and often misquoted) exchange with the Algerian student in Stockholm, where he said, "People are now planting bombs in the tramways of Algiers. My mother might be on one of those tramways. If that is justice, then I prefer my mother." Acutely sensible to pain and suffering, Camus could not condone it anywhere: "I am not made for politics," he wrote in his notebooks in November 1945, "because I am incapable of wanting or accepting the death of the adversary."

Daniel's other point is less frequently made, but just as important. Someone from circumstances as humble as Camus's "cannot consider himself the inheritor of a long history of colonial oppression. He is humiliated, oppressed, exploited like the other little poor people."

I would go further still. As a fatherless child of poverty, like my own grandfather, Camus was taken in hand by crucial pater-

---

[*]   Jean Daniel, *Avec Camus: Comment résister à l'air du temps* (Paris: Gallimard, 2006), p. 66. My translation.

nal figures: first by his schoolteachers, Louis Germain (who pressed his grandmother to allow the young Camus to attend the lycée rather than going to work) and, at the lycée, Jean Grenier, to whom he would remain gratefully indebted all his life, and to whom he would dedicate both his first book, *L'Envers et l'endroit* (1937), and *L'Homme révolté*.

Through these teachers, it was France itself that lifted the most humble from their poverty and afforded them every opportunity: it was France that made them. For my grandfather—the very opposite of *"l'homme révolté"*—there is no question that the French republic was a kind of father. In joining the navy, he was able to serve that father faithfully. For Camus, to be the rebellious child of France made him no less its passionate son. Writing about Camus's influence at the end of the war, Tony Judt in *The Burden of Responsibility* nicely describes the writer's tone: "It combined a traditional, romantic view of France and her possibilities with Camus's own reputation for personal integrity." Camus's traditional idealization of France as perhaps flawed in its actions but fundamentally noble in its intent did not waver, even in the face of the Algerian uprising. Daniel argues that "both [Tillion and Camus] were convinced that you couldn't exclude the possibility of erasing the sin of colonization with sincere repentance and extensive reparations."

Daniel's use of the terminology of sin and redemption is not irrelevant: whereas my grandfather remained all his life an ardent Catholic, Camus was a Catholic atheist. He rejected religion, but was nonetheless formed by its codes. His university thesis was a study of Saint Augustine and Plotinus, and his engagements always seemed to Czesław Miłosz "marked by a suppressed theological bent." That he was not wholly ready to dismiss a core of Christian values is further recorded in his *Notebooks*, when, at a gathering with Koestler, Sartre, Malraux, and Manès Sperber, he urged:

> Don't you believe we are all responsible for the absence of values? And that if all of us who come from Nietzscheism, from nihilism, or from historical realism said in public that we were wrong and that there are moral values and that in the future we shall do the necessary to establish and illustrate them, don't you believe that would be the beginning of a hope?

If France was Camus's father, Algeria was his mother; and for their adoring son, no divorce could be countenanced. He wrote frequently, in both nonfiction and fiction, about the bifurcated nature of his spirit: "The Mediterranean separates two worlds in me, one where memories and names are preserved in measured spaces, the other where the wind and sand erases [*sic*] all trace of men on the open ranges." This carnal, wordless, unmeasured world (the world of his illiterate, nearly mute mother) was also one of his life's great riches: "I grew up with the sea and poverty for me was sumptuous; then I lost the sea and found all luxuries gray and poverty unbearable." In his hymn to his birthplace, "Summer in Algiers," Camus writes:

> Between the sky and these faces turned toward it, there is nowhere to hang a mythology, a literature, an ethic or a religion, but rather stones, flesh, stars, and those truths that the hand can touch.

It is difficult to overestimate the importance of this landscape of coastal Algeria—the sun, the sea, the stones, the heat—in Camus's imagination; and as with the effects of his poverty and his gratitude to France, to appreciate this aspect of his character is better to understand his position on the Algerian question. The end of French Algeria—the demise of an Algeria in which he might belong—implied not simply the loss of his youth, but more perilously the disappearance of his creative wellspring and his joy.

Upon the publication in France of *L'Envers et l'endroit* in 1958, he explained in his preface:

> Every artist thus keeps within himself a single source which nourishes during his lifetime what he is and what he says. When that spring runs dry, little by little one sees his work shrivel and crack. . . . My source [in these essays] is . . . in the world of poverty and sunlight I lived in for so long.

At the time he wrote this, Camus was already at work on *The First Man*, his final, unfinished novel, the manuscript of which was retrieved from the trunk of the crumpled Facel Vega after he died. It is a fiction unlike all his others, grounded in "stones, flesh, stars, and those truths the hand can touch." It is Camus's return to the source:

> This night inside him, yes these tangled hidden roots that bound him to this magnificent and frightening land, as much to its scorching days as to its heartbreakingly rapid twilights, and that was like a second life, truer

perhaps than the everyday surface of his outward life; its history would be told as a series of obscure yearnings and powerful indescribable sensations, the odor of the schools, of the neighborhood stables, of laundry on his mother's hands, of jasmine and honeysuckle in the upper neighborhoods, of the pages of the dictionary and the books he devoured, and the sour smell of the toilets at home and at the hardware store, the smell of the big cold classrooms where he would sometimes go alone before or after class, the warmth of his favorite classmates, the odor of warm wool and feces that Didier carried around with him, of the cologne big Marconi's mother doused him with so profusely that Jacques, sitting on the bench in class, wanted to move still closer to his friend . . . the longing, yes, to live, to live still more, to immerse himself in the greatest warmth this earth could give him, which was what he without knowing it hoped for from his mother.

No "rootless cosmopolitan"—a label inaccurately applied to Camus by Tony Judt—could re-create with such impassioned nostalgia the visceral evocations of home. Camus lived much of his life in exile, to be sure, and that sense of exile was central to his perspective. His intellect and his spirit were double, straddling the cultures of France and Algeria. But he was the opposite of "rootless": he knew absolutely what and where his home was, and he knew what it meant to him. From the 1930s onward, Camus recognized the moral claims of the indigenous Algerian people and was explicit about the need to satisfy those claims. But his insistence on justice would not permit him to abandon Algeria's other citizens: he tried to propose solutions that might protect the rights of all Algerians. Having failed, he chose to be silent.

When my father died, an exile to the last, he left behind an enormous library, thousands of volumes accumulated over a lifetime, dispersed in various unlikely places. The books of his youth had been stored for twenty years in forty cardboard boxes in a dusty concrete lockup just off Highway 401 in Napanee, Ontario: first editions of Ionesco and Max Jacob, French versions of the classics, histories of the Middle East. Among them, I knew I would find my father's copy of *Noces*, Camus's rapturous love letter to their shared home, one of just 225 copies printed by Edmond Charlot in Algiers in 1939. He had told me to look for it.

Noces contains the vivid and sensual essay "Noces à Tipasa," in which, recounting a day trip to the Roman ruins at Tipaza on Algeria's north coast, Camus lingers on the almost erotic pleasures of the natural beauty around him:

> I understand here what is called glory: the right to love without measure. There is only one love in this world. To embrace the body of a woman is also to hold to oneself this strange joy that descends from the sky toward the sea.[*]

It seems right that this, of all Camus's books, would hide in the heart of my father's collection. Elsewhere in his libraries, he had all the others, too, but this one, this little text so full of passion-

---

[*]   My translation.

ate emotion, my father carried with him, all the way, all his life, from the source.

Fairly foxed, its binding weak, it stands on my shelf alongside the book I discovered in the box beside it—a copy of *La Nouvelle Revue Française* from February 1960, its pages largely uncut, containing a hasty tribute to the recently deceased Camus. Unsurprisingly, it is his honesty—an honesty that amounts to modesty—that the editors praise:

> One recognized in him—as in Saint-Exupéry—a writer who was also, who was above all, a guide. To which: "Me, a guide?" he would reply. "I'm just learning every day how to walk."

A NEW *L'ÉTRANGER*

One of the most widely read French novels of the twentieth century, Albert Camus's *L'Étranger* carries, for American readers, enormous significance in our cultural understanding of mid-century French identity. It is considered—to what would have been Camus's irritation—the exemplary existentialist novel. Millions have read this short novel as a set text in school: more than eighty years after its initial publication, it remains centrally important.

Growing up, I never considered the oddity of this fact: that one of the seminal French texts read by American students does not, in fact, take place in Metropolitan France but in Algeria. A French colony in North Africa from 1830 to 1962, Algeria was Camus's homeland and that of my father and his relatives. Just as Camus, as a boy, read stories in which characters moved through the snow, without any idea of what snow might look, feel, or taste like, so, too, young North American readers have surely conflated Camus's Algiers with an imaginary sense of France and Frenchness, largely oblivious to the complex realities behind the text. That's to say, *L'Étranger* as experienced by many Anglophone readers and by many readers generally, especially with the passage of time, is a text translated and yet simultaneously untranslated, perhaps even in some measure untranslatable, drawing as it does upon the long-defunct social configurations of French colonial life.

In spite of the moral quagmires and false hierarchies of colonialism (not only French colonialism, but all colonialism)—the Europeans' oppression of individuals, societies, and cultures around the globe, resulting in untold deaths and disfigurements of history—there were, embedded within it, ideas we discard at our peril. Among them, centrally important, is a belief in translation itself, a faith that communication between widely disparate languages and cultures is possible, and to be encouraged. Around the Mediterranean basin, millennia of conquest and movement of peoples resulted, for centuries, in hybrid societies and languages: whether in Salonica, Malta, Alexandria, or Tunis, diverse populations with different religions and languages lived prosperously and often in peace.

My paternal great-grandfather, Maltese in origin, the son of a Maltese miller who immigrated to Algeria, served as an Arabic-French court translator. Malta, from the early nineteenth century until after the Second World War, was a British colony; its citizens, of Phoenician origin, speak a language that mingles North African Arabic dialects with Italian, French, and English words. My great-grandfather, raised in Algeria by Maltese parents, straddled Algeria's indigenous and colonial cultures in his professional life; but, already doubly a colonial subject, he bequeathed, to his children, an empowering sense of their full Frenchness—the equivalent, at the time, of the gift of social advancement. This was curious in part because his wife's, my great-grandmother's, family hailed, on her father's side, from Naples, Italy, and Majorca, Spain, and only on her mother's from

France. My grandfather, only one-quarter French by blood, was all his life patriotically French in spirit. That said, when defining himself, he asserted himself to be, in this order: Mediterranean, Latin, Catholic, and French. His kinship was simultaneously national and transnational. His kinship was translatable.

Nuance is often lost in translation. My French father, who first came to the United States on a Fulbright scholarship in 1952 at the age of twenty-one, bridled when his American room-mate scoffed at his accent, and vowed to speak perfect English; which he did, with the exception of a few tiny traces—the words "nuisance" and "monk" gave him away. But we, his children, eventually came to understand that translation was a source of complication in our lives, a matter of register or tone that didn't cross easily from one language to another. Humor is particularly challenging; but so, too, are throwaway expostulations. For example, in French it is possible to say, *"T'es bête"* with light-hearted affection; whereas the English translation, "You're stupid," carries more of a wallop. Or you might say, *"Qu'est-ce qu'il est con!"* without the insult being devastating—rather like saying, "Jeez, he's an idiot!"—whereas the literal translation—"What an asshole he is!"—has a distinctly different valence. My father, who rarely swore beyond the occasional "damn," never used this latter term in English, but he deployed the former with some regularity; and it was only when I grew up that I realized he had not, perhaps, intended it as harshly as it sounded. Then, too, as my mother used to say (when annoyed with my father), there's no word in French for "fun"—the German word *"spass"* is equivalent; but the given French translation is *"amusement,"* which we all know is not remotely the same thing. These vagaries, widely known, may seem trite—like the much-bruited fact that the Inuit have fifty words for snow—unless of course you experience their consequences in daily life, in which case they are real and particular.

We live constantly, of course, in translation—from experience into language, from one language to another, from one culture to another, or even one idiom or region to another. Even the most precise translators cannot fully drag clouds of connotation or shades of refinement across the chasm between lived worlds. In varying degrees, all translations are faulty and partial. (Then again, all language is faulty and partial, too.) But translation is also, as people once believed, amazingly possible, even within the Beckettian understanding that we must "fail again, fail better." And there is such a thing as an excellent translation, one that is truer than another.

With regard to Camus's canonical text, for many years, Stuart Gilbert's 1946 version was the standard English text. In the 1980s, it was supplanted by two new translations—by Joseph Laredo in the UK and Commonwealth, and by Matthew Ward in the U.S. Ward's highly respected version rendered the idiom of the novel more contemporary and more American, and an examination of his choices reveals considerable thoughtfulness and intuition.

Each translation is, perforce, a reenvisioning of the novel: a translator will determine which Meursault we encounter, and in what light we understand him. Sandra Smith—an American scholar and translator at Cambridge University, whose previous work includes the acclaimed translation of Irène Némirovsky's *Suite Française*—published in the UK in 2012 an excellent and, in important ways, new version of *L'Étranger*.

To begin with, she has changed the book's English title: no longer *The Stranger*, Smith's version is called, rather, *The Outsider*. She explains in her introduction:

> In French, *étranger* can be translated as "outsider," "stranger" or "foreigner." Our protagonist, Meursault, is all three, and the concept of an outsider encapsulates all these possible meanings: Meursault is a stranger to himself, an outsider to society and a foreigner because he is a Frenchman in Algeria.

Then, too, Smith has reconsidered the book's famous opening. Camus's original is deceptively simple: *"Aujourd'hui, maman est morte."* Gilbert influenced generations by offering us, "Mother died today"—inscribing in Meursault from the outset a formality that could be construed as heartlessness. But *maman*, after all, is intimate and affectionate, a child's name for his mother. Matthew Ward concluded that it was essentially untranslatable ("mom" or "mummy" being not quite apt), and left it in the original French: "Maman died today." There is a clear logic in this choice; but as Smith has explained, in an interview in the *Guardian*, *maman* "didn't really tell the reader anything about the connotation." She, instead, has translated the sentence as "My mother died today."

"I chose 'My mother' because I thought about how someone would tell another person that his mother had died. Meursault is speaking to the reader directly. 'My mother died today' seemed to me the way it would work, and also implied the closeness of 'maman' you get in the French."

Elsewhere in the book, she has translated *maman* as "mama"—

again, striving to come as close as possible to an actual, collo-quial word that will carry the same connotations as *maman* does in French.

Smith has made a similarly considered choice when con-fronted, later in the novel, with the ever-ticklish French contrast between *vous* and *tu*. Central to the novel's plot is Meursault's burgeoning friendship with his unsavory neighbor, Raymond Sintès, a friendship that develops as a result of Sintès's inter-est rather than Meursault's. In the course of a long conversation, Meursault recalls:

> *Je ne me suis pas aperçu d'abord qu'il me tutoyait. C'est seulement quand il m'a declaré, "Maintenant, tu es un vrai copain," que cela m'a frappé. . . . Cela m'était égal d'être son copain et il avait vraiment l'air d'en avoir envie.*

Ward's translation is as follows:

> I didn't notice at first, but he had stopped calling me "monsieur." It was only when he announced "Now you're a pal, Meursault" and said it again that it struck me. . . . I didn't mind being his pal, and he seemed set on it.

This is a rather curious choice: to replace the *tu/vous* distinc-tion with, in English, a reference to the address *monsieur*—which appears in French in the English. It suggests that an Anglophone reader will understand that, while saying "Mister" or "Sir" in English isn't quite comparable to the formalities of the French, we can infer, from the supposedly retained (but actually inserted) French, the nature of Sintès's forwardness. In other words,

Ward is presuming upon an English reader's cultural fantasy of Frenchness.

Smith's translation is much more straightforward:

> At first I didn't realize he'd started addressing me in a very personal way. It only struck me when he said: "Now, we're really pals." . . . It didn't matter to me one way or the other whether we were friends or not, but it really seemed to matter to him.

When I read this, I understood at once that Smith was referring to the *tu/vous* difference—as would any reader with even a minimal knowledge of French—but even without that knowledge, the passage makes perfect sense.

Again, with the last sentence of this quotation, Smith's translation differs tellingly from Ward's. I myself would have been tempted to translate it in yet a different way: "It was all the same to me to be his friend, and he really seemed to want it." Smith's translation is unquestionably more elegant than mine; but it also comes closer to the French than Ward's does. This amounts to a matter of characterization, both of Meursault and of Sintès: in Camus's formulation, we understand that Meursault's attitude is chiefly complaisant. Sintès has a strong desire for friendship; Meursault, far from being cold, senses that strong desire and, having no contrary desire of his own, is willing to go along.

Ward's translation implies something more like obdurate determination on Sintès's part—"he seemed set on it"; whereas the French *envie*, meaning "desire," suggests an almost importunate element. It certainly implies something close to compassion on Meursault's part. Smith's translation, while somewhat more oblique than "he really seemed to want it," nevertheless crucially conveys the extent of Meursault's accommodating nature: having truly no opinion, he will not pretend to one; and may as well, at that point, accede to Sintès.

Smith is throughout attuned to such subtleties. She has a precise literary understanding of Camus's creations, and her Meursault emerges, in the crisp clarity of her prose, emphatically not as a monster, but as a man who will not embellish or elaborate. His insufficient demonstration of emotion at his mother's funeral and the fact that he does not believe in God will count for much in his condemnation to death by the court; but we are not to understand thereby that Meursault is unfeeling or heartless. He is, rather, painfully without pretense.

Consider the moment when Marie, Meursault's girlfriend, asks him if he loves her: "I told her that didn't mean anything, but I didn't think so." This unsettling frankness is not willfully hurtful; it is simply the truth. "She looked sad then. But while we were making lunch, she laughed again, for no apparent reason, and the way she laughed made me kiss her."

The emotions of this exchange are repeated a thousand times a day in domestic relationships, but they are not usually this openly expressed. The telling difference, in Meursault, is that he eschews pretense, and proves almost idiotic—or perversely noble—in his transparency. Smith's translation portrays him thus, granting him kinship with the likes of Prince Myshkin—albeit as the black sheep of the family.

Camus famously said that "Meursault is the only Christ that we deserve"—a complicated statement for an avowed atheist. But Camus, of course, was more complex in his atheism than we might commonly expect: he was an atheist in reaction to, and in the shadow of, a Catholicism osmotically imbued in the culture (of the French certainly, but of the *pieds-noirs* in particular). The inescapable result is that his atheism is in constant dialogue with religion; in *L'Étranger* no less than in, say, *La Peste*.

Sandra Smith has, in her admirable translation, plucked carefully upon this thread in the novel, so that Anglophone readers might better grasp Camus's allusions. Here is but one key example: the novel's last line, in French, begins *"Pour que tout soit consommé . . ."* which Ward translates, literally, as "For everything to be consummated." But as Smith points out, the French carries "an echo of the last words of Jesus on the Cross: *'Tout est consommé.'*" Her chosen rendition, then, is "So that it might be finished," a formulation that echoes Christ's last words in the King James translation of the Bible.

Translation is inevitably to a degree subjective. The quality of a translator will depend, then, not merely on her understanding of the mechanics of a language, or on her facility as a writer of prose, but also on her capacities as a reader of texts, her sense of subtext, of connotation, of allusion—of the invisible textures that give a narrative its density and, ultimately, shape its significance. Sandra Smith is a very fine translator indeed.

THE BROTHER OF THE STRANGER:
KAMEL DAOUD

Kamel Daoud's novel *The Meursault Investigation* may have attracted more international attention than any other debut in recent years. The Algerian writer's book, first published in French in Algeria in 2013, then in France in 2014 (where it won the Goncourt First Novel Prize and was runner-up for the Prix Goncourt itself), then admirably translated into English by John Cullen and published in the United States in 2015, has been widely acclaimed in France, North America, and the UK as an "instant classic" (to cite the *Guardian*).

Daoud is an influential and controversial journalist who writes for *Le Quotidien d'Oran*, in the city on Algeria's Mediterranean coast where he lives. From December 2014 onward he has been under a fatwa declared, on Facebook, by the Salafist cleric Abdelfatah Hamadache. This followed an interview on French television in which Daoud criticized Muslim orthodoxy and said that he considered himself Algerian rather than Arab.[*] Azadeh

---

[*] For an excellent commentary on Daoud's political ideas and his journalism, see "Stranger Still," Adam Shatz's profile in the *New York Times Magazine*, April 1, 2015.

Moaveni, writing for the *Financial Times*, called Daoud's book "perhaps the most important novel to emerge out of the Middle East in recent memory."

The Meursault Investigation—called in French *Meursault, contre-enquête*, or counter-investigation—is a response to Albert Camus's *The Stranger*. Narrated by an aging drinker named Harun, the account conflates Meursault and his creator and presents the infamous fictional murder of "the Arab" on a sun-drenched beach as if it were a real crime worthy of a police inquiry. Harun's aim is to tell the "true" circumstances of that story and its legacy, from his own perspective. In Camus's book, he points out, "the word 'Arab' appears twenty-five times, but not a single name, not once." Harun wants his listener to understand that the dead man had a name and a family, neither of which figure in Camus's novel. "Just think, we're talking about one of the most read books in the world," he muses. "My brother might have been famous if your author had merely deigned to give him a name."

Meursault's victim was in fact, Harun explains, his older brother Musa (Moses). Harun himself was only seven at the time of the crime (in 1942), and recalls that "everything revolved around Musa, and Musa revolved around our father, whom I never knew and who left me nothing but our family name." As a result of the tragedy, his mother "imposed on me a strict duty of reincarnation"; serving the memory of his lost brother and his mother's need to preserve it, he writes that he "had a ghost's childhood."

The novel is the poignant account of a man whose life has been warped, from the beginning, by his mother's legacy of rage and grief. This is a familiar theme of postcolonial literature and one that Daoud will shape into a critique of revolutionary and post-revolutionary Algeria, a country that, in Harun's view, is not much better off than in its previous incarnation. Harun, sitting on a barstool and chatting with a foreigner, speaks openly about Algeria, his brother, and his own life story. His secularist, sophisticated reflections would seem to echo those of his creator. Daoud's complex and thoughtful analysis is inescapably tied to the thought and work of his French colonial predecessor—also a controversial journalist, whose youthful work forced him into exile in France.

From Daoud's first sentence—"Mama's still alive today"—the novel is a dialogue with Camus; the first sentence of *The Stranger* is *"Aujourd'hui, maman est morte."* But Daoud, who is both erudite and playful in spirit, samples and riffs upon not only Camus's most celebrated novel but on his entire work and his life. Unburdening himself over several nights to his unnamed interlocutor at a bar, Harun recalls Jean-Baptiste Clamence, the protagonist of *The Fall*; he laments "the absurdity of my condition, which consisted in pushing a corpse to the top of a hill before it rolled back down, endlessly," a reference to Camus's philosophical essay *The Myth of Sisyphus*. Even Harun's fatherless childhood in Algiers echoes that of Camus, who had no memories of his father, killed in the first days of World War I when Camus was an infant.

But the novel engages primarily with *The Stranger*, the outlines of which define Harun's story. Not only is Musa Meursault's victim; Harun himself, like Meursault, has a murder to deal with, as well as a difficult mother and a firm hostility to organized religion. Harun's childhood was shaped by his mother's mythmaking about her lost elder son:

> She wouldn't describe a murder and a death, she'd evoke a
> fantastic transformation, one that turned a simple young

man from the poorer quarters of Algiers into an invincible, long-awaited hero, a kind of savior.

She was, as Harun puts it, a peasant "snatched away from her tribe, given in marriage to a husband who didn't know her and hastened to get away from her." She inhabited a different world from that of the French colonials who ruled Algeria or of the Algerian government that has followed: "I don't know my mother's age, just as she has no idea how old I am. Before Independence, people did without exact dates; the rhythms of life were marked by births, epidemics, food shortages, et cetera." The cultural gulf between Harun's mother's perspective, based on myths, and the Western views of Meursault/Camus is vast, reminiscent of the gulf between Petrus, a black, polygamous South African farmer, and the white Lurie family in J. M. Coetzee's *Disgrace*. In Coetzee's book, as in Daoud's, this separation results in a violent act that casts doubt on the new order.

Harun serves as a bridge between two mutually uncomprehending societies—"that's the reason why I've learned to speak this language [that is, French], and to write it too: so I can speak in the place of a dead man, so I can finish his sentences for him," he explains at the outset—and herein lies his importance.

In a telling passage, Harun reflects more expansively on the difference between the world of his childhood and what came later, claiming that his mother's dramatic grief

pushed me to learn a language that could serve as a barrier between her frenzies and me. Yes, the *language*. The one I read, the one I speak today, the one that's not hers. Hers is rich, full of imagery, vitality, sudden jolts, and improvisations, but not too big on precision. Mama's grief lasted so long that she needed a new idiom to express it in. In her language, she spoke like a prophetess, recruited extemporaneous mourners, and cried out against the double outrage that consumed her life: a husband swallowed up by air, a son by water. I had to learn a language other than that one. To survive. And it was the one I'm speaking at this moment.... Books and your hero's language gradually enabled me to name things differently and to organize the world with my own words.

More than that, Harun will explain that Meursault's story was first brought to him by a young woman, a scholar named Meriem, who traced "the Arab's" origins to Harun and his mother, both of them then living in the village of Hadjout, formerly Marengo. "I was held as if spellbound. At one and the same time, I felt insulted and revealed to myself.... It was like reading a book written by God himself."

The genius and the limitation of Daoud's novel lie in the directness of this engagement with Meursault/Camus. It's not hard to grasp why a fiction that so deliberately and so intimately binds itself to Camus's classic should excite attention and admiration from Western readers. As Nick Fraser wrote in the *Guardian*, Daoud "has created the ultimate Camus mixtape." Harun expresses equal parts awe and frustration at Meursault/Camus ("a book written by God himself"). Camus's admirers, then, in identifying with Harun's admiration, are also more able to understand his dismay.

Daoud, for his part, takes the opportunity to criticize the post-colonial Algeria from which Harun finds himself increasingly alienated. During the first days after liberation, Harun murders a Frenchman (again in a direct echo of Meursault; although the Frenchman is, importantly, granted a name: Joseph Larquais). Harun's interrogation by the police is as farcical as was Meursault's. Whereas Meursault was convicted because he didn't behave like a loving son, Harun is criticized because his timing was off: "This Frenchman, you should have killed him with us, during the war, not last week!" the local colonel explains. Still, Harun says, "At the time when I did that killing, God wasn't as alive and heavy in this country as he is today."

Fifty years later, Harun is saddened at the disappearance of women like Meriem ("free, brash, disobedient, aware of their body as a gift, not as a sin or a shame"), and ruefully amused that producing wine—let alone drinking it—is now "considered *haram*, illicit." Above all, he is profoundly affronted by the dominance of religion in Algeria, horrified by a neighbor who recites from the Koran all night long: "As far as I'm concerned, religion is public transportation I never use," he quips. "I alone pay the electrical bill, I alone will be eaten by worms in the end. So get lost! And therefore I detest religions and submission." And further, "I'll go so far as to say I abhor religions. All of them! Because they falsify the weight of the world."

As Moaveni observes in the *Financial Times*, "Harun represents the alienation of millions of Arabs struggling to occupy that secular middle ground in their societies, struggling to live among their neighbors in peace and write in safety." Daoud is giving literary voice, in a language intelligible to the West—both literally, in French, and also within a familiar philosophical tradition—to a point of view that the West longs to hear but that tends to be drowned out by other voices from the Middle East.

It's a perspective that Daoud articulates also in his journalism, putting himself at considerable risk while doing so. One of his newspaper columns from *Le Quotidien d'Oran*, entitled "Meursault," was translated for the online magazine *Guernica*:

> Try to remember the last time there was anything like a national will: twenty years ago. Since then some people have died, others can't manage to be born, and still others have that faraway look in their eye. In short, we're all just spectators, like when you see people quarreling in a train station, but you're worrying about your luggage, your sandwich or your ticket. This feeling is universal with us now: the campaign for reform finally breaks down into an individual struggle to get by. Our country is no longer a project we all share, it's an obstacle each of us confronts alone.

This insight reverberates in many ways: most simply, it suggests—originally to Algerians themselves, and more broadly to readers outside his country—why Algeria took no more than a small part in the Arab Spring. But it also illuminates the psychological state that keeps the silent millions to whom Moaveni refers from speaking out. It suggests why Harun would need to be half drunk in a bar in order to confess his thoughts to an outsider. This insight expresses an increasingly widespread state of affairs: in the U.S. as much as in Daoud's country, we stand by apparently inured to mass shootings, widespread surveillance, and unchecked police brutality, instead worrying, as it were, about our luggage and our sandwiches.

Daoud is bold to explore, in journalism and in fiction, the true complexity of the Algerian experience as he and others see it. Roger Cohen, in an op-ed in the *New York Times*, celebrates the similarities between Daoud and Camus:

> There is more that binds their protagonists than separates them—a shared loathing of hypocrisy, shallowness, simplification and falsification. Each, from his different perspective, renders the world visible—the only path to understanding for Arab and Jew, for American and Iranian, for all the world's "strangers" unseen by each other.

Daoud's voice is particularly telling for its subtlety and tolerance. He sees Camus more clearly than do many of his enthusiastic European and North American critics, and appreciates the irony that "*The Stranger* is a philosophical novel, but we're incapable of reading it as anything other than a colonial novel." Describing his *Meursault* project, he says: "I'm not responding to Camus—I'm finding my own path through Camus."

> [Camus] was an Algerian writer. My own "Algerianness" is not exclusive and does not exclude others: I assume everything that enriches me, including the monstrous wound of colonization. Camus is Algerian because Algeria is larger and older than French Algeria, Ottoman Algeria, Spanish or Arab Algeria.

Daoud neither rejects Camus and his colonial legacy outright nor accepts his work uncritically. His resulting meditations are rich and thought-provoking, both for Algerian and for Western readers. He lets no one off the hook, including Harun himself.

The claims for the novel's international importance are, in this sense, well founded. That said, the book cannot be read meaningfully without *The Stranger* behind it: for all its vitality, the novel's skeleton is Camus's. Harun's actions and meditations exist in counterpoint to Meursault's.

This puts Daoud, ironically, in an irretrievably postcolonial position—always in response, always post facto—that is both philosophically and literarily discomfiting. Yet it enables North American readers as much as French ones to enter, using Camus's fiction as a filter or funnel for Daoud's, into a contemporary Algeria otherwise largely inaccessible to outsiders.

Daoud has cited *The Fall*, rather than *The Stranger*, as his favorite Camus novel, lauding it as "a literary, philosophical, and religious exercise all at once." In Europe and North America at least, *The Fall* is now much less widely read than most of Camus's work, and its form—the narrated confession—can seem didactic and often abstract. It has precisely the effect of an exercise, to use Daoud's word. More than *The Stranger* or *The Plague*, *The Fall* now feels dated. The self-accusing monologues of the former Parisian lawyer who ends up in Amsterdam raise issues that are still germane; its literary form is less convincing. Indeed, one could argue that the force of Camus's fiction (unlike that of, say, Balzac or Proust or Marguerite Duras) is tied to his philosophical essays; that the sum of his works amounts to more than themselves.

By the same token, *The Meursault Investigation*, fascinating and important as it is, is not of itself an especially interesting work of art. Cleaving as it does to the substance of *The Stranger*, taking *The Fall* as a literary model, it, too, has the quality of an intellectual exercise—albeit one expertly executed and replete with significance; one that should, even must, be read for its fierce and humane intelligence.

Like Camus before him, Daoud is an intellectual, deploying the novel for philosophical and political purposes. His voice and his presence are what many—in Algeria, in Europe, and around the world—have been yearning for. He dares to speak his mind, and is keen to speak in such a way that strangers—in this case, most of his readers—can understand him. In order to assert this freedom, he is prepared to risk his life. As he has said:

> The intellectual is the unbending witness to his era, one that leads to liberty or surrender. He's the voice that carries and proclaims, but also reminds. In the face of the rising totalitarianisms of our new century, it is a question of witnessing on behalf of what is human, on behalf of humanity, but especially on behalf of liberty—its value and necessity.

KAZUO ISHIGURO

The consolations of literature are many and vaunted: Who hasn't found delight in rereading *Pride and Prejudice* or in a production of *The Tempest*? Rarer and more challenging is the thin but intense literary vein that runs from *King Lear* to Beckett and beyond, works that lay bare the human condition in its stark fundamentals, and pose thereby the hardest existential questions. Dostoyevsky's *The Possessed* is such a novel, as Beckett's *Endgame* is such a play. Camus's *The Plague* is another example. Such art explores the agony of, and the choices available in, our human struggle toward the certainty of death; it questions how we might proceed without any ultimate hope; and finds in the absurd darkness glimmers of human dignity, and of the beauty of the human spirit in adversity.

Without fanfare or Dostoyevskian histrionics, *Never Let Me Go* joins the ranks of these abiding works. Camus's *The Plague* portrays a world dominated by disease (on the one hand, an allegory for the German occupation of France in World War II, but also an allegory for the human condition), in which characters just like us must choose their courses of action in the face of infection and imminent death. So, too, *Never Let Me Go,* set in 1990s Britain, posits a race of clones living alongside us, bred with the sole purpose of repeated organ donation (presumably to cure our ills) and early death. As they grow up and come into the knowledge of their fates, how will each of them live? This vision casts a searing light upon ordinary life: we are, to the novel's characters, Baudelairean doubles (*hypocrite lecteur, mon semblable, mon frère*), equally mortal, and hence less distanced than we would wish ourselves to be.

Thirty-one year old Kathy H., the novel's narrator and protagonist, makes no claims for herself as an individual, and yet believes profoundly in her exceptionalism: she tells the stories of her adolescence first at Hailsham, a boarding school, and then in a group home with, among others, her closest friends Ruth and Tommy, as if they were the most important in the world. For most of her short life, she hopefully believes that their love—a passion somewhat fluidly distributed among the three of them—may be strong enough to triumph over their fate, and to avert death itself. In this, albeit more literally, she resembles most of us. She recounts for us (and the narrative is very explicit in addressing an audience: she doesn't simply tell her story, she tells it *to us*) her relatively brief life, replete with the details of a privileged childhood and the spats and reconciliations of teenage society; but her deceptively superficial account is, ultimately, a reckoning with mortality—that of her friends, and her own.

As Tolstoy observes in *The Death of Ivan Ilych*, "The example of a syllogism which he had learned in Kiezewetter's *Logic*: 'Caius is a man, men are mortal, therefore Caius is mortal,' had seemed to him all his life to be true as applied to Caius but certainly not as regards himself." The horror that human life must end in death is comprehensible, even tolerable, *as long as it is not my death*. Who, really, can conceive of her own annihilation? Against this unbearable truth, art has long been considered a bulwark: *Ars longa, vita brevis*, as Hippocrates succinctly put it; or, more cynically, *selon* Eliot, "These are the fragments I have shored against my ruins." Kathy H. tells her story also with this hope. In the novel, Ishiguro renders that hope concrete: poignantly, the children at Kathy's Hailsham are encouraged to create artworks, the finest of which are selected for a mysterious "gallery" held by one of the school's senior administrators, a woman known only as "Madame": it is bruited about that the finest young artists may be offered a reprieve from their inexorable life's course, which is to become first "carers" (looking after other clones as they are stripped, one by one, of their vital organs) and then "donors" themselves.

Ishiguro first makes literal this fantasy about art's power, only then to reveal, inevitably, its vanity and inadequacy. In a culminating confrontation between Kathy and Tommy and their former school leaders, Madame and Miss Emily, the young couple (and we along with them) are forced to accept that their art, regardless of its quality, is no defense against fate. It doesn't really matter who wields the power—whether it is Society, as for Kathy and her kind, or Nature, or God, for the religious: the result, for clones and humans alike, is the same.

I FIRST READ *Never Let Me Go* in proofs, before its official publication. In my plain-jacketed copy, its central conceit was neither advertised nor explained. When Kathy H. announces, in the novel's first paragraph, that "I've been a carer now for over eleven years . . . I'm not trying to boast . . . My donors have always tended to do much better than expected," there were no immediate explanations for her terms. Rather, the parameters of Kathy H.'s parallel world emerged only over time, through her account of an upbringing both familiar and subtly but profoundly awry.

Kathy is not a flamboyant figure, not the sort who dominates—unlike her friend Ruth, repeatedly the leader in their youthful antics. Retiring, even timid, Kathy is emphatically ordinary, down to the almost weary flatness of her tone: "While we're on the subject of tokens, I want just to say a bit about our Sales, which I've mentioned a few times already. The Sales were important to us because that was how we got hold of things from outside . . ." Her autobiography is necessarily comprised of anecdotes about special pencil cases and lost cassette tapes, rather than feats of bravery or politically significant adventures.

Against this banality of adolescence—which could, crucially, be *anybody's* adolescence—Ishiguro's juxtaposition of radical strangeness is deeply unsettling. The effect is not unlike that of Ishiguro's canonical early novel, *The Remains of the Day*, in which he sets the unquestioning quotidian devotions of the butler, Stevens, against the abhorrent appeasement politics of his master, Lord Darlington. Both Stevens and Kathy are pawns in life's larger games, but this apparent insignificance only fortifies the tenderness of their humanity. These creations insist, by their very existence, that you do not need to be a member of Parliament or a celebrity or even a headmistress in order for your life to matter. Ishiguro is always mindful that while History may unfold around us—or allegorical Science Fiction, as the case may be—each individual is passionate in the pursuit of his or her small existence, a life made up precisely of pencil cases and cuff links, of light bulbs, scissors, sore throats.

This ability to convey life's ironic, even agonizing, palimpsestic quality is a particular strength of Ishiguro's, essential to the force of his fiction. But no literary appreciation of this capac-

ity could have prepared me for the novel's long visceral afterlife, for the way it would inhabit my psyche and enter my lexicon
as shorthand for a particular type of soul-altering experience.
In the years since its publication, I've had many conversations
about this book, and have discovered that almost without exception other readers have shared my experience: we may initially
have been bemused by the smallness of Kathy's memories, by
the carefully detailed parameters of her sheltered life; but in
an appreciation—a sympathetic understanding—of her doomed
struggles, we have allowed the novel's characters and their fates
to enter us, reminders of the simultaneous value and futility of
existence itself. As we journey through our own lives—sooner or
later inevitably, ourselves, carers, like Kathy, and/or the cared-
for, like the novel's donors—we hold Kathy and her cohort uneasily
in mind. Indeed, Ishiguro's haunting novel proves eponymous.

This is a particularly acute discomfort, surely, for those who've
enjoyed the privilege of education, who've pursued knowledge in
the passionate belief that we are "improved" by it. We may not
have lounged in pavilions on the playing fields of posh boarding schools, as do Kathy and her friends in their youthful days at
Hailsham; but if we're readers at all, chances are we've taken on
faith the idea that our education is *for* something, and not merely
a means to pass the time. We trust that our lives are more meaningful, more useful, or more profoundly lived—that in some way
we will live better, if not longer—as a result of our enriching
education. But what if, at life's heart, there is only death? From
a certain long-term perspective, this will always be true; but for
Kathy and her ilk, destined to die young, this swiftly becomes
unignorable fact.

As Kathy will discover only at the end of the novel, she and her Hailsham friends are the result of an experiment within the broader social experiment of cloning. In their burning confrontation with Madame and Miss Emily, Kathy and Tommy learn the specifics of what she had always murkily grasped: that Hailsham—at this point in the novel defunct—was separate from the mainstream, a special place. It was conceived by a few liberal zealots, who insisted that the clones, or "students" as they are euphemistically called, be given rigorous instruction and a fine quality of life; that they be encouraged to study, to reflect, and to create art; that, in sum, their lives thereby be granted some meaning beyond the purely utilitarian. It is a belief that has, by the time of the novel's telling, lost its currency; just as in our own times, society's pendulum has swung strongly toward support of the strictly purposeful, and the value of a liberal arts education—of reading history, or classics, or art history for their own sake—is increasingly in question.

We understand almost before Kathy herself the passionate nostalgia that she experiences for her school days—a nostalgia that she experiences even before she leaves Hailsham, and that she suffers markedly more than do her intimates Ruth and Tommy. She senses, from the outset, the importance of clinging to the pleasures of the present, or the past; while they, naïvely, are focused on the future. As she observes with hindsight, "I never appreciated in those days the sheer effort Ruth was making to move on, to grow up and leave Hailsham behind." Kathy may not at first see hers to be a nostalgia for faith, but this is essentially what it is: this willed transition to adulthood that all the "students" undergo—moving from the hermetic safety of institutions like Hailsham first to the Cottages, a sort of halfway house, and thence into the wider world—will involve accepting that their life's purpose is either to die (or to attain "completion," as the clones' death is delicately termed) or to ease that path for their fellows. The "students" must make this transition as soon as they reach maturity—at little more than seventeen or eighteen years old; whereas we ordinary mortals, in our equally strange contemporary reality, are often able to deny its truth for much of our long lives.

Given this, the "students" are left to look back upon their childhoods—that brief, halcyon time—as most of us, in age, may look back upon our lives entire. In Kathy's recollection, small incidents take on great meaning, are interpreted and reinterpreted, and yearning—the unlived life—becomes paramount. She reads her life *like a book*, searching for signs, for explanations of why it must be as it is, or for ways in which it might have been different. Unlike Ruth, and ultimately Tommy also (certainly after the dramatic encounter with their former guardians in which he comes to accept his fate), Kathy H. remains an analyst, a true student, to the last—as if making sense of her senseless trajectory could help her, could imbue it with significance: "These are the fragments I have shored against my ruins."

THAT THE "STUDENTS" are incapable of reproducing is essential to the novel's power: as Cicero famously observed, "Of all nature's gifts to the human race, what is sweeter to a man than his children?" And indeed, children, more profoundly even than art, protect us from being overwhelmed by the ubiquity of decay and loss. As we face the deaths of our parents, and then those of our peers, it is the pressing needs of our children—the faith in their futures—that keep us *in life*. The irony of course is that our desire, then, is to protect them precisely from this adult knowledge of the inevitability of death, just as Kathy, at Hailsham, is held by the teachers and staff in blissful ignorance; and in this sense, what provides our lives with meaning is the perpetuation of a lie.

One of the novel's central images—and that which gives the book its indelible title—is of Kathy as a young girl, dancing by herself in her dormitory to her favorite pop song, "Never Let Me Go":

> What was so special about this song? Well, the thing was, I didn't used to listen properly to the words; I just waited for that bit that went: "Baby, baby, never let me go . . ." And what I'd imagine was a woman who'd been told she couldn't have babies, who'd really, really wanted them all her life. Then there's a sort of miracle and she has a baby, and she holds this baby very close to her and walks around singing: "Baby, never let me go . . ."

As Kathy is miming this fantasy, "swaying about slowly in time to the song, holding an imaginary baby to my breast," Madame passes in the corridor and witnesses the sight:

> She just went on standing out there, sobbing and sobbing, staring at me through the doorway with that same look in her eyes she always had when she looked at us, like she was seeing something that gave her the creeps. Except this time there was something else, something extra in that look I couldn't fathom.

This is but one of many moments that Kathy attempts, much later, to "read," hoping thereby to gain some understanding of her life. These recalled incidents comprise the novel, puzzle pieces held up to the light. (In this, she is the polar opposite of Ishiguro's Stevens: to the last, he is someone who willfully refuses to "read" the incidents that have defined him, leaving us to read them for him, and to feel a pain that he cannot consciously allow.) When finally Kathy meets Madame, they will discuss this encounter, and Kathy will know what was in Madame's mind.

But as the novel makes clear, there is a value in her lifelong uncertainty. The impulse to interpret, to attribute meaning to events and to the actions of others, is what impels us, ourselves, to act in certain ways. It is, quite simply, what gives us hope, even though our own deaths are as certainly inscribed as Kathy's or Tommy's or Ruth's. The demystification of our human storytelling—the moment of certainty, when we know *for sure* what was intended, or what actually happened—is also the end of that hope. In the novel, it leads Tommy to run out into a night field, "raging, shouting, flinging his fists and kicking out"; and subsequently, devastatingly, to be resigned to his fate.

This is not the case for Kathy, for all the calm flatness of her narration. Even as she approaches her own end, she does not renounce—she does not rail, but nor does she go gently. Rather, she illustrates that to imagine a truth and to know a truth aren't mutually exclusive, but that the dance between the two—a life spark that could be called "reflection"—proves in itself a certain, other, kind of hope. The fragments that Kathy has collected are not, in the end, negligible, even if they cannot prevent her physical annihilation. The pictures she drew and sculptures she made while a child at Hailsham may have proven worthless (like any drawerful of child's drawings, years later), but the creation that is her story—a story strangely truer than any truth—has its hold upon us, and will never let us go.

JANE BOWLES

Two Serious Ladies came into my life in my junior year in college, when, while perusing the tables at the university bookstore, I found myself drawn to a slim paperback with a striking—and ugly—front cover, a drawing of two women in cloche hats, one wearing a fox stole, set against a black background; and with, on the back, a black-and-white photograph of the author, Jane Bowles, seated amid what appears to be tropical foliage, her hand upon her hip, her rather arch, elfin gaze over her right shoulder, while a black-and-white kitten climbs her shirt-front and a bright-eyed parrot prepares to whisper in her ear.

I can't say whether it was the odd but appealing photograph or the odd but unappealing drawing that prompted me to open the book. I think, perhaps, it was their unlikely combination. Even before I got to the novel's first page, I encountered other writers' encomia: John Ashbery called Jane Bowles "one of the finest modern writers of fiction in any language"; Alan Sillitoe anointed the novel "A landmark in twentieth-century American literature"; Truman Capote deemed her "One of the really original pure stylists"; James Purdy said she was "an unmatchable talent"; Tennessee Williams announced that she was "the most important writer of prose fiction in modern American letters."

Why hadn't I heard of her? With the arrogance of youth, I thought I'd laid out the map of twentieth-century letters. There was a great deal I hadn't yet read; but I believed—in my ignorance— that at least I knew what there was to read. I flipped to the back for her biography, and there discovered that she'd been married to the writer Paul Bowles (best known, of course, for *The Sheltering Sky*)—a committed, but unconventional union, as both of them were gay; that she'd been peripatetic, and had lived, among other places, in Mexico and Morocco; that she was Jewish but died in a Spanish convent, in 1973, at the age of fifty-six. Her "flamboyant" life was described as "short" and "stormy."

The signs were propitious, enticing. (Now in mid-life, I feel a deep sadness at the brevity of her life that I could not, when not yet twenty myself. Then, "short" and "stormy" sounded glamorous.) But it was upon reading the first page of the first chapter of the novel—standing in the aisle sweating in my winter coat with my book bag weighing on my shoulder—that I knew I couldn't leave the shop without it. I simply could not put it down.

I would soon learn to my dismay that *Two Serious Ladies* was the only novel Jane Bowles ever completed. It was not especially well received upon its publication in 1943. Her play *In the Summer House* was produced in 1954, again, to mixed reviews. Her complete oeuvre, published as *My Sister's Hand in Mine: The Collected Works of Jane Bowles*, with an introduction by Truman Capote, amounts to fewer than five hundred pages, and includes, in addition to the novel and the play, several short stories and some fragments.

In part this small output is a result of her brief life: Bowles died at fifty-six, but at the age of forty suffered a stroke that left her significantly impaired and unable to write. In part, too, it is a result of her tormented, self-critical nature and of her reliance on alcohol. Like many mid-century writers, she drank a good deal. In part, arguably, her husband's greater success as a fiction writer (when first they met he was an up-and-coming composer, rather than a writer) proved a further obstacle—although she would vehemently have denied this.

But the fruits we do have of her thoroughly original mind—a mind at once profoundly witty, genuinely unusual in its apprehensions, and bracingly, humanly true—are eminently worth savoring. As Francine du Plessix Gray wrote in her 1978 introduction to the Virago Modern Classics edition of the novel, "Mrs. Bowles's oeuvre is all the more unique because of its Grand Guignol hilarity, its constant surprises, and a blend of realism and grotesqueness . . . [her] lithe, feverish dialogue has a blend of childlike integrity, surreal candour and deadly precision often worthy of Lewis Carroll."

❦

MILLICENT DILLON, Jane Bowles's biographer, writes in *A Little Original Sin: The Life & Work of Jane Bowles* (1981) that "From the first words, something of what she told, something of what she withheld, her style and her language touched me as if I'd come upon a world I'd once known but had forgotten." This was my experience also.

When, on the novel's first page, we are introduced to Christina Goering—a character whose religious bent is enfolded in her first name; and whose tyrannical nature alluded to in her last— we learn that:

> As a child Christina had been very much disliked by other
> children. She had never suffered particularly because of

this, having led, even at a very early age, an active inner life that curtailed her observation of whatever went on around her ... Even then [at the age of ten] she wore the look of certain fanatics who think of themselves as leaders without once having gained the respect of a single human being.

Upon reading these sentences, spritely in tone but rapier-sharp, I thought, first, *But I know exactly that girl Christina*—as we have all known such a girl—and second, *I want to know this writer, who sees the world as I know it to be, but with a sly new clarity.* I thought, too, *Here is a new and abiding companion for my literary journey.* It was, for me as for Millicent Dillon, a *coup de foudre*.

As a child, Christina Goering, we learn further, "was in the habit of going through many mental struggles—generally of a religious nature—and she preferred to be with other people and organize games. These games, as a rule, were very moral, and often involved God." When she ropes her little sister Sophie's friend Mary into just such a game—a bitter, mucky baptismal lark called "I forgive you for all your sins"—Mary asks, "Is it fun?" and Christina answers—oh, how well I know her now!—"It's not for fun that we play it, but because it's necessary to play it."

Herein lies the seriousness of Jane Bowles's *Two Serious Ladies*, Miss Christina Goering and her friend Mrs. Frieda Copperfield. Superficially, their lives may appear whimsical, even rackety—they drift from place to place, from acquaintance to acquaintance—but in fact, each woman is embarked on a tremendously earnest quest: their apparently frivolous movements are prompted by invisible codes of ethics, shaped by perilously constructed moralities. For each woman, her seemingly bizarre actions are not undertaken for fun, but because they are, in the service of those moralities, absolutely necessary.

Christina Goering, who is wealthy (she explains to her companion, the truculent Miss Gamelon, that each of us has a guardian angel, who "comes when you are very young, and gives you special dispensation . . . Yours might be luck; mine is money"), decides to sell her fine home and move to a small, uncomfortable house in the farther reaches of what appears to be Staten Island. Her reasoning is that "in order to work out my own little idea of salvation I really believe that it is necessary for me to live in some tawdry place and particularly in some place where I was not born."

This she does, in the company of Miss Gamelon, a creature as unexpectedly discordant as the Balinese orchestra of similar name, and whose interest in Christina is in significant part financial; and of Arnold, a "stout, dark-haired man" in his late thirties who propositions her at a party (where she also sees her friend Mrs. Copperfield), and with whom her life becomes entangled. Both of these hangers-on are uncomplainingly financially supported by Christina Goering: as Mrs. Copperfield wisely points out, in a different context, the rich "want to be liked for their money too, and not only for themselves." Christina has her eye on greater things, and preserving her fortune appears to be of no more importance than her own physical comfort. Of their move to the island, a frustrated Miss Gamelon observes to Arnold, "There are certain people . . . who turn peace from the door as though it were a red dragon breathing fire out of its nostrils and there are certain people who won't leave God alone either."

Mrs. Copperfield, meanwhile, sets off for Panama with her husband, even though she has announced to her friend that "I

don't think I can bear it . . . Really, Miss Goering, it frightens me
so much to go." Having landed at the port of Colon and arrived at
a seedy hotel of her husband's choosing in the red-light district,
she is alarmingly disoriented, and decides, "I must try to find a
nest in this outlandish place." Bowles explains that "Mrs. Copperfield's sole object in life was to be happy, although people who
had observed her behavior over a period of years would have been
surprised to discover that this was all."

The "nest" Mrs. Copperfield finds for herself—to her husband's grave dismay—is in another red-light establishment, the
Hotel de las Palmas, where she settles in the company of a teenage prostitute named Pacifica and the hotel's owner, an older
woman named Mrs. Quill. The reassurance that Pacifica provides (as with the others, her name is not irrelevant) has to do,
in part, with her enviable fearlessness. As Mrs. Quill observes,

> when I got married, I felt like a scared rabbit. As if I was
> going out into the world. Mr. Quill was like a family to
> me, though, and it wasn't until he died that I really got out
> into the world . . . Pacifica's really been out in the world
> much longer than I have. You know, she is like an old
> sea captain . . . It isn't so much a question of age as it is a
> question of experience. The Lord has spared me more than
> he has spared Pacifica. She hasn't been spared a single
> thing. Still, she's not as nervous as I am.

In one of the novel's most moving scenes, Mrs. Copperfield
accompanies Pacifica to the beach, where Pacifica offers to teach
the older woman to swim. There ensues an echo of Christina
Goering's childhood baptism of Mary; but one in which Mrs.

Copperfield feels successfully protected—even, in Christina's terms, "saved." Afterward, "Mrs. Copperfield collapsed on the sand and hung her head like a wilted flower. She was trembling and exhausted as one is after a love experience."

For Mrs. Copperfield, who often must resort to gin to find her happiness—"At a certain point gin takes everything off your hands and you flop around like a little baby. Tonight I want to be like a little baby"—Pacifica's companionship proves indispensable. When Mrs. Copperfield elects to stay with Pacifica and Mrs. Quill rather than leave Colon with her husband, her decision feels both enormously difficult and inevitable:

> She trembled so violently that she shook the bed. She was suffering as much as she had ever suffered before, because she was going to do what she wanted to do. But it would not make her happy. She did not have the courage to stop from doing what she wanted to do. She knew that it would not make her happy, because only the dreams of crazy people come true. She thought that she was only interested in duplicating a dream, but in doing so she necessarily became the victim of a nightmare.

Mrs. Copperfield surmounts at least one of her great fears, and takes control of her own life. If you will, she becomes "Frieda" rather than "Mrs. Copperfield." The outcome of her courage looks, to the world, like a disaster: when she encounters Christina Goering in New York some months later, the latter, alarmed, suggests that her friend has "gone to pieces." Mrs. Copperfield, however, is unrepentant:

I *have* gone to pieces, which is a thing I've wanted to do for years. I know I am as guilty as can be, but I have my happiness, which I guard like a wolf, and I have authority now and a certain amount of daring, which, if you remember correctly, I never had before.

Christina Goering, meanwhile, having set up house uncomfortably and in self-imposed poverty, has continued to push herself not to new heights but to new depths: ultimately she is not simply mistaken for a prostitute but employed as one. In making solo excursions to the mainland from her new island home, in forcing herself to go where she least wants to, "She even felt a kind of elation, which is common in certain unbalanced but sanguine persons when they begin to approach the thing they fear."

As she explains to a young woman named Bernice in a dive bar on the mainland:

It wasn't exactly in order to have a good time that I came out. I have more or less forced myself to, simply because I despise going out in the night-time alone and prefer not to leave my own house. However, it has come to such a point that I am forcing myself to make these little excursions.

The same idiosyncratic ethical code that prompted her religious games as a child now shapes her actions in adulthood. Not long after abandoning Miss Gamelon and Arnold to become the girlfriend of a down-and-out fellow named Andy that she meets in the bar, she abandons Andy in his turn for a gangster named Ben:

For several days it had been quite clear to Miss Goering that Andy was no longer thinking of himself as a bum. This would have pleased her greatly had she been interested in reforming her friends, but unfortunately she was only interested in the course that she was following in order to attain her own salvation. She was fond of Andy, but during the last two nights she had felt an urge to leave him.

At the novel's conclusion, Miss Goering has a rare, fleeting moment of insight: " 'Certainly I am nearer to becoming a saint . . . but is it possible that a part of me hidden from my sight is piling sin upon sin as fast as Mrs. Copperfield?' This latter possibility Miss Goering thought to be of considerable interest but of no great importance."

The parallel trajectories of Miss Goering and Mrs. Copperfield—from financially comfortable bourgeois lives to impoverished isolation in a world of gangsters and prostitutes—hardly seem, from the outside, like paths towards sainthood or salvation. On the one hand, they may appear to be merely the indulgent playacting of women of privilege (I'm reminded of the late-'90s Pulp song "Common People": "You wanna live like common people . . . you wanna sleep with common people, you wanna sleep with common people like me . . ."). Seen thus, they may seem at no great remove from Christina in autocratic and disagreeable childhood, insisting upon her selfish fantasies without concern for others.

But these two women are, at the same time, in deadly earnest. Mrs. Copperfield really *does* leave her husband for Pacifica. Christina Goering really *does* sleep with unsavory strangers she picks up in bars. They do not subscribe to a common or readily recognizable morality (indeed, they may by some lights be "piling sin upon sin") but each has carefully outlined her morality nonetheless. One pursues a path of asceticism, the other of a more intangible but no less dramatic renunciation. If this is a game, everything is at stake.

❦

IN A LETTER to Paul Bowles in early August, 1947, Jane wrote: "Certainly Carson McCullers is as *talented* as Sartre or Simone de Beauvoir but she is not really a serious writer. I am serious but I am isolated and my experience is probably of no interest at this point to anyone." She goes on to refer to an article by de Beauvoir entitled "New Heroes," of which she says, "It is what I have been thinking at the bottom of my mind all this time and God knows it is difficult to write the way I do and yet think their way."

A great deal is explained in this short passage. Jane Bowles was exactly the same age as Carson McCullers, whose work shared a similar penchant for so-called grotesque characters— both can be compared to their slightly younger contemporary, the photographer Diane Arbus, focusing their artwork on socially peripheral lives. But whereas McCullers was widely acclaimed and fashionable, Bowles had received only mixed notices for her work and worried that "really *Two Serious Ladies* never *was* a novel." She felt "isolated" in various ways—having battled tuberculosis of the knee as a teenager, she walked with a limp and jokingly called herself "Crippie the Kike Dyke"— and apparently assumed that McCullers did not. Her calibrated envy is both palpable and understandable. If she and McCullers both wrote about neurotics and freaks, she felt that what distinguished her from McCullers was a seriousness of purpose, a philosophical underpinning.

Reading Sartre and de Beauvoir, Bowles found kinship with their existentialist philosophy: the ultimate question of how to forge a self in a Godless world *is* the question with which Miss Goering and Mrs. Copperfield are grappling. The writer Lorna Sage has rightly pointed out the connection between Jane Bowles and the philosopher, mystic, and ascetic Simone Weil. Bowles's women are simultaneously existential paragons and thoroughly feminist protagonists, women in search of elusive, meaningful self-determination, inhabiting at once a concrete world of shabby hotel rooms and dark bars, and a more spiritual, nebulously Godless, plane of sin and salvation. They are by no means familiar heroines; nor are their choices easy to fathom; but it would be wrong to dismiss them as trivial neurotics or mere game-players. The consequences of their choices are very real: paradoxically, each of them, in attempting to make a self, must "go to pieces."

Millicent Dillon observes that Bowles's novel is "autobiographical . . . but not in the confessional sense. It is autobiographical in that in every moment of the novel Jane is present in each of her characters." Bowles was famously indecisive, in part because she fretted that each decision, however small, might have lasting moral implications. She was also, in youth, extremely fearful, constrained by an impressive catalogue of anxieties and phobias. But she pushed hard against her nature. According to one friend, "Jane was vulnerable and strong. She was always testing herself and she kept on testing to see how it would come out if she put herself in danger."

To Dillon, Paul described Jane early in their marriage staying out late, returning home barefoot. When he'd ask where she'd been:

> She'd answer that she'd been wandering around the docks all by herself at four or five in the morning.
>
> "Why?"
>
> "Because that was the one place I didn't want to be. I'm terrified of it."
>
> "Then, Jane, why did you go?"
>
> "Don't ask me. You ought to know why. I had to or I couldn't face myself in the mirror tomorrow if I hadn't gone because that was the one thing I was afraid of."

As with her characters, there is, here, on one level an element of whimsy: there was no call for Jane Bowles to wander the docks before dawn, when she had a safe home and a partner awaiting her return. But by the same token, there was a deadly earnestness in her endeavor: in pursuit of her own code, this tiny woman *did* put herself in danger, without seeking support, in order to justify something to herself—in order, like Christina Goering, to find her own salvation.

Jane Bowles is a writer of surprises and contradictions. Acerbic, willfully unsettling, she renders the familiar new, undercuts our social and emotional expectations. Her work, ironic and complex, alternately oblique and direct, defies categorization. Tennessee Williams wrote, of her play *In the Summer House*, that it was "a piece of dramatic literature that stands altogether alone, without antecedents and without descendants, unless they spring from the one and only Jane Bowles." Her friend the academic Wendell Wilcox concurred, saying: "God knows Jane's stories were exotic but the really exotic element was Jane herself. Both the story and the telling are completely natural in Jane and come from nowhere outside herself. No one but Jane could have written a line of them." He went on: "I talked in this way to her and tried to make her feel less desolate about her work."

Jane was temperamentally and artistically original. She was herself a misfit; if you will, a grotesque. Lesbian but married; American but living most of her life abroad (as a teenager in France and Switzerland; later in Mexico; and then, for the longest stretch, Morocco); friends with many artists but truly intimate with none, except her husband Paul, with whom her relationship became increasingly complicated and whose reputation superseded and overshadowed her own. Never fashionable, she had a passionate small following—but she expressed her anxiety about this situation in a *Vogue* interview after the production of *In the Summer House*, when she said, "There's no point in writing a play for your five hundred goony friends. You have to reach more people."

There is great, even unbearable, sadness in the unfolding of Jane Bowles's life, just as there is considerable darkness in her fiction. But there is also much delight, vivacity, and even joy in her work. There is a reason that, in spite of her small oeuvre, generation after generation returns to her novel, her play, and her stories. Those "five hundred goony friends" have multiplied exponentially. She has influenced now generations of writers; and for many of us, her voice has felt as special, as intimate and cherished, as that of a close and particularly beloved relation.

ITALO SVEVO

Italo Svevo's third and final novel, *Zeno's Conscience*, is most famously a novel about quitting smoking. It is obviously more than that, an extraordinary and slippery liar's memoir; but when all else is forgotten, Zeno's addiction and its ramifications remain. The Triestine idler Zeno Cosini, and through him the Triestine writer Italo Svevo, make a life's philosophy not simply of smoking, but of the joys of the last cigarette: "I believe the taste of a cigarette is more intense when it's your last," Zeno announces in the book's opening section, "Smoke." "The last one gains flavor from the feeling of victory over oneself and the hope of an imminent future of strength and health." Inevitably, we will learn that neither strength nor health is Zeno's forte. With a pessimist's optimism, he aspires forever to these states, even as he is grateful to be spared them. "Who knows? If I had stopped smoking, would I have become the strong, ideal man I expected to be? Perhaps it was this suspicion that bound me to my habit, for it is comfortable to live in the belief that you are great, though your greatness is latent."

Encapsulated in this dance of resolution and resignation are many of the novel's, and the novelist's, themes. Zeno Cosini is a modern antihero, the bourgeois nephew of Dostoyevsky's nameless narrator of *Notes from Underground*—seething, oppressed, suffering, but with a veneer of manners and social pretension, and a comical haplessness. In his supposed search for health, Zeno is in the process of psychoanalyzing himself: this is the novel's premise. Psychoanalysis is perhaps the ultimate bourgeois luxury, and the very notion of an illness that requires analysis is an indulgence. In short, the ailments of the *malade imaginaire* are the diseases of the rich.

Unlike his Dostoyevskian counterpart, Zeno would seem to want to shed his disease, just as he would seem to want to stop smoking. But both undertakings are merely feints: he wants above all else to keep smoking, just as he wants to remain "ill," and thereby—as he confesses—to persist in the belief in his potential, or latent, greatness and health. His relationship to analysis, to the writing of the manuscript that we are to read, is that of his bond to the cigarette: an engagement with disease in the pretended hope of health, but in truth for the greater delight of the disease.

"Health doesn't analyze itself, nor does it look at itself in the mirror. Only we sick people know something about ourselves," muses Zeno, with regard to the good health of his wife Augusta. Consciousness—one of the meanings of the novel's Italian title, *La Coscienza di Zeno*—is itself a disease. Zeno goes so far as to assert that "Life does resemble sickness a bit . . . [although] unlike other sicknesses, life is always fatal." If being alive, and being conscious, is to suffer ill health, then ill health is clearly a state to be prolonged. To have ostensible faith in the cure, even while knowing that the cure will be lethal and is thus, at all costs, to be avoided: this is the only way forward for Zeno. To be smoking, and yet on the cusp of not smoking, is physically to enact that same paradox. The morbidity of this enterprise reflects, as do his earlier novels, Svevo's devotion to a Schopenhauerian bleakness. But the novel resists the fin-de-siècle decadence of its predecessors; its comedy and its modernist structures make Zeno's antivitalism almost joyful, and thoroughly new.

Desire is at the heart of Zeno's acrobatics: the desire to believe always in the future instead of the past, or even the present. And in the willed heat of passion, the object of desire—the last cigarette, the latest woman—will always be an invention, whose resemblance to the actual is vestigial. Thus Zeno makes ample use of signs and symbols as he plans his last cigarettes—on Napoleon's birthday! on his father's death day! on the day he left studying chemistry for the law, or left studying the law for chemistry!—and thereby grants a particular flavor, a Proustian conjuring power, to each of them.

Zeno drums up his desire for women, and its meaning, as deliberately and arbitrarily as he wills significance into his cigarette-stubbing resolutions. On the eve of consummating his first marital infidelity with the aspiring opera singer Carla, Zeno writes in his dictionary, next to "C," "last infidelity." His apparent hope would seem to be that the words, like a magic spell, would stop him from taking a mistress; but they have only an inverse and titillating effect, like the words "last cigarette." Indeed, when Zeno ultimately breaks off his affair with Carla, he does so unintentionally, by announcing that they will make love "for the last time": "It was a delightful moment. The resolution made by both of us had an efficacy that canceled all guilt. We were innocent and blissful! My benevolent fate had reserved for me an instant of perfect happiness." But Carla does not know the pleasures of living ironically, of speaking as if she meant it: "All of a sudden, with no pity at all, I was forced to maintain such a resolution. I felt ill, really ill. I limped, and I struggled also with a kind of shortness of breath."

Zeno is a man who has taken to his simultaneously ironic and innocent heart the adage "live every day as if it were your last." Paradoxically, only this presumption enables him to live each day as if it were his first, as a new beginning. His resolutions—like his cigarettes—are a sense-enhancing drug; but being forced to keep them causes him physical pain.

Svevo's novel itself reflects, in its structure, the circular logic by which Zeno orders his life. An autobiography, it is not strictly linear. It is divided into sections covering different aspects of his history: his relationship to smoking, his relationship to his father, his courtship and relationship to his wife and mistress, and his business partnership with his brother-in-law. None of these connections is simple; nor is Zeno's telling of them simple. He confides in us the lies that he has told those around him, and yet we can discern that he also lies to us, his readers (his doctors), without admitting it.

In one spectacular fiesta of mendacity, he leaves his sister-in-law's engagement party to see his mistress, under the auspices of paying a visit to a dying friend named Enrico Copler. In order to keep up his alibi, Zeno stops in on Copler on his way back to the party, only to find that his friend has died. Uncertain whether to disrupt the festivities with sad news, he lies and pretends to his relatives that Copler is still living; then, in a fit of pique, reveals that he is dead; then recants this announcement; so that all are ultimately confused and amused over an event that ought to have been tragic. He provides conflicting information about his opinions and emotions. Although he sometimes seems to see himself clearly—and is unabashed about the baseness of his motives and the cowardliness of his behavior—at other moments he reveals a profound incapacity for self-knowledge. In short, he is that slippery fish, the unreliable narrator, whose comedies unnerve us and whose inconsistencies troublingly resemble our own.

Yet the fundamental outlines of his life are not as elusive as all that. Zeno Cosini is the ne'er-do-well son of a prosperous Triestine businessman, a mama's boy whose relations with his father were never close. Upon his father's death—and this early section, along with the opening section about smoking, is one of the strongest in this marvelous book, bleak and hilarious and above all humanly true—Zeno decides that he needs a wife. He takes, instead, a surrogate father, Giovanni Malfenti, a businessman unlike himself, a "man of health *imaginaire*," and the father of four daughters whose names all begin with the letter *A*.

Ada and Augusta are the two elder girls of the foursome, and it is upon Ada that Zeno fixates, proceeding to imagine his own Ada into being, with little attention to the reality before him: "She was the woman I had chosen, she was therefore already mine, and I adorned her with all my dreams, so that the prize of my life would appear more beautiful to me. I adorned her, I bestowed on her all the many qualities I lacked and whose need I felt, because she was to become not only my companion but also my second mother, who would adopt me for a whole lifetime of manly struggle and victory." Zeno's idealized Ada bears no necessary relationship to Ada Malfenti; and with comparable whimsy he dismisses her sister Augusta on account of her squint.

Of course, it is not Ada but Augusta whom he marries, after a series of darkly comic errors. Ada—whom Zeno protests hollowly to have renounced for the remainder of the novel, while frequently revealing through his actions that his passion still burns—marries the dapper Guido Speier, who can play the violin beautifully, who "spoke Tuscan fluently, while Ada and I were condemned to our horrid dialect," and who sports a fine head of hair, in painful contrast to Zeno, who comments that "a good deal of my head had been invaded by my brow." Guido is his second self, his alter ego: the man of action to Zeno's man of thought, the supposed success to Zeno's failure (in business, in art, in sex). Guido will prove ultimately the less solid and resilient of the two, a gambler and a weakling. But this does not stop Zeno from hating him, and even from fantasizing about killing him.

Into this grouping of two couples—Zeno and Augusta, Ada and Guido—enter mistresses (Carla for Zeno, Carmen for Guido) and children and unfortunate business ventures. Eugenio Montale rightly said that "*La Coscienza di Zeno* is a strange book, stagnant and yet continually in motion." It is a novel without plot, in spite of its events; an intricate portrait of Zeno and his relationships rather than a progressive narrative; scrupulously true in spite of, or because of, its innumerable and repeated falsehoods.

Svevo's language is the practical businessman's Italian of Trieste, as distinct from elegant Tuscan as Zeno is from Guido. This accounts at least in part for the lack of enthusiasm with which Svevo's work was initially met in Italy. According to William Weaver, "from the beginning of his career critics have insisted that his Italian is clumsy. 'The Italian of a bookkeeper' is a recurrent jibe." Renato Poggioli called it "the least literary and even the least literate, certainly the least polished, Italian ever used by a man of letters in our time."

An embrace of this clumsiness, an effort to render the infelicities of the Italian, is one of the strengths of Weaver's new translation. Beryl de Zoete's version, called *Confessions of Zeno*, has been the only available one in English until now, and it is also fine; but where Svevo is ragged, de Zoete's tendency is to smooth the prose, whereas Weaver is pleasingly unafraid of the cumbersome or colloquial. Weaver's translation is the fresher for this, and clear also. Its unadorned style highlights the fact that Zeno's Trieste could be anywhere, anytime: there is virtually no physical description of place, and very little physical description whatsoever, in this book; and very little to tie it to the period in which it is set. This is one reason why the novel is no less powerful today than it was seventy-five years ago.

The struggle for a public that dogged Svevo's life has continued after his death: *Zeno's Conscience* is acclaimed as a classic, but it is not typically known or read in the way of, say, *Buddenbrooks* or *Portrait of the Artist as a Young Man*. Rather like the late W. G. Sebald, Svevo came to public attention late in life, and barely had time to enjoy his success before being killed in an automobile accident in 1928. Born in Trieste in 1861 to a German Jewish father and an Italian Jewish mother, Ettore Schmitz was educated in Germany but felt his allegiance to be with the Italian irredentists in his hometown. He adopted the pen name Italo Svevo (Italus the Swabian) to reflect both his Italian and his German heritage.

He wanted always to be a writer, but found himself pressured by family and financial necessity to take work in a bank. His brother Elio was his confidant and support, and believed absolutely in his literary talents: "No historian admired Napoleon as much as I admired Ettore," Elio wrote in his diary, before his early death of nephritis at the age of twenty-three, in 1886. Without his brother's support, Ettore continued to pursue his literary ambitions and, while still working in business, published his first novel, *Una Vita*, at his own expense, in 1892. (It is available in English as *A Life*, translated by Archibald Colquhoun.)

The dark and meticulously observed account of a humble bank clerk with literary aspirations, *Una Vita* gained some favorable local reviews and sank without a trace. In truth, the book is long and plodding, with moments of psychological understanding and agonizing truth but without the compelling voice of Zeno or the structural elegance and compactness of *Senilità*, Svevo's second novel. A work of apprenticeship, it is of interest largely in relation to Svevo's succeeding novels, for his oeuvre reads rather like a palimpsest, repeatedly addressing the same questions and presenting the same patterns. Alfonso Nitti, the hapless protagonist of *Una Vita*, pursues his boss's daughter in a manner not unlike Zeno at the Malfentis; just as Emilio Brentani, the hero of *Senilità*, has a close and complicated friendship with a sculptor, Stefano Balli, which echoes in Zeno's relationship to Guido.

Senilità was issued in English in a new translation by Beth Archer Brombert, re-titled *Emilio's Carnival*. (This was the title that Svevo envisioned for the novel; the English title of Beryl de Zoete's earlier translation, suggested by James Joyce, is *As a Man Grows Older*.) Like Alfonso Nitti in *Una Vita* and Mario Samigli in Svevo's delightful late work *The Hoax*, Emilio Brentani is a modest businessman with literary aspirations and fantasies of greatness. In his mid-thirties he falls in love, for the first time, with a young woman named Angiolina, who is in fact something of a trollop, but whom Emilio insists on seeing as a paragon of beauty and virtue: "He had a certain literary prejudice against the name Angiolina. He called her Lina; but when this abbreviation did not please him he turned her name into French and called her Angèle; or, if he wanted her to be more tender still, he changed it to Ange."

Just like Ada in Zeno, this Angel is a fiction—the untruthful fantasy of a narcissistic soul. So bound up is Emilio with this fantasy life that he fails to notice the disintegration of his sister Amalia, whose unrequited love for Balli runs alongside Emilio's passion. Amalia's love is so repressed, however, that she can indulge it only while dreaming, and Emilio overhears her speaking to her beloved while she sleeps. The cost of this thwarted love will be Amalia's life.

In this novel, the despair that subsumes Alfonso Nitti is passed on to Amalia rather than to her brother, while Emilio persists in his amiable but pernicious delusions to the point where, after Amalia's death, he conflates his sister and Angiolina, making of the latter a beauty with moral virtue. *Emilio's Carnival* is a novel about lies: the lies that Angiolina tells Emilio, but more reprehensibly the lies that he cheerfully and persistently tells himself. Zeno, too, is an account of hypocrisy and dishonesty, even if Zeno is a more self-knowing self-deluder than Emilio. Indeed, all three of Svevo's novels are about delusion and lying, although the tenor of each tale is markedly different.

By the time Svevo published *Senilità*, again at his own expense, in 1898, he had fallen in love with and married his cousin Livia Veneziana, whose parents owned a military paint factory. According to Livia's highly readable and poignant memoir of her husband's life, "No Italian paper mentioned the novel at all, apart from the *Independente* in a supplement. Shaken by public silence and indifference, Ettore wrote: 'I don't understand this incomprehension. It means that people don't understand. . . . Write one must; what one needn't do is publish.' " And so Ettore Schmitz went to work in his in-laws' business, and Italo Svevo was not publicly heard from for twenty-four years. In 1906, however, Schmitz sought English lessons from an unknown Irishman then living in Trieste, the young James Joyce; and a friendship was formed that eventually proved life-changing for the older man. Joyce read and admired both *Una Vita* and *Senilità*, and particularly praised the latter. In turn, he showed his work to Schmitz, and perhaps drew upon his friend in the shaping of Leopold Bloom. Certainly Livia's name and mane of blond hair inspired Anna Livia Plurabelle.

Schmitz continued to write fables in secret—not unlike Mario Samigli, the aging businessman in *The Hoax*; and not unlike Zeno himself. Of Samigli, Svevo observes, with the wry and deprecating humor typical of all his work, "He often wrote fables on the disillusion which follows every human activity. It was as if he sought to console himself for the poverty of his own life by saying: 'I am all right. I cannot fail, because I attempt nothing.'" Livia's memoir recalls her husband's years in business, when—touchingly or foolishly, depending on your point of view—he placed his bourgeois duty to his family above his desire to create art. The man who emerges from her pages is wry, self-deprecating, and resigned: a comic nihilist.

But Svevo finally could not resist what he called his "literary demon," and immediately after World War I he started work on what was to become *La Coscienza di Zeno*. A first draft was written in a matter of weeks in 1919, but the novel took three years and many drafts to complete. "He was surprised by the force of inspiration, which gave him no peace," writes Livia. The book was published—once again, at his own expense—in 1923. Without Joyce's intervention, it seems entirely possible that *Zeno's Conscience* would have disappeared without a trace, in the manner of its predecessors; but with the assistance of his now-celebrated supporter Svevo found himself not only published but feted across Europe. In these last years, Svevo told an acquaintance: "Until last year I was the . . . least ambitious man in the world. . . . Now I am overcome by ambition. I have become eager for praise. I now live only to manage my own glory. I went to Paris . . . and all I could see was Italo Svevo. . . . The *ville lumière* . . . seemed to exist only as a function of my glory."

Svevo makes mock of this old man's youthful zeal for fame in *The Hoax*, in which Mario Samigli, now sixty, has a practical joke played upon him by a friend, who pretends to him that the long-forgotten novel of his youth is to be published in German. Samigli believes that "he had simply got what he deserved, surely the most natural thing in the world. The only extraordinary thing was that it had not happened before. The history of literature was full of celebrated men who had not been famous quite from birth. At a given moment would appear among them the really great critic (white beard, heavy brow, penetrating eye) or maybe an intelligent businessman . . . and immediately they rose to fame." And this naïve fantasy is followed by an astute satirical observation: "For one does not win fame merely by deserving it. The inert mass of the people must be influenced first by one or more powerful minds who choose for them what they shall read. It seems rather absurd, but there is no way out of it. Even if the critic understands nothing but his own job, and the publisher (the businessman) does not even understand that, the result is the same. Once the two get together, even a quite undeserving author is made for the time being."

This capacity to indulge naïveté and yet clearly to see through that indulgence is central to Svevo as a writer: he sympathizes powerfully with the importance of fantasy in the little man's dreary existence, having himself lived so long upon the mere fantasy of literary success; and yet he is also aware of its dangers. Samigli may be a cheerful fool, but Svevo's other protagonists are, in their narcissistic preoccupation, dangerous to themselves and to others—indeed, lethal. Alfonso Nitti commits suicide; Emilio Brentani is indirectly responsible for the death of his sister; and Zeno, in spite of all his protestations, is implicated in the suicide of his brother-in-law, partner, and rival, Guido Speier. Lies and delusion may be essential for happiness, Svevo seems to say, but, like smoking, they can have nasty consequences.

In *Zeno* in particular, Svevo goes still further: if the novel begins by asserting that "disease is a conviction, and I was born with that conviction," the last pages of Zeno's manuscript see him cured of his imaginary illnesses—not by medicine, but by the presence of death in life, by World War I. Having pursued good health without success throughout his life, Zeno finds that his imaginary malady evaporates when the world around him is engulfed in death and destruction. "I do not feel healthy comparatively. I am healthy, absolutely," he insists. "Sorrow and love—life, in other words—cannot be considered a sickness because they hurt." With uncanny pre-atomic prescience, he goes on to predict the apocalypse, the world's end at the hands of "an ordinary man" who invents "an incomparable explosive": "And another man, also ordinary, but a bit sicker than others, will steal this explosive and will climb up at the center of the earth, to set it on the spot where it can have the maximum effect. There will be an enormous explosion that no one will hear, and the earth, once again a nebula, will wander through the heavens, freed of parasites and sickness."

Thus ends Zeno's account, a narrative shaped from the fantasy of his birth to the fantasy of his death, from his first introduction to disease to its last banishment from the earth. It is both comedy and horror that that banishment will entail the end of the earth itself; it is also simply life. As Zeno aptly observes to Guido in the midst of their financial troubles, a discovery he makes to his surprise: "Life is neither ugly nor beautiful, but it's original!"

The arc of Svevo's own life was that of a black comedy that he himself might have written: a man's progress from youthful literary aspiration through failure and despair to late, unanticipated literary success, only then to find himself brutally punished for that success by the hand of fate. Svevo anticipated such absurdity: from a very young age, he knew better than most what life is really like. He deserves to be read in order that we might better understand our weak and desirous selves, laughing and suffering at once. *Senilità* is a fine tale, in its precise and tightly structured portrait of a weak man and the toll of his fantasy life upon the reality of others; but *Zeno's Conscience* is a masterpiece, a novel overflowing with human truth in all its murkiness, laughter, and terror, a book as striking and relevant today as it was when it was first published, and a book that is in every good way—its originality included—like life.

TEJU COLE

In our age of rapid technology and the jolly, undiscriminating ephemeralizing of culture and knowledge, an insistence upon high stakes—a desire to ask the big questions—can seem quaint, or passé, or simply a little embarrassing. How to reconcile Philip Roth's observation about American life, in his essay "Writing American Fiction" (written now an astonishing fifty years ago), that "the actuality is continually outdoing our talents," with a writer's lofty aim, to quote J. M. Coetzee's *Elizabeth Costello*, of "measuring herself against the illustrious dead"?

Teju Cole, in his lauded debut novel *Open City*, has perhaps found a way forward. This economical account of a young African man's year in New York lays no overt claim to greatness; indeed, it revels in banal digression: the narrator, Julius, riffs on the closing of Tower Records and Blockbuster stores, and fusses a great deal over his forgotten ATM PIN number. The novel relies on small, almost self-indulgent observations ("In recent years I have noticed how much the light affects my ability to be sociable"), and peculiar detail ("One of the characteristics of the bedbug, Campbell wrote, is its cannibalistic nature. He presented evidence that engorged bugs were sometimes slit open and consumed by their young"). But Cole nevertheless addresses vital human issues more astutely than do most contemporary works of fiction. What is knowledge? What is self-knowledge? What is responsibility? What is the value of witness alone? What is the weight of history upon us? How do we move through it? And what are the costs of remaining an outsider?

Questions such as these are not subjects for theory, although Cole's narrator, a young psychiatrist, occasionally refers to theorists in his wide-ranging musings. Rather they are lived, through passing conversations and fragmented memories, or, obliquely, through the lacunae in Julius's story.

In this way, Cole creates a more nuanced, visceral, and unsettling realism than that produced by so-called practitioners of the form: there are, in this flaneur's narrative, hardly any scenes, few characters, and no plot as we would traditionally understand it. We are furnished, on the other hand, with startling observations and juxtapositions, memorable aperçus, and the complicated portrait of a narrator whose silences speak as loudly as his words—all articulated in an effortlessly elegant prose that convinces of itself, without recourse to pyrotechnics.

There are, in *Open City*, strong echoes of European writers such as W. G. Sebald, in the book's form and sometimes, too, in its syntax; and an un-American, unabashedly mandarin sensibility, unafraid of literary, musical, and artistic references. Julius confesses early on that he cannot listen to American classical radio because of the commercials—"Beethoven followed by ski jackets, Wagner after artisanal cheese"—and instead relies on the internet for stations "from Canada, Germany, or the Netherlands." It is a cosmopolite's detachment from his American experience that will haunt the book: here is a worldly foreigner's New York, colored by simultaneous curiosity about and recoil from the city's history and

essences. Cole's enterprise is not in itself new—it has a long literary history, stretching back at least to Baudelaire—but its American setting is novel, not least because it presumes that New York,
like Paris, London, or Berlin, has sufficient history, sufficient
sedimentation, to warrant an almost archaeological approach.

It is also important that Cole's narrator is Nigerian—African,
rather than African-American; and notably, given that his interior world is illuminated by Roland Barthes, Gustav Mahler,
and J. M. Coetzee, black rather than white. As Julius reflects, on
attending a concert at Carnegie Hall:

> I am used to it, but it never ceases to surprise me how easy it
> is to leave the hybridity of the city, and enter into all-white
> spaces, the homogeneity of which, as far as I can tell, causes
> no discomfort to the whites in them. The only thing odd, to
> some of them, is seeing me, young and black, in my seat or
> at the concession stand.

At Carnegie Hall, Julius is distinctive in his blackness, a reality for a long time both familiar and dismaying to liberal white
readers; but this is just one of many experiences that are shaped
by Julius's skin color, or, sometimes more specifically, by his
Africanness.

This characteristic determines his passing exchanges, not just
with the white tourist children on the subway who observe, one
to another, "He's black . . . but he's not dressed like a gangster,"
but also with an African taxi driver ("The way you came into my
car without saying hello, that was bad. Hey, I'm African just like
you, why you do this?"); with a dignified Haitian shoeshine man
who recounts his life story in a strangely antiquated language

("The years of yellow fever were the most difficult. It fell on us like plague, and many were those who died in this city"); or with the African-American postal worker named Terrence McKinney, who, confiding, "I could see you were from the Motherland," volunteers his own poetry:

> We are the ones who received the boot. We, who are used for loot, trampled underfoot. Unconquered. We, who carry the crosses. Yes, see? Our kith and kin used like packhorses. We of the countless horrific losses, assailed by the forces, robbed of choices, silenced voices. And still unconquered.

These are but a few of the instances in which Julius's quotidian experience is shaped by what others presume at the sight of him; and his consistent resistance to this African identification is striking. He says, of the taxi driver, "I was in no mood for people who tried to lay claims on me"; and of the encounter with McKinney, "I made a mental note to avoid that particular post office in the future."

And yet, over the course of the novel, this same dispassionate young man eagerly explores Manhattan from the Customs House and Wall Street to Pinehurst and Cabrini, making careful note not only of the peculiar minutiae of city life—marathon runners, art exhibitions, park musicians, and so forth—but also, memorably, of the forgotten atrocities that lie, in palimpsest, beneath the city's current geography. It is almost as if these pilgrimages are an act of witness, however haphazard, for history's downtrodden—for the very predecessors of the present-day taxi driver or postal worker whose advances Julius is at such pains to resist. He reflects upon the massacre of the Canarsie Indians by Cornelis van Tienhoven, a seventeenth century "schout" in New Amsterdam. He visits the Customs House far downtown, noting that:

> Trading in slaves had become a capital offense in the United States in 1820, but New York long remained the most important port for the building, outfitting, insuring, and launching of slavers' ships. Much of the human cargo of those vessels was going to Cuba; Africans did the work on the sugar plantations there.

He happens upon the site of an African burial ground on and around Chambers Street in Lower Manhattan:

> What I was steeped in, on that warm morning, was the echo across centuries, of slavery in New York. At the Negro Burial Ground, as it was then known . . . excavated bodies bore traces of suffering: blunt trauma, grievous bodily harm. Many of the skeletons had broken bones, evidence of the suffering they'd endured in life. Disease was common, too: syphilis, rickets, arthritis. In some of the palls were found shells, beads, and polished stones, and in these scholars had seen hints of African religions, rites perhaps retained from the Congo, or from along the West African coast, from which so many people had been captured and sold into slavery. One body had been found buried in a British marine officer's uniform. Some others had been found with coins over their eyes.

This marking of the city's forgotten sites of violence attempts a redemption through retrieval, an act vital given the truth—

articulated by Professor Saito, Julius's mentor and former teacher of early English literature at Maxwell College—that:

> There are towns whose names evoke a real horror in you because you have learned to link those names with atrocities, but, for the generation that follows yours, those names will mean nothing; forgetting doesn't take long. Fallujah will be as meaningless to them as Daejeon is to you.

Human memory, even for the unspeakable, is short; and without efforts such as Julius's, an entire violent legacy will remain, unaddressed, beneath the bustling and plausible surface of that bastion of tolerant hybridity that is New York.

We have, then, in Julius, a new and particular guide to a familiar world: he awakens us to the city as we had not heretofore seen it; and in so doing, thrillingly follows Pound's literary exhortation to "make it new." That such an almost taxonomical impulse—a desire to locate the patterns in life's chaos, and in these patterns, meaning—is more complicated, and more compromised, than at first it appears, is, perhaps, the book's central, unarticulated "story."

Just as Julius's random walks somehow provide a rich map of the island from end to end, so, too, do his apparently serendipitous encounters combine to create a very particular sense of the city itself and of its observer. Alongside this narrative, Julius gradually reveals a series of apparently unrelated memories of his childhood, first in Lagos and then at the Nigerian Military School in Zaria, and a smattering of facts about his family, in particular about his estranged German mother and her own estranged mother, his grandmother.

It is as if, in his choices of what to retell, Julius is providing us with the superficial historical plaques that gesture toward his life's central traumas. When we walk past a monument or marker in the city, we cannot, unless we seek further, know all that may have occurred there in its full significance; and so, too, we cannot apprehend simply from Julius's description of facts—of, for example, a frustrated afternoon of sexual awakening, in which his abortive childhood attempt at masturbation was punctuated by the theft of a bottle of Coca-Cola and an epic downpour—what actually, in its fullness, took place on a given day. What happened and what it means remains beneath the surface, where we can only glimpse its psychological magnitude.

There is perfect logic in this obliquity for a young psychiatrist like Julius, who learned from his beloved Professor Saito "the art of listening . . . and the ability to trace out a story from what was omitted." So we, too, Cole's readers, must operate like psychiatrists or like archaeologists; and in so doing, we find beneath Julius's calm but fragmented account of the "open city" another, darker topography, of neurosis, rupture, and violence.

Open City's loose frame is a year in the life of a young psychiatric resident on the verge of qualifying. Half German, half Nigerian, and American-educated, Julius is in his early thirties when the story unfolds, from the fall of 2006 into 2007—old enough to be an adult with a web of social and familial responsibilities, but young enough, too, to be without them. He has recently broken up with his girlfriend, Nadège (although this seems to have been a relatively short-lived liaison); he is under stress in his work; not only far from his Nigerian family, he has long been estranged from his mother (his father died when he was fourteen). He starts, in this time, his walks around the city:

The walks met a need: they were a release from the tightly regulated mental environment of work, and once I discovered them as therapy, they became the normal thing, and I forgot what life had been like before I started walking. Work was a regimen of perfection and competence.... The streets served as a welcome opposite to all that. Every decision . . . was inconsequential, and was for that reason a reminder of freedom.

THE FREEDOM JULIUS seeks is precisely detachment: untethered by family or relationships, undecided in most things, he is most comfortable in the role of voyeur. He is so busy seeing—and showing us what he sees—that he hopes, himself, to remain unseen.

Insofar as any of us can present a clear outline, it is shaped by our connections to, or disconnections from, others. Only tenuously attached to the American city around him, Julius has willfully broken with his African past. Central to his account of the year are his ex-girlfriend Nadège (who, now in California, remains a figure in his mind rather than a presence in his world); his mentor Professor Saito, in failing health at the novel's outset and dead well before its close; and an unnamed jazz-loving, divorced academic friend, who ultimately leaves the city for a position at the University of Chicago. Others who intermittently penetrate the boundaries of Julius's well-defended consciousness include his psychiatric patients, among them the young woman V., a Native American assistant professor of history at NYU, and the author of a book about Cornelis van Tienhoven; and, increasingly, in apparent friendship, a young Nigerian woman named Moji Kasali, the sister of Julius's high school friend Dayo, upon whom he has stumbled in New York and with whom he has renewed acquaintance.

Beyond this already somewhat remote human layer lies the spectrum of passing encounters that give fundamental shape to Julius's solitary days: conversations not only with taxi drivers and postal workers, but also with the illegal immigrant Saidu, from Liberia, whom he visits in a detention center in Queens as part of Nadège's church group outing—a visit that hints at the conflicts within Julius himself. After hearing—and reporting—Saidu's extraordinary tale of exodus from war-torn Liberia, via Guinea and Morocco to Spain and Portugal, only to find himself immediately detained upon arrival in the U.S., Julius takes his leave, knowing at some level that he has no more wish to be associated with Saidu than with Terrence McKinney. As he goes, Saidu says, "Come back and visit me, if I am not deported."

I said that I would, but never did.

I told the story to Nadège on the way back into Manhattan that day. Perhaps she fell in love with the idea of myself that I presented in that story. I was the listener, the compassionate African who paid attention to the details of someone else's life and struggle. I had fallen in love with that idea myself.

Julius, of course, has so fallen in love with this idea that he has become a healing listener by profession, someone who can proudly relay the reverent remark of one of his patients:

Doctor, I just want to tell you how proud I am to come here, and see a young black man like yourself in a white coat, because things haven't ever been easy for us, and no one has ever given us nothing without a struggle.

Tellingly, though, Julius is no psychotherapist; and perhaps not as good a listener as he would purport to be.

His ultimate indifference to Saidu's fate is far more egregiously echoed in his friendship with Professor Saito, to whom he insists, after a long hiatus, "You'll see more of me in the next few months, now that things are stable again"—a comment made during what proves his penultimate visit, and in anticipation of a memorable failure of intimacy:

> I wish I had asked what his late partner's name was. He would have told me. . . . But in spite of myself, unable to be fully present to our conversation, I could not lead it in this new direction.

Instead, Julius is suddenly obsessed by the bedbugs that have infested Professor Saito's apartment: in this chapter, his thoughts about these creatures simply supplant the professor altogether.

Similarly and fatally, Julius, while on vacation in Brussels, fails to heed the call of his patient V. ("I can't be reached, I said, have her call Dr. Kim, the resident covering for me"); and it is only just in passing, as something barely noticeable, that we learn of V.'s subsequent suicide:

> The *Times* had said, in the obituary I read that day, that V. wrote of atrocity without flinching. They might have said, without flinching visibly, for it had all affected her far more deeply than anyone's ability to guess.

This parenthetical observation about V.'s intolerable pain and the act to which it drove her—the pain for which Julius was the supposed healer—is sandwiched between his persistent distress about having forgotten the PIN number for his ATM card when on his way to meet his accountant.

This pattern, an unmasterable solipsistic irresponsibility largely invisible to Julius himself, recurs fiercely but not heavy-handedly, a red thread in the book's superficially muted weave. What Julius can see of it—an awareness only of the internal ticks of his moods, moments of happiness or sadness dependent on such small things—he judges from an almost haughty distance:

> How petty seemed to me the human condition, that we are subject to this constant struggle to modulate the internal environment, this endless being tossed about like a cloud.

But these are, like so much in his story, symptoms rather than a cause.

Julius the unhealed physician is both the most reliable and the most unreliable of narrators, and it is in his terrifying failures of self-knowledge—no more disturbing, we might think, than anyone else's: a solipsistic failure of which we are all, with our PIN numbers and sudden fear of diseases, more or less guilty—that he proves a dark and possibly broken soul, someone for whom the role of flaneur is a hermetic one, rather than open at all.

Just like the city, Julius, in moving on, has buried much, and more than he is aware. He insists that:

> Each person must, on some level, take himself as the calibration point for normalcy, must assume that the room

of his own mind is not, cannot be, entirely opaque to him. Perhaps this is what we mean by sanity: that whatever our self-admitted eccentricities might be, we are not the villains of our own stories. In fact, it is quite the contrary: we play, and only play, the hero, and in the swirl of other people's stories, insofar as those stories concern us at all, we are never less than heroic.

And yet his heroism, even at its most shining, is of a curiously passive sort. In the middle of his year, Julius takes a long trip to Brussels. It is at the heart of Cole's novel (in itself a fascinating decision: at the core of the "open city" lies an escape from it), and serves as a microcosmic reconfiguration of his relation to New York.

Julius makes the journey to Brussels supposedly to search for his lost maternal grandmother, of whom he has only one boyhood memory. She is a German war widow whose daughter, Julius's mother, was born in May 1945, a survivor of great hardship (including, he surmises, rape at the hands of the triumphant Russian army). This woman was last known to be living in Brussels.

But what he tells us of his time there would suggest that his grandmother was all along a diversionary tactic; or else that she is too great a trauma for him to confront. He makes no apparent effort to locate her at all. Instead, he re-creates his loose web of random connections, befriending first his neighbor on the airplane, a woman surgeon, grandmotherly in aspect, named Madame Maillotte; and subsequently a Moroccan student, Farouq, who works in the local internet café. Julius has a fleeting but lovely intimate encounter with a middle-aged Czech woman met in a café—"we were simply two people far away from home,

doing what two people wanted to do. To my lightness and gratitude was added a faint sorrow. . . . I returned to my solitude"—but
then, typically, he retreats to his rented room to read Barthes's
Camera Lucida.

In this loose, limpid wandering, Julius's "oma," as he calls his
grandmother, becomes only the faint memory of the day

> she had visited Olumo Rock with us in Nigeria, and had
> wordlessly massaged my shoulder. It was in these thoughts
> that I began to wonder if Brussels hadn't somehow drawn
> me to itself for reasons more opaque than I suspected, that
> the paths I mindlessly followed through the city followed a
> logic irrelevant to my family history.

In short, in order to avoid introspection Julius turns outward
yet again, a chronicler of his environment rather than of his own
soul. But in Brussels, he shows himself capable of more active
human pursuit than at home in New York, and the focus of his
attention is Farouq, with whom he has several intense conversations. As a scholar and thinker, Farouq is passionately engaged—
he reads Walter Benjamin in the internet café, and drops terms
like "the victimized Other: how strange, I thought, that he used
an expression like that in a casual conversation"—even while, as
a citizen, he is passionately disenchanted: "He, too, was in the
grip of rage and rhetoric. . . . A cancerous violence had eaten into
every political idea, had taken over the ideas themselves. . . ."

Together, the young men discuss literature (Tahar Ben Jelloun
versus Mohamed Choukri), the value of Edward Said, nonvio-
lence, the importance of the Middle East conflict, the role of al-
Qaeda, and the existence of a genuine political left in the United

States. Then, too, Farouq tells his tale of embittered woe, of his failed Ph.D. and of the academic conspiracy against him, of how he is reduced by fate from his ambition to be a thinker, and will be instead merely a translator.

Here, in Farouq, is the man to whom Julius most readily feels a connection, and also the man he most dreads becoming. He is at once impressed by and contemptuous of the young Moroccan, whose political engagement has propelled him to autodidactic feats, and has at the same time rendered him a furious victim. Far better to be Julius, in his cool isolation and his white doctor's coat, earning the respect and admiration of remote but grateful patients, than to be the doomed Farouq:

> How many would-be radicals, just like him, had been formed on just such a slight [as the failed Ph.D.]? . . .
>
> There was something powerful about him, a seething intelligence, something that wanted to believe itself indomitable. But he was one of the thwarted ones. His script would stay in proportion.

So saying, Julius passes a white man's judgment upon Farouq, and dismisses him. He, like all the others, will vanish henceforth from the story.

It is immediately hereafter that Julius awakens from a dream set in Lagos, and, upon hearing the rainfall, is visited by the childhood memory of stealing a bottle of Coca-Cola and attempting, unsuccessfully, to masturbate. Long but very precise, this memory has itself the quality of a dream; and like a dream, it seems to point to, rather than to elucidate, its import. Of the sexual aspect of the recollection Julius notes:

For many years, I had been tempted to overinterpret the other events of that day, but what happened afterward, between my mother and myself, was due as much to any other day in my boyhood as to the day the rain began.

This, unexpectedly and yet (given his temperament) inevitably, is the most direct accounting of their rift in the entire book. Other later signs, more disturbing, involving Moji Kasali, may point us toward an interpretation; but there will be, in *Open City*, no closing of the case.

Teju Cole has achieved, in this book, a rare balance. He captures life's urgent banality (think of Victor Klemperer, in his diaries of his life as a Jew in Nazi Germany, fretting endlessly about toothache or how to procure cigarettes), and he captures, too, the ways in which the greater subjects—violence, autonomy, selfhood, life and death—glimmer darkly in the interstices between bedbugs and Tower Records. The foreground and the background are, in the end, equally important; but by shifting perspective, we can greatly change the story that we tell. Each of us, no matter how clearly we see others, is guilty of potentially criminal blindness with regard to ourselves. The violence that we do and that is done to us remains, like the violence of our culture itself, often invisible. New York City itself is built upon bones, and the fact that we do not see them—that we cannot bear to see them—will not make them disappear.

MAGDA SZABÓ

Magda Szabó, who died in 2007, was one of Hungary's most important twentieth-century writers. Not that most of us Anglophones would have known it, as until recently little of her work had been translated into English. *The Door*, her best-known novel, which appeared in Hungary in 1987, was initially translated by Stefan Draughon and brought out in the United States by an academic publisher in 1995. Subsequently translated into French, the book won the Prix Femina Étranger in 2003 and was beautifully retranslated by Len Rix for British publication in 2005. A decade later, New York Review Books Classics—acting, yet again, in its capacity as the Savior of Lost Greats—delivered this version to an American audience.

It's astonishing that this masterpiece should have been essentially unknown to English-language readers for so long, a realization that raises once again the question of what other gems we're missing out on. The dismaying discussion of how little translated work is available in the United States must wait for another time; suffice it to say that I've been haunted by this novel. Szabó's lines and images come to my mind unexpectedly, and with them powerful emotions. It has altered the way I understand my own life.

A work of stringent honesty and delicate subtlety, *The Door* is a story in which, superficially, very little happens. Szabó's narrator, like the author a writer named Magda (in interviews, Szabó suggested that the novel was only thinly veiled personal history), follows the intricacies of her intimate filial relationship with her housekeeper, Emerence. In doing so, it exposes the rich inadequacies of human communication even as it evokes the agonies of Hungary's recent history.

When Emerence first comes to work for Magda and her husband, they have recently moved into a large apartment, following Magda's political rehabilitation in Communist Hungary: "For ten years my writing career had been politically frozen. Now it was picking up again and here, in this new setting, I had become a full-time writer, with increased opportunities and countless responsibilities." Emerence chooses Magda and her husband, rather than vice versa—"I don't wash just anyone's dirty linen"—and while it emerges that the two women are from the same rural region, the formidable Emerence remains a mystery, of near-mythical proportions. At their first encounter, "she was washing a mountain of laundry with the most antiquated equipment, boiling bed linen in a caldron over a naked flame, in the already agonizing heat, and lifting the sheets out with an immense wooden spoon. Fire glowed all around her. She was tall, big-boned, powerfully built for a person of her age, muscular rather than fat, and she radiated strength like a Valkyrie. Even the scarf on her head seemed to jut forward like a warrior's helmet."

Emerence's strength is imposing (in addition to her housecleaning, she sweeps the snow for eleven buildings on their shared street), as is her reserve. Animals of all kinds gravitate to her; people in the neighborhood rely on her, look up to her, and are grateful for her charity. But in return, she remains stern and aloof. "Although she looked after us for over twenty years," Magda recalls, "during the first five of them it would have taken precision instruments to measure the degree to which she permitted real communication between us."

Eventually, however, through a series of exchanges both emotional and material, the two women become close in spite of their differences. Emerence sustains Magda through her husband's grave illness. She encourages the couple when they adopt a dog, then names him (Viola) and trains him so that she is his real mistress. She relies on Magda for help when awaiting an undisclosed but important visitor. She introduces Magda to her trio of close friends, who surround her like the three Fates. She bestows upon Magda and her husband a number of gifts that they resist at their peril. And, through all of this, tempestuous, the two women repeatedly argue and reconcile.

The greatest intimacy Emerence shares with Magda is to permit her to cross the threshold of her home, to witness her secrets. It is a unique privilege: Although Emerence entertains a great deal on her porch, she never allows anyone beyond the front door. "You're going to see something no one has ever seen," she explains, "and no one ever will, until they bury me. But I've nothing else you would value . . . so I'm going to give you the only thing I have."

Even before Magda enters what she terms "the Forbidden City," she is past the point of no return: "It wasn't easy to accept that from now on I would always have to consider Emerence. Her life had become an integral part of my own. This led to the dreadful thought that one day I would lose her, that if I survived her there would be yet another addition to those ubiquitous, indefinable shadow-presences that wrack me and drive me to despair."

Emerence is as practical, anti-intellectual, and hostile to the church as Magda is abstracted, literary, and religious, but in spite of their radical dissimilarities, both women are aware that friendship has its costs. Magda's dead mother hovers over the narrative, the clearest of her "shadow-presences." Emerence's life has been marked from early childhood onward by brutal losses, a trail of tragedy and sacrifice that may explain the locked front door. Questions linger, too, about Emerence's own shadow, about what she may have done, or not done, through Hungary's darkest years. The dog Viola—as vivid and fully realized a character as any human, a truly great literary dog—is essential to their love for each other. Their treatment of this creature is a manifestation of their disparate experiences.

Throughout the novel, Szabó sows plentiful allusions—to Book 6 of Virgil's *Aeneid*, to Shaw and E. T. A. Hoffmann, to the Fates of Greek myth and to the Bible, even to *Gone with the Wind*—that lend Emerence a superhuman significance. She may be a mere housekeeper, but she is also an indomitable icon. It is a stature, Szabó implies, of which Emerence is not unaware, which makes the onset of her human frailty, the advent of true old age, perilous and tragic. When that time comes, Magda and Emerence understand differently what it means to care lovingly for an ailing friend. An unintended, heartbreaking betrayal inevitably ensues.

WHEN I FIRST read this novel, not long after the death of my only aunt, the book spoke particularly to that experience; even as it resonated with relationships, earlier in life, with women who had worked for my Canadian grandmother and for my French grandparents. Anyone who has either been, or had a long-standing connection with, a family retainer knows the complexities of such relationships; others have written powerfully about the experience, from Proust's housekeeper Céleste Albaret to Kathryn Stockett, the author of *The Help*. Szabo's Emerence, however, is mythic in her forcefulness, which renders particularly wrenching both her eventual vulnerability and Magda's failure properly to protect her.

My Canadian grandmother's housekeeper Rosa, crinkle-eyed, ruddy-skinned, and wiry, was a presence not only in my childhood but well beyond: Raised on a collective farm in the Ukraine, taken by the Germans as a teenager for forced labor in a factory, she arrived in Canada as a Displaced Person shortly after the Second World War, along with her Polish husband and new baby. Barely literate in English—or in her native Ukrainian, or in Russian, or in German, for that matter, though she spoke all these languages—she and her husband nevertheless enabled their son to go to university: he became an engineer and built a successful business. Widowed young, Rosa didn't seek to remarry: instead, she spent her vacations traveling to the Caribbean, and her weekend evenings dancing at a supper club on the Toronto waterfront. She walked miles each day, and continued to work well into her eighties—coming to clean once a week for my mother and, for a time, for my sister also, after my grandmother died in the mid-1990s.

Having come to work with our family in 1947, having watched my mother grow up, Rosa was, by the time of my childhood, fully a part of my maternal family: my grandmother, too, was widowed early, and my mother her only child. The two aging women relied on one another, confided in one another, bickered, and at times quarreled outright, like blood relatives. Their emotional bonds were contorted by the underlying transactional relationship: my grandmother felt responsible for Rosa, and Rosa for my grandmother, but they irritated one another, and over time, complained volubly to my mother about one another. Their points of friction were embedded in their weekly routines, and after forty years they reached a point of furious rupture—over a trifle, of course (my grandmother was at fault)—which my mother, the peacemaker, worked for months to repair.

Twenty years younger than my grandmother, fifteen years older than my mother, Rosa proved stronger than both of them. When my mother was in the grip of the Lewy body dementia that would kill her, but first robbed her of access to her will and her memories, we took her to visit her old caregiver. "Oh," my mother exclaimed, her voice filled with wonder, as if her life were restored to her, "It's you! It's *Rosa*!" And Rosa, undiminished at ninety, tears in her eyes, wrapped her arms around the husk of the young girl she'd known so long ago.

My French grandparents relied on Odet, a Portuguese woman who had immigrated in youth to France with her *fainéant* husband Francisco. Small and round like a loaf, meticulous in all things, she spoke French with a singsong lilt, and wore patterned pinafores over her nylon dresses. When I was a child, she hurried from the kitchen across the hallway's marble tiles, slippers slapping, when my grandmother rang the little brass bell with a maid for a handle; until Odet told her employers how she hated it, and they put it away forever. She worked for my grandparents for almost thirty years, from eight a.m. till one p.m., six days a week, and she, too, was as much a part of our family as any blood relation. When we were small, she spoiled my sister and me with cakes and treats, and when we were teenagers she pressed upon us, when we arrived each summer, a five-hundred-franc note apiece, a great deal of money at the time. We were aware of how long it must have taken her to earn it. While there, we were largely idle—"you're on vacation," she'd insist, often shooing us from the kitchen, "go enjoy yourselves!"—but unlike the adults, we sometimes moved in her domestic world: we made the beds, and set and cleared the table, and dried the dishes and put them away. In the evenings, as we grew up my sister and I did the washing-up, knowing that otherwise Odet would arrive to a mountain of crusted plates and cutlery in the morning. She, rather than our grandmother or aunt, taught us the family recipes, had us from an early age salting sliced cucumbers or eggplant and pressing them between layers of paper towel to drain, scalding and peeling tomatoes and scooping out the seeds, preparing elegant platters of wafer-thin prosciutto and Charentais melon.

For my antique grandparents, Odet had, as far as I know, only affection. She claimed to love them with a fairy-tale simplicity, and acceded to the family myth that my grandmother was, in fact, a lay saint. (My grandmother, born in the nineteenth century, died at ninety-one while eating an orange madeleine, having taken only a small bite: Odet and my grandfather sequestered the biscuit in a glass jar in the cereal cupboard, where it remained, like a saint's relic, for easily a decade. Tellingly, it did not decompose.) My grandparents treated Odet like a daughter, she used to say; and before Madame lost her memory, she taught Odet everything she knew.

But their actual daughter, Denise, my aunt, posed challenges. Unmarried, she lived initially in another apartment in the same complex, even though she spent much of her free time with her parents. After my grandmother's death, however, my aunt moved in with my grandfather, ostensibly to care for him, though perhaps also to protect her own fragile sanity; and this made Odet's life a misery. Herself working long hours, nerves frayed, always a woman with a short fuse, Denise treated Odet neither as daughter nor as sister, but as a maid, an underling, the domestic help; which, after decades with the family, baffled and infuriated Odet. "*C'est une garce*," Odet muttered to my sister and me, irate in a way we'd never seen her, and once, agonizingly for all, to Denise's face: "*Vous êtes une garce*." Our grandfather attempted, with only moderate success, to salve all wounds; but his daughter, his blood, remained his first responsibility. Odet's loathing for Denise seeped into the fabric of her days: the unmade bed, laundry left on the floor, the spattered bathroom sink, overflowing ashtrays with their filthy, ashy reek—even when she wasn't at home, Denise was ubiquitous. Eventually, Odet and her husband decided to retire early and return to Portugal: "I wanted to wait till your grandfather died," she told me, "but I couldn't stand it."

It was my Tante Denise, recently deceased when I read Magda Szabó's novel, of whom *The Door* put me most powerfully in mind; or rather, of my own failings with regard to her. Always idiosyncratic, often difficult (she had a history of depression and a bipolar diagnosis), Tante Denise became, with age, impossible. After her father's death, in addition to her lifelong chain-smoking, she took rather pointedly to drink; but after my father's death, she threw herself wholeheartedly into the project, and deteriorated rapidly from an elegant if frail bourgeois lady into a rough-skinned haggard sot, increasingly rebarbative and vexatious, prone to insults, rages, and physical collapse. Because my sister and I lived far away, we didn't for some time grasp the extent of the problem; but were set straight by the building's concierge and eventually by the neighbors, more than one of whom had been called upon to rescue Denise after a drunken fall.

We had long been aware that our largely secular, liberal North American mind-set was a far cry from Denise's: an exhaustingly devout *pied-noir* Catholic, she was a staunch cultural and political conservative who firmly embraced hierarchies and traditional roles. She believed, too, that our failings are God-given—her temper, for example, and eventually her drunkenness—and hence to be accepted by those who love us, like the color of our eyes. My sister and I, meanwhile, with our Emersonian belief in agency, in the capacity to change, and with a perhaps naïve optimism for the future—we sought to help our aunt get a grip on things. We believed, we wanted to believe, that she had a whole chapter of her life still ahead. We arranged for her to dry out in rehab, which she resisted until we suggested we might enlist her doctors' help and formally oblige her. But she got so drunk the night before her departure that when she fell, broke her hip, and was rushed to hospital, they couldn't operate for over fifteen hours. We cheered the fact that on account of the surgery and its aftermath, she'd quit smoking; for which she cursed us roundly, and with venom. In the rehab hospital (of a different sort altogether than had been planned), she had me wheel her out onto the deck with her oxygen tank so she could light up: she went to considerable inconvenience to restart her habit. Just as she couldn't wait to smoke again, she couldn't wait to slake her thirst; she engaged a neighbor's loose-tongued housekeeper (with whom she'd spent many afternoons tippling) to slip her bottles on the sly in her hospital bed. When finally back at home, albeit with around-the-clock care, she set about her self-destruction in a spirit of almost exuberant vengeance against us, the nieces—her only nieces—who had so impertinently and egregiously bucked the generational hierarchy, disrespected her desires, and ruined her life. In her last weeks—because after that return home, she was diagnosed with terminal lung cancer almost at once, and lived less than three months—she often refused to speak when one of us called, instructing her caregivers to say that she was busy, or didn't feel well enough. When I visited, she glared at me with an expression of terror and desolate aloneness that haunts me still: unlike the eyes of the others I've known dying, hers afforded an unconsoled glimpse of the abyss. Her Catholic faith apparently provided no solace. She refused to discuss her cancer, or her drinking, or to acknowledge her imminent death. In the last days, she turned her face to the wall and fell silent.

READING *THE DOOR*, I was again painfully aware of having failed my aunt. What does unconditional love entail? Tante Denise's Catholic version and Emerence's stoical one—to accept a person's flaws, to respect their desires, and to continue to love them, without judgment—are surely closer to the answer than were our self-righteous attempts to reform Denise "for her own good." Just as Magda betrays Emerence by following society's supposedly benevolent rules, I, too, had betrayed my lonely aunt, who, after the long-distant death of her beloved mother, and the more recent death of her beloved father, and the intolerable death, at the last, of her beloved brother, had wanted only oblivion, the oblivion that whiskey offered, or death itself. She wanted to be permitted to obliterate herself, and she wanted to be neither abandoned nor condemned for doing so. This would never have been an easy wish to grant; but in the event, I failed until too late even fully to understand her wishes. I failed to see her, alone on her darkling plain; I failed to accompany her as far as the gate—which is all, and the best, we can do.

There is nothing simply ordinary about the friendship between Magda Szabó's two women characters. Set on the stage of a single street in mid-twentieth-century Budapest, theirs is nothing less than the account of humanity's struggle to love fully and unconditionally, a struggle that is perhaps always doomed. As Szabó's narrator reflects: "Humankind has come a long way since its beginnings and people of the future won't be able to imagine the barbaric early days in which we fought with one another, in groups or individually, over little more than a cup of cocoa. But not even then will it be possible to soften the fate of a woman for whom no one has made a place in their life."

RACHEL CUSK

Rachel Cusk has been a prominent novelist for well over twenty years in Great Britain, since her first book, *Saving Agnes*, won the Whitbread First Novel Award in 1993. She has since published nine more novels, including her acclaimed trilogy, *Outline*, *Transit*, and *Kudos*. Until these, however, it was for her three memoirs that she was chiefly known in the United States.

The first of these, *A Life's Work* (2001), is a witty and unsparing—some might say harsh—examination of the demands of new motherhood. *The Last Supper: A Summer in Italy* (2009) chronicles her family's two-month sojourn in Tuscany: Adam Begley, reviewing the book in the *New York Times*, likened it to "a sour, highbrow pastiche of Peter Mayle's books about Provence." Her most recent personal chronicle, *Aftermath* (2012), was written after the breakup of her marriage. Frank, personal, and fierce in its critique of the underlying dynamics of the institution of marriage, the controversial book earned her passionate supporters and detractors both. She said, in an interview with Kate Kellaway in the *Guardian*, that "without wishing to sound melodramatic, it was creative death after *Aftermath*. That was the end. I was heading into total silence—an interesting place to find yourself when you are quite developed as an artist."

Cusk, in this interview, speaks of frustration with the novel form, and of a concomitant sense that her autobiographical forays were finished, even though "I'm certain autobiography is increasingly the only form in all the arts. Description, character—these are dead or dying in reality as well as in art," she said. As a writer, her response was to forge a new form for her work, a sort of semiautobiographical novel in which the first-person narrator is largely absent or erased, serving chiefly as the recorder of the lives—or, more accurately, the stories of the lives—of others.

Outline (2014) was the first to take this form, followed by *Transit* (2017), and then, swiftly, *Kudos* (2018). All are narrated by a writer named Faye as we track her experiences from soon after the breakdown of her marriage to a time, several years later, soon after remarriage. *Outline*, set in Athens where she teaches a summer writing course, recounts Faye's encounters with friends, acquaintances, students, and an unnamed Greek man she meets on the plane from London, who takes her out on his boat and shares with her his complicated family history. *Transit* takes place in London, where Faye renovates the former council flat she has purchased, to make a new home for herself and her two young sons. Here, too, the reader encounters the life stories of former lovers, of her friends and relatives, of her hairstylist and the builders working on her flat—but in *Transit*, glimmers of Faye herself emerge more clearly than they do in *Outline*, perhaps in part because in London—as opposed to Athens—she has a place in the city and a history; and perhaps because just as her flat is undergoing renovation, so too is Faye's spirit: she is in transition, to be sure, but hers is no longer a fully "annihilated perspective," to use Cusk's own language from the *Guardian* interview. In the third novel, *Kudos*, we accompany Faye to a literary festival on the

Continent (or possibly to two literary festivals), where she meets publishers, journalists, and other writers who, as in the earlier books, tell her their life stories—divorce and parenting are again a primary theme—but also discuss the role and nature of the literary enterprise. These disquisitions include a winking self-referentiality, as when an interviewer remarks to Faye that "He had noticed . . . that my characters were often provoked into feats of self-revelation by means of a simple question, and that had obviously led him to consider his own occupation." In this volume, Faye herself opines on topics such as justice and suffering, arguably still less "annihilated" than in *Transit*; and yet she is no more clearly visible to the reader than before.

In *Aftermath*, Cusk writes:

> Form is both safety and imprisonment, both protector and dissembler: form, in the end, conceals truth, just as the body conceals the cancer that will destroy it. Form is rigid, inviolable, devastatingly correct; that is its vulnerability. Form can be broken. It will tolerate variation but not transgression; it can be broken, but at what cost? If it is destroyed what can be put in its place? The only alternative to form is chaos.

She refers here to the institution of marriage, but her meditation applies also to artistic endeavor: navigating the tension between formal constraint and freedom is at the center of a writer's undertaking. Familiar forms, shaped by convention, allow a certain flexibility ("it will tolerate variation," as Cusk observes), but only within limits. Dissatisfaction with the form of the realist novel is not new (consider Flaubert, who wanted to write a book "about nothing," and who claimed to "detest what is conventionally called 'realism'"), but it is currently widespread, and includes intolerance for artificial structures of character development, the willful machinations of plot, and the presumption of authorial omniscience. Attempts to find new ways of telling, and of telling more "honestly," have turned, sometimes exhilaratingly, to the "autobiography" to which Cusk refers—notably in the fictions of Karl Ove Knausgaard or Sheila Heti, or in literary memoirs like Maggie Nelson's, or Cusk's own.

Outline, *Transit*, and *Kudos*, however, turn away from self-involvement and draw formal inspiration from a particularly powerful antecedent: the work of W. G. Sebald, whose revolutionary fictions eschew the familiar pleasures of animated characters in action and a rising narrative arc with a climax and denouement; they rely, instead, on self-consciously crafted summaries of individual life stories. Sebald's *The Emigrants*, published in English in 1996, is comprised of four such narratives, thematically linked in an illumination of the legacy of World War II and its trauma and loss. Sebald's semiautobiographical narrator is both incidental and essential, largely self-effacing. He emerges—as does Cusk's Faye—chiefly through what he chooses to relay about others.

Cusk's primary concern is familial relationships—the constant, impassioned, and often agonized dance between men and women, between parents and children—and, secondarily, in all three novels but in *Kudos* in particular an appraisal of the current state of literary discourse and literary forms: workshops, panels, festivals, and interviews recur throughout the trilogy, offering both direct and enacted commentary on the theme. Cusk deploys Sebaldian techniques (without adopting his distinctive use of old photographs) to explore these broad concerns. In *Outline*,

Faye's own life is almost entirely absent—with the exception of phone and text communications from her absent sons ("Where's my tennis racket?") and from Lydia, the mortgage broker calling from the UK about Faye's application to increase her loan (and tellingly the only person in the novel to utter the narrator's name). Faye, in a rare moment of self-revelation, asserts:

> I had come to believe more and more in the virtues of passivity, and of living a life as unmarked by self-will as possible. One could make almost anything happen, if one tried hard enough, but the trying—it seemed to me—was almost always a sign that one was crossing the currents, was forcing events in a direction they did not naturally want to go. . . . There was a great difference, I said, between the things I wanted and the things that I could apparently have, and until I had finally and forever made my peace with that fact, I had decided to want nothing at all.

In *Transit*, the reader becomes more acutely and recurringly aware of Faye as a particular individual. Her two sons are no less remote than they were in *Outline*, in this case sent to their father's house for the novel's duration, present once again only on the phone; but in this instance, their absence seems to lend Faye a more, rather than less, distinct sense of self. While she remains largely in the background—in an entertaining section about her participation on a panel at a literary festival (which of course prefigures the world in which *Kudos* fully takes place), she recounts over almost twenty pages the self-indulgent autobiographical bloviating of her two male counterparts, and concisely records her own contribution thus: "I read aloud what I had written"—she nevertheless emerges as a person with a will, opinions, and a capacity to act.

She buys a flat against the advice of her real estate agent and embarks on its renovation. She encounters Gerard, a former boyfriend, and as he tells her about his life in the intervening years and about his family, she declares that "it seemed to me that most marriages worked in the same way that stories are said to do, through the suspension of disbelief," thereby acknowledging her distinct perspective. She asks Dale, her hairstylist, "whether he could try to get rid of the grey." And out on a date with a man ("someone I barely knew"), she portrays her vindictive downstairs neighbors in ways that imply that she herself is, indeed, as much a character in a story as are any of the others in her narrative:

> On top of that, I said, there was something in the basement, something that took the form of two people, though I would hesitate to give their names to it. It was more of a force, a power of elemental negativity that seemed somehow related to the power to create. Their hatred of me was so pure, I said, that it almost passed back again into love. They were, in a way, like parents, crouched malevolently in the psyche of the house like Beckett's Nagg and Nell in their dustbins.

This gesture toward the mythical is palpable elsewhere also: whereas in *Outline*, Faye seemed to be filtering the stories of her friends and acquaintances through the lens of their marriages, with a particular focus on the repeated failure of those relationships, both romantic and familial, in *Transit* she elicits accounts of coping, of the ways in which, in spite of limitations, her subjects have managed to persevere and even upon occasion transcend their failings. Dale the stylist explains a recent period of crisis "in which every time he saw someone he knew or spoke to them . . . he was literally plagued by this sense of them as children in adults' bodies." He dates this state from a New Year's Eve gathering where he felt "there had been something enormous in the room that everyone else was pretending wasn't there." Faye asks what it was: " 'Fear,' he said. 'And I thought, I'm not running away from it. I'm going to stay right here until it's gone.' "

While Dale's story is one of apparent triumph—he has come to feel at ease in his skin, alone—others are less unequivocal. But any grain of self-awareness has about it a feeling of triumph, as when Faye's tutorial student Jane describes her flirtation with an older, married photographer, and, pressed by Faye, explains that its allure lay in "the feeling of being admired . . . by someone more important than me. I don't know why, she said. It excited me. It always excites me. Even though, she said, you could say I don't get anything out of it."

By the third novel in the trilogy, as Faye continues to record her interlocutors' revelations, the reader may feel considerable familiarity with the pithy and apposite nature of these exchanges. In *Kudos* there is a risk, as we move with Faye from one studiously bland venue to another (the plane ride; the hotel bar; the group dinner at a restaurant) and one literary contact to another (editors, interviewers, publicists, etc.), that Cusk's enterprise will come to seem a parody of itself. Through these novels she has so carefully walked the line between quotidian banality and willed meaning; here, Faye seems almost to offer a nod and a wink regarding the meaning ("Suffering had always appeared to me as an opportunity, I said, and I wasn't sure I would ever discover whether this was true and if so why it was, because so far I had failed to understand what it might be an opportunity for"). At the same time, the banality becomes, in the aggregate, both genuinely and willfully banal.

When Cusk concludes the novel (and the trilogy) with Faye's sighting, while walking along the beach, of a "huge burly man with a great curling black beard and a rounded stomach and thighs like hams" pissing into the ocean, it is an exhilarating return to form, a scene in which a thoughtless everyday action becomes imbued with mythic significance.

This, of course, is the only way in which we come to know Faye—by the imprint of others upon her. She unstintingly brings others' personal stories to the reader: in *Transit*, she offers us Gerard, her long-ago lover, who still lives in the flat they once shared, now with his professionally driven Canadian wife Diane and their daughter, Clara, the focus of his life. We encounter Faye's old friend Amanda and her troubled builder-boyfriend Gavin, who keeps promising to move in but keeps living instead with his sister in Romford because "it's easier to run his business from there, but I know it's because he can watch telly and eat a takeaway and no one expects him to talk." There is, too, Pavel the Polish builder, whose wife and family are back in Poland in the dream house in the forest that he built for them, a house that is the cause of a painful rift with his father. Finally, there is Faye's cousin Lawrence, his second wife Eloise, and the guests at their fogged-in rural dinner party—each of them prepared, in spite of the brouhaha and distractions of children and their bickering, to divulge their personal stories. As a woman named Birgid puts it to Faye, " 'I like it that you ask these questions,' she said. 'But I don't understand why you want to know.' "

The stories in *Kudos* are either literary or familial, and in some instances both. Women discuss the malice of their ex-husbands or their disappointments in love; a young man tells Faye about being witness to his parents' divorce. Characters debate whether or not a parent's role is to protect their children. Relationships are seen as relentless terrains of battle, power play. What of the self, in this vision?

Faye initially casts an acerbic and uncharitable eye on her fellow novelist Linda ("Her hair was dishevelled and fell past her shoulders in matted-looking hanks, and her skin had the pastiness of someone who rarely goes outdoors"), but records Linda's account of an encounter on a plane with a woman who'd survived a near-fatal skiing accident: "I guess it reminded me of having a kid," Linda says. "You survive your own death . . . and then there's nothing left to do except talk about it." Linda elaborates that childbirth was, for her, "a process of being broken and then reassembled into an indestructible, unnatural and possibly suicidal version of herself."

Faye may tease out these confessions in order to feel less isolated, or better to understand her own situation, or in the hope that she may find courage or wisdom heretofore unimagined, or indeed as part of a broader morality play for her own edification and the reader's. Or again, perhaps Faye records these stories in order simply to hide behind them, using this literary form, too, as "both protector and dissembler," obscuring herself in the superior safety of the listener (which is, of course, always the position of a book's reader).

It is hence powerful—and pleasing, for the reader as for Faye—when, in *Transit*, the man with whom Faye is on a date finally takes her arm, and she steps out at last from behind the emotional arras:

A flooding feeling of relief passed violently through me, as if I was the passenger in a car that had finally swerved away from a sharp drop.

Faye, he said.

Later that night, when I got home and let myself into the dark, dust-smelling house, I found that Tony had put down the insulating panels. . . .

Just as, in *Outline*, Lydia the mortgage broker was the first and only person to call Faye by her name, almost at the novel's end (and in a question: "Is that Faye?"), so, too, late in *Transit*, this suitor is the first and only person to name our protagonist. That he does so not as a question nor in a larger sentence, and not even in quotation marks, feels significant: here, at last, Faye is seen for herself. Which of course in turn implies that she has a self to see—that she is no longer "annihilated."

In *Kudos*, it is Faye's adolescent son who calls her by name, surprisingly, just at the novel's end. He rings her from the UK to appeal for her maternal care. Having inadvertently started a fire in a pool changing room, he has for hours expected the police. Faye reassures him: "You didn't do anything wrong." Consolation is all she can offer; it feels at once paltry, insufficient, and probably true. In this trilogy, Faye is willfully an observer above all, a vessel rather than an agent.

In *Transit,* she tells her future husband about her shifting understanding of her own agency:

> For a long time, I said, I believed that it was only through absolute passivity that you could learn to see what was really there. But my decision to create a disturbance by

renovating my house had awoken a different reality, as though I had disturbed a beast sleeping in its lair. I had started to become, in effect, angry. I had started to desire power, because what I now realised was that other people had had it all along, that what I called fate was merely the reverberation of their will, a tale scripted not by some universal storyteller but by people who would elude justice for as long as their actions were met with resignation rather than outrage.

Faye's ruminations pertain to her own life, but like much in these novels, they echo outward, articulating wisdom about human experience more universally. Faye's adopted passivity in *Outline* is not more or less true than her apprehension of willfulness (her own and others') in *Transit*, or the ambivalence around moral questions of action or inaction in *Kudos*: these concerns affect not only her own choices but those of all whose stories she records. In this way, Cusk pulls off a rare feat: richly philosophical fiction—addressing nothing less ambitious than how to live in relationships with others—in which ideas are so successfully and naturally embedded in the quotidian that the reader can choose whether or not to acknowledge them.

With the culminating volume *Kudos* in hand, it proves inaccurate to suggest that *Outline* and *Transit* have no traditional narrative arc. While subtle, couched in scintillating, substantive digressions—summaries of decades in adult lives, potted histories of famous artists, explanations of dog breeding, painfully accurate renditions of family squabbles—Faye's evolution emerges: a woman undone by the end of her marriage, painstakingly reconstructing a new, ever-contradictory, self, and then looking outward, to question her role as a writer and the place of literature and of herself to broader contemporary society.

In *Outline*, Faye reflects, watching a family enjoy a day's outing on a boat:

> When I looked at [them], I saw a vision of what I no longer had: I saw something, in other words, that wasn't there. Those people were living in their moment, and though I could see it I could no more return to that moment than I could walk across the water that separated us. And of those two ways of living—living in the moment and living outside it—which was the more real?

Whereas, by *Transit*'s conclusion, there is the prospect of a new beginning:

> Through the windows a strange subterranean light was rising, barely distinguishable from darkness. I felt change far beneath me, moving deep beneath the surface of things, like the plates of the earth blindly moving in their black traces.

This is a considerable distance from the ending of *Kudos,* with its phallic Dionysian vision—that pissing man, "cruel, merry," so vital, replete with "malevolent delight"; while Faye, looking on, merely "waited for him to stop." Much remains intractable, the final novel suggests, and for women in particular the challenges may appear insurmountable. But the movement at the conclusion of *Transit* is not false. Faye's cousin Lawrence, in that volume, deems it "truth": "Fate, he said, is only truth in its natural state. When you leave things to fate it can take a long time, he said, but its processes are accurate and inexorable."

SAUL FRIEDLÄNDER

We have understood, at least since Aeschylus, that wisdom is attained through suffering. But it is a truth powerfully reinforced by the experiences of Saul Friedländer's generation: born into a prosperous, assimilated Jewish family in Prague in 1932, Friedländer had experienced by the age of sixteen more trauma, upheaval, and grief than many do in a lifetime. *When Memory Comes*, a memoir of his youth, written in a moment of comparative hope (at the time of Anwar Sadat's visit to Israel in 1977, in the run-up to the Camp David Accords of 1978), is valuable not simply for Friedländer's inspiringly vivid and elegant account of his youthful travails, but also for his Tiresian clarity of vision, and for the forthrightness of his narrative. It is, if anything, only more relevant forty years after its initial publication.

Few have inhabited such diverse personae as did the young Friedländer: born Pavel, a Czech boy, he became "Paul" when his family fled to France in 1939, settling in Néris-les-Bains, "Vichy on a smaller scale minus the government plus the Jews." Subsequently, placed in a Jesuit boarding school, Saint-Béranger, by his parents (who would themselves die in Auschwitz), he was known as "Paul-Henri Ferland." Immediately after the war, having come to understand for the first time his Jewish identity, he was sent to a Russian-Jewish guardian in Paris, where he attended the Lycée Henri IV. From there, in the spring of 1948, he ran away to join Betar, "a youth movement with ties to Menachem Begin's Irgun." As a new Israeli, he took the Hebrew name "Shaul," the French transliteration of which is Saul.

Internal confusion was inevitable along his journey, as was a sense of isolation. As a teenager, he refused meat at his first Passover Seder because it was Good Friday. Of his Catholic years at Saint-Béranger, he recalls that, unaware of his Jewishness, "I soon felt a vocation: I wanted to become a priest"; "I liked the austere simplicity, the intense devotion of the early mass at which I sometimes served." He remembers, too, being part of the school's majority, "faithful to the Marshal [Pétain] in every way," that ostracized a young boy named Jean-Marc on account of his Gaullist views: "how happy I was to be able to share this fraternal warmth and look upon this proscribed youngster with scornful eyes!" Even in midlife, he acknowledges that "I still feel a strange attraction, mingled with a profound repulsion, for this phase of my childhood."

From this unlikely extreme, with the revelation of his heritage and of his parents' fates he turned, in 1947–1948, to fervent Zionism. As he abandoned his French schooling and his known world, he did so for reasons not wholly dissimilar to those behind his earlier enthusiastic embrace of Catholicism: "I was all alone in the world . . . To leave for Eretz [Israel] meant merging my personal fate with a common lot, and also a dream of communion and community." Ultimately, an unmitigated sense of belonging would continue to elude Friedländer as an adult, and it is this very not-belonging that affords him so crucial a perspective.

He recalls a moment when, as a newly Jewish-identified teenager, he sought to conjure imaginatively an experience of the camps Belzec and Majdanek (which of course he had not seen):

> It was only much later . . . that I understood that what was missing was not literary talent but rather a certain ability to identify. The veil between events and me had not been rent. I had lived on the edges of catastrophe; a distance— impassable, perhaps—separated me from those who had been directly caught up in the tide of events, and despite all my efforts, I remained, in my own eyes, not so much a victim as—a spectator. I was destined, therefore, to wander among several worlds, knowing them, understanding them—better, perhaps, than many others—but nonetheless incapable of feeling an identification without any reticence, incapable of seeing, understanding, and belonging in a single, immediate, total movement. Hence—need I say?— my enormous difficulty in writing this book.

THE LONELINESS OF the stateless, the singularity of fractured experience, is beautifully evoked in Friedländer's prose. For this reader, his experiences afford a glimpse of the irretrievable lostness of the past that resonates in my own history, and more potently still, gives me some understanding of the loneliness of my father, just a year older than Friedländer, a colonial Catholic French child crisscrossing the Mediterranean during the war, even as Friedländer was forced into hiding in a Catholic boarding school in France. There exist, of course, countless versions, though few as harrowing, of the radical dislocations of which

Friedländer writes: many people carry vividly intense early memories that cannot be shared.

Having been born in the United States, having paused briefly in Toronto at the age of four, I spent the chief of my childhood in Sydney, Australia, and we returned to Toronto, Canada, in early 1976. I recall powerfully the last taxi ride to the airport in Sydney, on December 27, 1975, squashed next to my sister and mother, running my fingers over the cracked black leatherette of the seat beneath my sticky thigh, breathing the hot summer air, looking out the half-open window at our neighborhood passing away, and thinking: *Remember this: This is the end. You will never live here again, never be this person in this place again.*

After several years in Toronto, where we learned all over the codes and ways of being, not just a new geography but the idioms, slang, clothing, and social orders of another culture, we moved once more to the United States, where, as I discovered, everything was different again: Australia and Canada, both Commonwealth countries, shared a common colonial heritage, however rebellious they felt themselves to be, and with that heritage, a particular awareness of the world beyond their borders. The U.S., on the other hand, philosophically distinct, proved an entity wholly absorbed in itself and its myths, a desire to welcome and ultimately subsume all who come here into a passion for its ideals. Above all, in coming to this country, we understood that we were to embrace this country, to let go of all that had come before.

It would be more than a decade before anyone in my life other than my sister understood about my lost life: when I first met him, I discovered with joy that my now-husband, being British, shared certain long-undisclosed ways that I had of seeing things, imprinted early in my Australian childhood. More than that, we understood each other's classroom memories, television jingles (*H.R. Pufnstuf!*), particular snacks or characters in children's books that had formed me, and that in the intervening years had seemed not only invisible but possibly imaginary. But the places of my childhood still existed, at least. I could go back, and did eventually, to walk the same streets and parks, speak to people I'd once known, and revisit a world that, while it had moved on without me, spoke of the constancy and solidity of life.

My father, on the other hand, whose childhood was shaped by the war, by the Before, During and After, could no more return to the sites of his memories than he could visit heaven. From the ages of almost five to nine, he was a boy in Beirut and, for some months, Salonica (now Thessaloniki); but Beirut was the home he remembered, all his life, as the home of his unquestioned happiness. Returning to Algiers in 1940, he could not fit in at school: he threw himself into his schoolwork, determined to succeed, but his mother wrote to my grandfather that he was lonely, and he himself wrote asking whether the family could move back to Lebanon. From Algiers, he would eventually move to Paris to study; from there to the United States, first for a fellowship year and then for his graduate degree. The summer that he and my mother married in Toronto —1957— saw the worst of the Battle of Algiers: his parents and sister had left Algeria also, by then, and none of them would ever set foot there again. My father's legacy to us was rootlessness; my sister's family and mine are dispersed across continents, probably forever. We have had instilled in us, as primary as breathing, that you can never go back.

FRIEDLÄNDER, SEEKING IN part to rend the veil, in part to understand his past—having fruitlessly attempted a Proustian conjuring with a strawberry milkshake in the Paris milk bar he'd frequented with his mother as a small boy: "though it brings back memories, [it] doesn't summon up what I am looking for ... No, really not ..."—turned, with ardor, to history. His memoir's title is the inversion of a quotation from Gustav Meyrink (author of *The Golem*, an Austrian writer and Prague resident who died in the year of Friedländer's birth): Meyrink wrote that "When knowledge comes, memory comes too"; for Friedländer, in life's path of self-discovery, "when memory comes, knowledge comes too."

The essential and abiding lesson is that "Knowledge and memory are one and the same thing." To bear witness to his multiple, incongruent selves amounts, for Friedländer, to acknowledging the experiences of others, whether they are fellow Jews or Palestinians or his Czech nanny Vlasta, who went on to work for the family of a German general. He has had the fortitude to examine clearly even the acts of the Nazis themselves. To bear witness is to recognize, in his young daughter's face, the echo of his lost mother's; or simply to evoke, with magnificent Tolstoyan precision, the details of a distant memory:

> I must have been no more than three and ... [my grandmother Cécile] was busy at the stove. I could hear her talking, I could hear the little repeated sounds of a wooden spoon tapping the sides of a pot and in the background the noise of flies circling the immense table; from time to time a brief silence announced that one of them had just gotten stuck on the ribbon of yellow flypaper, already studded with black dots, which hung from one of the beams overhead.

In a moment of self-doubt, Friedländer asks, "what are the values that I myself can transmit? Can experience as personal, as contradictory as mine rouse an echo here, in even the most indirect way?" This, surely, is a question for each of us, but all the more pressingly so for those with hybrid or complex identities. In a historical moment when many seem all too eager to revert to primitive tribalisms, the answer, unreservedly, is yes. Friedländer's incapacity wholeheartedly and unthinkingly to "identify" is also his great gift. His liminal sensibility has enabled him, as a historian of the Nazi era, to seek out truths in their full horror and in their nuanced complexity; and as a citizen of Israel, to speak out for dialogue and justice even when—especially when— these calls have been unpopular. He records, too, the moments when, as with the young Jean-Marc in boarding school, he did not speak out, and has compassion for those failures also. That he sees the gamut of perspectives enables him to write, and to think, without vanity or superiority. *A priori*, to be aware of the "enormous difficulty in writing this book" is to insist upon a truthfulness that is all too rare.

MUCH HAS CHANGED since Friedländer wrote *When Memory Comes*, as becomes clear in its powerful new companion volume, *Where Memory Leads*; and yet inevitably, much has remained the same. Contemporary culture's apparent unwillingness to embrace memory, and with it knowledge, risks leading us anew down dark paths. Jingoism and hate-filled rhetoric threaten in Europe and the United States, stirred by demagogues of scant, or nonexistent, moral character. Even in the face of these perils, Friedländer— the outsider who has chosen to embrace community—offers perspective and an individual course of action:

It took me a long time . . . to admit that a living community follows paths that are often impossible to predict and map out in advance, that dilemmas and contradictions are part of this journey, that at best the role of each individual remains to affirm certain principles that are essential to him, in an attempt to erect dikes along the shores, and guardrails along the edges of history.

Edgar's words at the close of *King Lear* come inevitably to mind: "We that are young / Shall never see so much, nor live so long" (Act V, Scene 3). But just as Friedländer inverts Meyrink's words, so, too, his book plays upon Shakespeare's: in youth, he had already seen so much. And through his testimony, those experiences, and the wisdom born of them, will live on, hopefully for a long time.

YASMINE EL RASHIDI

The unnamed narrator of Yasmine El Rashidi's short first novel, *Chronicle of a Last Summer*, records her conversation in 2014 with a young Cairene record salesman named Mohamed:

> He tells me the revolution has connected us to a past that preceded us. I nod, tell him I've gone back into our history books to understand. I've read everything. I can't believe all this I didn't know. You might not believe me, he says, but I have too. He's learning that history is repeating itself. We talk about Nasser. The first revolution. 1919. The Wafd revolting against the British.

What El Rashidi attempts in her deceptively quiet, adamantine novel is no less than to suffuse the present with the past, to convey the way in which a walk through Cairo and the purchase of vegetables are acts filled not only with vivid present detail but also with echoes of historical and political significance. Language, too—whether Egyptian Arabic or English—means more than itself, and in the novel's three sections, El Rashidi's narrator builds a small lexicon of freighted words: "listless," "lethal," "*Tadmeer*" or "devastation," "*Kifaya*" or "it's enough," "truth." An entire nuanced world emanates from these apparently offhand recollections.

The novel's title is, like the book itself, artfully simple, carrying as it does the echo of Jean Rouch and Edgar Morin's famous 1960 documentary, *Chronicle of a Summer* (in which the then-ongoing Algerian War and reminders of the Second World War are never far from the surface): *Chronicle of a Last Summer* suggests the presentation of a single, meaning-filled summer, the one final season in which perhaps all becomes clear. In fact, however, each of the book's three sections relates the events of a different summer—1984, 1998, and 2014—and even within these, the narrator recalls other summers, too. Each might be the last (i.e., final) in a different respect—the narrator's last summer with her father, the last summer of her innocence, the last summer in her childhood home, etc. Or El Rashidi could also intend the title in the sense of the stock student assignment "what I did last summer," which would account for the near-diaristic element of the later two segments. In any event, the title's ambiguity hovers over the novel: we, like the narrator herself, seek elucidation, resolution, and change where there may be none to find. It is not only the character's plight, but that of her very nation: not for nothing is the book's subtitle *A Novel of Egypt*.

In the first section—in its details, the most vividly rendered—the narrator is a small girl. She tells us she was just three and three-quarters when Anwar Sadat was assassinated, which puts her at six and a half in the summer of 1984. El Rashidi finely conjures the world through a child's eyes, with the abruptness and near-surreality of that perspective. For a child, everything is normal, or potentially so. *"I am sitting with Mama waiting for the power to cut,"* she writes in her school notebook, then explains

that everyone in Cairo—except their most important friends—
endures daily power cuts of an hour or two: "Mama also says
the Sadats never have them. They are related to us, but not close
enough for our power cuts to stop too."

The narrator lives with her mama in an architecturally notable modern house by the Nile, where her mother was also raised.
The household has suffered painful attrition: the deaths of her
maternal grandmother and her aunt Nesma, who had Down's
syndrome; and, most bafflingly, the disappearance of Baba, her
father. "I loved the way Baba smelled. . . . Even when he went on
trips his smell would still be there. It had gone away this time.
I was waiting for him to come back." She doesn't know why or
where he has gone: "I didn't know why nobody talked about Baba
even though everyone missed him. I still counted every day but
didn't know anymore what I was counting to."

Beyond this intimately unsettled domesticity lies an analo-
gously unstable world:

> There are some things that are never there the next day.
> There are some things that are always there. Like the
> billboard with the president on it. There are some things
> that are there for a very long time then disappear.

The cityscape changes constantly; shops and people vanish overnight; nobody explains any of it. "I told Grandmama there were
too many things I was waiting to understand. She laughed and
patted my head. She said it's better not to know too much anyway."

The narrator's mother remains largely a cipher, at no time
more so than in these early years. Her expression, when we're
privy to it, is a lament—"Mama lost many friends because of

Nasser. Her best friend was the daughter of the king and had to leave. Her other best friend was Jewish and also had to leave." The narrator knows that her parents' politics diverge:

> They would only ever fight about Nasser and money. Mama would scream about all the things that Nasser took from Grandpa. Baba shouted back that he gave *his* father his *whole* life.

Any social education the narrator receives will come not from her mother but from two very different father figures: her young cousin Dido, staunchly rebellious, and her "Uncle," a close family friend of her parents' generation. Dido, a Communist ("It means he keeps to the left," she explains), disapproves of her enrollment at the British School: he "says my school will repress me. It is the only thing left of the monarchy and colonialism. Mama and Baba are antirevolutionary for sending me there. *Where did their nationalism go?*" Uncle, on the other hand, older, an architect and a traditionalist, rails that "*everything Nasser did was a failed idea.*"

These two stand on opposite sides of an intellectual divide. Uncle is closer to the narrator's mother. Mama's social world was, in youth, that of a pre-1952 cosmopolitan elite about which excellent memoirs have been written (such as André Aciman's *Out of Egypt*). In Mama's case, being neither Jewish nor of the royal family, she has remained ensconced in an ever-shrinking aristocratic world, between her beautiful but increasingly decrepit house and "the club," which

> used to belong to the king. Then Nasser came and gave half of it to the people. He made it free. Half the fields and half

the horse-racing track and half the golf course. The other
half is for other kinds of people, like us.

Baba, although a regular at the club before his disappearance, came from a different background than his wife: a successful businessman (he owns a tile factory), he is descended from
one of Nasser's close associates, presumably a military officer of
middle-class origins catapulted to prominence by the 1952 revolution. The novel is rich in its quiet implications—we learn, for
example, that Baba's cousin was one of Sadat's assassins, which
makes clear that "rebellion" can take the form of the Muslim
Brotherhood as easily as it can communism.

By 1998, the narrator is a university student at the American
University in Cairo. She aspires to be a filmmaker, in itself a
radical act in a country in which visual memory has been created by the state-controlled television, in the form of frequently
replayed political hagiographies showing great moments in the
lives of Nasser and Sadat. "I begin to realize the power of these
montages, these visual narratives of my childhood. We had all
seen these scenes innumerable times. Images imprinted on us
through repetition." Inspired by Rouch and Morin's *Chronicle of a
Summer*, the narrator proposes to make a documentary in which
she asks people in the street a single question: while Rouch and
Morin asked, "Are you happy?" El Rashidi's narrator suggests,
"Maybe I could ask people if they are angry." But she is well aware
of the wariness of her compatriots when faced with a camera:

The only people who are allowed to film on the streets are
the TV. They work at the Egyptian Radio and Television
Union. If you work there, you are also *the TV*. You are

also, maybe, someone with ties to the surveillance state. Someone it might be better to stay away from.

For the newly adult narrator, questions arise about how appropriately to position herself in society. Her cousin Dido still pushes her to overt rebellion; her friend Habiba educates her in Egyptian political correctness:

> She didn't buy anything made in Israel or America. Didn't drink coffee because the money benefits Israel. Didn't wear certain kinds of shoes because the soles are made in Israel. . . . She didn't use the term *Middle East* because it is a creation of the British. To use it is to remain colonized. I used *Middle East* all the time.

In this situation, she says, "I think about Baba more and more." Her father still has not returned. "At a point the idea of someone long absent turns from emotion into something of a mental exercise in remembering and deduction." Figuring out who her father actually was and who she herself may be are endeavors linked, too, to figuring out the reality of her nation, and nationality: "I felt deceived too, cheated out of a life, but I wasn't sure why, or by what. I wondered. Was that also inherited, our listlessness, our sense of resignation?" Baba's stories and opinions glitter in her memory:

> Much he had said had been true, the things I remembered anyway. The things he told me. There was much I didn't know, and many things I imagine I had inherited, borrowed, maybe even imposed on him, the man I wanted him to be, pieced together, fading memories held tight by strands.

This imaginary Baba, "pieced together," offers the narrator a path between Dido's and Uncle's, a way forward that would account for both the past and the need to change the past. When the narrator sets off to the campus science building with her camera to shoot her film, she is accosted by a guard who tries to shoo her away. Seeing the name on her ID, he practically falls at her feet: "He . . . asks if I need anything. What a great pleasure to meet you. Your Baba was a great man. If ever you need anything. *Anything at all.*"

One might surmise that Baba's return—were it possible—could provide a solution to the many irreconcilable elements in the narrator's life. Her mother's nostalgia, Uncle's frustration, Dido's rage—all swirl around and within her. It's as if Baba, so mysteriously and so long vanished, holds the key.

But the novel's third section proves this hope to be false. By 2014, Uncle has died (in 2010); Baba, miraculously, has returned (in the same year); Mama has become a social activist; the 2011 revolution has taken place; poor Dido is in prison awaiting trial. And yet, in spite of so much change, there is only the slightest sense of progress. The narrator's own perspective has altered over time—"Ours wasn't a culture used to change. Permanency was valued. We lived in the same places we were born in. The less change, the less movement, the better. It was a view to stability, rather than the oppression I had internalized it to be"—and she has turned from filmmaking to writing a novel.

Instead of being filled with optimism, she has reinforced, through her father's return, the cyclical existential absurdity of the Egyptian situation: "I became less and less reactionary to Baba's pessimism when I fully digested all that he had been through," she records. Interestingly, we are never told what he has done or where he has been, although we understand that he was in hiding as a result of false criminal charges brought when he refused to become involved in corruption. "We have never really spoken about his years of absence," she says. "I have pieced together stories, but never ask questions, never raise the conversation. . . ." Instead, the cohort with which he surrounds himself explains all:

> Once an outer mourning had left and marked their faces, they all began to laugh, about the old days, how they used to live. . . . At this time one year ago I would be sitting down to drink tea with Mubarak and briefing him. And look at me now, practically in my boxers, being served stale bread. . . . Here is the former state security agent. He used to be the most successful currency trader. This man used to be the minister of foreign affairs. This man was Mubarak's adviser on Israel. This man was his photographer. . . . This woman used to be Miss Egypt. Once the most important newspaper columnist in the Arab world. This man used to own a bank. . . .

The members of the club, power brokers now obsolete, mill about as if in an allegorical scene from Dante.

In this third section, El Rashidi addresses, in fiction, some of the events she wrote about in her essays for the *NYR Daily*, the online edition of the *New York Review of Books*, collected under the title *The Battle for Egypt* (2011). Dated from January 26 to March 29, 2011, they recorded, as did her reports for the print edition, the heady unfolding of events in Tahrir Square and their aftermath; the divisions that emerged almost immediately; the sense that the vote for the new constitution was skewed by various factors. In a spirit of optimism, she wrote on February 12, 2011, that "this revolution, for the people of Egypt, may turn out to be less about a leader than about hope, pride and the sense of possibility"; but by February 23, she observed:

> The splintering of the movement feels familiar.... Many of the core activists who are still coming out belong to an upper-middle-class elite.... But the larger story at this point lies with the labor movements and unions— the broader public whose participation was so vital to the uprising, and whose long struggle for economic justice continues.

For the narrator of El Rashidi's novel, several years later in 2014, disillusionment is profound: her father "tells me that he knew a revolution would change nothing." She recalls clashes in which the Muslim Brotherhood and the police colluded: "At the morgue piles of young men had phone numbers scrawled on their arms.... They had left their houses knowing they might not return." Cairo's cityscape exists for her now in a palimpsest, the memories of recent violence inseparable from those that preceded them:

> My memories of crossing that street, of university, of my paralysis in the face of the city, have been overwritten. Then overwritten again. The scars of our most recent history are everywhere. I have to dig, consciously project myself back into an imagined past as I sit here now, writing, to recall going there with Baba. It was on the same street corner where Baba saw the Israeli jets [in 1967] that I first saw the square full, first experienced tear gas, saw my first dead body, shot from behind. I think of Uncle constantly and

the conversations we had. . . . He would tell me that to be a witness to history is a burden for the chosen.

El Rashidi's novel is elliptical, at times even oblique. Much is discreetly omitted from her text—the narrator's name; Mama's character; the circumstances of Baba's long absence. The book's three sections, each at so considerable a chronological remove from the others, have the effect of vivid but separate snapshots from a vast album. The book coheres instead around the trajectory of a rebellious energy, the struggle against that ingrained vocabulary of listlessness and defeat that permeates so much of the characters' discourse.

Uncle and Dido are, in this sense, the novel's central characters, more so even than the observing narrator herself. By 2014, Uncle is dead, and Dido is in prison, "on charges of inciting anarchy, disrupting the state." The narrator and Dido have been intermittently estranged over the years, but she visits him there—"he seemed to sit as if in obligation, answering me in monosyllables"—and eventually he asks to see her father. Baba's symbolic importance affects Dido, too, and the older man offers a version of a blessing: "I heard him [Baba] whisper that he was proud of him [Dido], that he was much braver than he had ever been."

Soon thereafter, the narrator has the realization, of her rebellious cousin, that "more and more he sounds like Uncle." Dido's personal journey—from youthful optimism (1984) to a fierce restlessness (1998), thence to a boil (the events of 2011), and on to disastrous deflation and despair—mirrors that of Egypt itself over these years. That trajectory, the book suggests, has been repeated over generations: it was also Baba's; in a different form, it was Baba's father's, too, by Nasser's side.

There is, at the novel's close, a meaningful shift in the narrator's family, at least: Mama finally decides to leave the beloved family home. Although she remains largely in the background, Mama is the character apparently most energized by the revolution of 2011, the person who has found purpose and focus, eschewing nostalgia even as the men who surround her have lapsed into rueful inanition. Whether her newfound vigor will prove effectual is unclear—the country's fateful defeatism is a strong adversary—but in the disheartening aftermath of the revolution, there is mercifully some modest sense of an opening to the future, the prospect of something new and possibly better.

Chronicle of a Last Summer wastes no words. Every sentence has meaning, though not portentously so. The novel can be read swiftly, as the personal narrative of a young girl growing into womanhood while her aristocratic family collapses around her and she tries to find her artistic path; or it can be read more slowly, as a domestic tapestry through which are threaded all the complexities of recent Egyptian society.*

As a small child visiting the Mugamma (a Cairo government building) with her mother in 1984, the narrator overhears a group of women talking about Ayman al-Zawahiri (one of the

---

* Fully to appreciate this evocative debut, some American readers may be grateful for a background account of modern Egyptian history. Afaf Lutfi al-Sayyid Marsot's brief volume, *A Short History of Modern Egypt* (Cambridge University Press, 1985; updated 2007), while it does not cover the last tumultuous decade, provides a succinct, engaging, and often witty account of the last century that puts El Rashidi's narrator's family history into enlightening perspective, and makes clear both the importance and the complexity of Egyptian national identity.

men arrested after Sadat's assassination and the current leader of al-Qaeda): *"He should be in jail forever, and they've now set him loose on us. Yalahwee."* In 2014, she remembers Uncle's last year (2010):

> He had been saying all year that it was untenable. *La faim.* He told me to watch for certain things. The price of tomatoes and okra. If the man carrying the bread on his head as he cycles is whistling or not.

Camus of course wrote about Algeria's famine in the 1940s as one cause of the war for independence; similarly, the famine in Syria has been cited as a cause of the civil war there.[*] On the one hand, the narrator simply records Uncle's passing conversation; on the other, she elucidates for us both the tenor of the times and its significance.

In El Rashidi's novel, as in life, the familial and the societal are ultimately inseparable. It is Uncle's melancholic perspective that provides the book with its abiding wisdom:

> Uncle said it was inevitable, eventually some change would come, but much more so he wished our lives were different. To fall in love, to build a life with a loved one, was the greatest freedom. He hoped I, we, would have that one day.

---

[*] See Albert Camus, *Algerian Chronicles*, translated by Arthur Goldhammer, with an introduction by Alice Kaplan (Belknap Press/Harvard University Press, 2013); and see also Ian Sample, "Global Warming Contributed to Syria's 2011 Uprising, Scientists Claim," the *Guardian*, March 2, 2015.

VALERIA LUISELLI

Although Valeria Luiselli lives in New York City, she isn't herself North American—not by birth (she was born in Mexico), nor by upbringing (her father was a diplomat, her international childhood nomadic), nor, to a significant degree, in her literary influences and style. But the five books she has written so far expand our understanding of North American literature. *Lost Children Archive*, her third novel, is the first that she has written in English (her first two were very well translated from the Spanish by Christina MacSweeney), and it is a passionate, if complicated, American novel—or, perhaps more accurately, a novel of the Americas.

For all their inventiveness, neither of her earlier novels could have led readers fully to anticipate this ambitious, somber, urgent new work. Her first, *Faces in the Crowd* (2014), is the artfully fragmented account of a young woman who, as she writes about her husband and small children, creates apocryphal translations of poems and extracts from an autobiographical narrative by the (actual) Mexican poet Gilberto Owen (1904–1952). Luiselli plays with reality and literary convention (in a manner familiar from European and Latin American fictions from Pirandello to Borges to Bolaño) and combines that play with an often ironic, intermittently autofictional recording of daily life's more banal moments, in a way popularized in contemporary North American fiction by women writers like Sheila Heti or Jenny Offill.

Luiselli's second novel, *The Story of My Teeth* (2015), is driven by the inimitable voice of Gustavo "Highway" Sánchez Sánchez, an auctioneer whose tall tales about the literary provenance of his own teeth (he claims one belonged to Saint Augustine, for example, and another to Virginia Woolf) and whose different styles of storytelling salesmanship engage the reader in a lively narrative dance. Filled with absurdist literary allusions ("My uncle Marcelo Sánchez-Proust once wrote in his diary . . ."), the novel was in fact commissioned by the Galería Jumex, an art gallery outside Mexico City, as a serial narrative for the workers at Mexico's Jumex juice factory, part of an exhibition exploring connections between the gallery and the Jumex empire. In an afterword, Luiselli explains that "many of the stories told in this book come from the workers' personal accounts—though names, places and details are modified." The almost frothy quality of the book's pacing arises in part, surely, from its conception as a serial: we are buoyed along by episodic comic surprise.

Between *The Story of My Teeth* and *Lost Children Archive*, Luiselli wrote a slim, memorable volume of nonfiction, *Tell Me How It Ends: An Essay in Forty Questions* (2017), expanded from an essay that appeared in *Freeman's* magazine in 2016. (This was her second nonfiction book: her first, *Sidewalks*, from 2010, is an allusive and, again, cleverly fragmented series of meditations on topics ranging from Joseph Brodsky's grave, to bicycling, to the empty spaces in Mexico City.) In the course of applying for permanent resident status in the United States, Luiselli and her family took a road trip in the summer of 2014, from New York to Cochise

County, Arizona, near the U.S.-Mexico border. The following year, back in New York, she became a volunteer interpreter in the federal immigration court. The essay reconstructs both Luiselli's initiation into the world of immigration courts (including the lives of several of the vast number of children seeking asylum) and her family's journey across the southern U.S. by car. As Latin Americans, they attract questions from policemen, one of whom remarks sardonically, "So you come all the way down here for *the inspiration*." She notes that "since 2006, around 120,000 migrants have disappeared in their transit through Mexico," and that "between April 2014 and August 2015, more than 102,000 unaccompanied children had been detained at the [U.S.] border." Horrified by the statistics and the dark realities they represent, Luiselli writes:

> Perhaps the only way to grant any justice—were that even possible—is by hearing and recording those stories over and over again so that they come back, always, to haunt and shame us. Because being aware of what is happening in our era and choosing to do nothing about it has become unacceptable.

The conceptual overlap between *Tell Me How It Ends* and *Lost Children Archive* is considerable. It is not new for a writer to address a subject in multiple forms. Camus famously did this when grappling with his theory of the absurd, writing three thematically linked but profoundly different works: *The Myth of Sisyphus* (a philosophical essay), *The Stranger* (a novel), and *Caligula* (a play). In his case the works are markedly distinct, however, and each is fully realized on its own terms; whereas here,

Luiselli's novel, framed, like the essay, by a family's road trip across the United States from New York to Arizona, repurposes both literal and thematic material in ways that don't feel fully realized in the novel.

The novel's unnamed characters—the mother, the father, the ten-year-old boy (the father's child from a previous relationship), and the five-year-old girl (the mother's child, also from a previous relationship)—reflect the configuration of Luiselli's own family in the essay. Specific details from the essay recur in the novel—from the idea of the mother in "the copilot's seat" to the policeman's quip about "the inspiration"—as well as the presence of two young sisters from Guatemala, whose "grandmother sewed a ten-digit telephone number on the collars of the dress each girl would wear throughout the entire trip." In the essay, Luiselli writes, "sometimes, when our children fall asleep again, I look back at them, or hear them breathe, and wonder. . . . Were they to find themselves alone, crossing borders and countries, would my own children survive?" This question will be posed, and then acted out, in *Lost Children Archive*.

In the course of Luiselli's work as an interpreter, helping children answer an NGO's intake questionnaire (hence the forty questions of her essay's subtitle), she learns that most children, coming from Mexico, Guatemala, El Salvador, and Honduras, have traveled "'on La Bestia,' which literally means 'the beast,' and refers to the freight trains that cross Mexico, on top of which as many as half a million Central American migrants ride annually." In *Lost Children Archive*, this journey—and the subsequent crossing of the border into the American desert—forms the subject of a fictional book within the novel that the mother is reading, *Elegies for Lost Children* by Ella Camposanto. The embedded narrative reaches toward myth, producing some of the most arresting prose in *Lost Children Archive*:

> They were all asleep and did not hear or see the woman who, also asleep, rolled off the side of the roof of their gondola. Tumbling awake as she went down the jagged ridge, she'd torn open her stomach on a broken branch, and kept on falling, until her body thumped flat, into abrupt emptiness. The first living thing to notice her, the next morning, was a porcupine, its spines erect and its tummy ballooned on larch and crab apples. It sniffed one of her feet, the one that was unshod, and then circled around her, uninterested, sniffing its way toward a bunch of drying poplar catkins.

Lost Children Archive contains many formal complexities, but its most basic structural feature is a division between the accounts of a mother and her young stepson. The novel's first half is recounted by the mother, a Luiselli-like figure who takes a road trip with her family to Arizona. She and her husband are both sound archivists, albeit of different sorts: "We'd say that I was a documentarist and he was a documentarian, which meant that I was more like a chemist and he was more like a librarian." The impetus for their journey is her husband's documentary project on the Apaches, for which he has received a grant: "The material he had to collect for this project was linked to specific locations, but this soundscape was going to be different. He called it an 'inventory of echoes,' said it would be about the ghosts of Geronimo and the last Apaches." Up till now the narrator has been more practical and journalistic in her own approach, but she, too, is pursuing a project, one she calls a "Lost Children Archive," the exact substance of which is initially unclear:

> I'm not sure that I'd ever be able to—or should—get as close to my sources as possible. Although a valuable archive of the lost children would need to be composed, fundamentally, of a series of testimonies or oral histories that register their own voices telling their stories, it doesn't seem right to turn those children, their lives, into material for media consumption.

The paradoxical nature of the endeavor is apparent: the lost children, being lost, cannot be heard. To hear these stories, the narrator must find the children, of course; next to this problem, her concern for potential media exploitation is surely secondary. The alternative is to invent their stories, in one way or another.

As the family travels westward the parents' relationship deteriorates, while the plight of the immigrant children at the border grows increasingly pressing. Availing herself of a grand American trope—the road novel—Luiselli turns it sideways: her protagonist is no footloose American man, but the immigrant mother of a nuclear family. They travel not between coasts but away from the city, from the center to the margins—their progress, if it can be called that, recalls *The Sheltering Sky* more than *On the Road*. The reader is privy to fairly little of their daily reality, beyond the occasional diner experience or reference to their audiobook choices (the opening sentence of Cormac McCarthy's postapocalyptic novel *The Road* recurs, ominously). While we are granted charming glimpses of the children, their gestures, questions, and games, the narrator's husband remains largely opaque, present chiefly in his pedagogical role, educating the children about the Apaches, a history of colonial violence and slaughter.

The second half of the novel is mostly narrated by the woman's unnamed stepson, addressing his younger sister. Dismayed by the parents' unraveling marriage and his stepmother's growing obsession with the lost children, he hatches a plan to run away: "I wanted to remind her that even though those children were lost, we were not lost, we were there, right there next to her. And it made me wonder, what if we got lost, would she then finally pay attention to us?" He successfully dragoons his sister into following him, and the two set off into the inhospitable landscape, armed only with maps, a compass, a flashlight, and other sundries filched from their parents.

This strand of the narrative is suspenseful, but its progression and resolution make clear that we are in the realm of consoling—and not entirely convincing—fantasy rather than in that of truth. The children's trajectory is interspersed, ever more heavily, with the fictional novel-within-a-novel, *Elegies for Lost Children*. Before the children's departure, their mother has realized that "they are the ones who are telling the story of the lost children. They've been telling it all along, over and over again in the back of the car"; appropriately, then, her stepson ultimately manages—as if, of narrative necessity, living out his stepmother's projection—to conflate his and his sister's story with that of the children in the *Elegies*. In embarking on their journey, they are seeking the actual lost children (the two young sisters from Guatemala); they have themselves become lost children; and the lost children in the *Elegies* seem real to the boy. This melding culminates in the boy's extended, highly literary first-person stream-of-consciousness section near the novel's end. The children walk following

> the same eagles the lost children now see as they walk north into the desert plain, beating muscled wings, threading in and out of black thunderclouds, they see them with their bare eyes, the five of them, as they walk onward, under the sun, keeping close together and silent, in a tight horde, deeper and deeper into the silent heart of light, saying nothing and hearing almost nothing, because nothing can be heard except the monotonous sound of their own footsteps, on and on across these deadlands, never stopping because if they stop, they will die, this they know, this they've been told . . .

This bow to modernism—the passage is drawn from a sentence that continues for almost twenty pages—is but one of the novel's many stylistic intricacies. Its intention is clear (to unite, through the boy's voice, all the lost children), yet its effect is not ultimately transcendent.

A commitment to formal innovation has been central to Luiselli's work; in this regard *Lost Children Archive* is clearly linked to its predecessors. *Faces in the Crowd* is made up of brief sections—fragments—told from shifting perspectives. More adventurous, *The Story of My Teeth*, divided into seven books (separated by marbled papers), includes epigraphs in various forms, auction lot descriptions, a series of photographs, and a timeline (compiled by Christina MacSweeney). The new novel, still more formally complicated, is divided into four parts, each subdivided into sections (among them seven archival "boxes," the contents of which are either listed or contained in the text, including photographs, maps, and news clippings), and further into subsections. Among these are fifteen parenthetical sections of the *Elegies* by Ella Camposanto, whose surname means "cemetery" in Spanish and is also the title of W. G. Sebald's posthumous book of essays. The majority of the subsections have less clearly directive titles—such as "MAPS," "INVENTORY," or "COPULA & COPULATION." The reader will understand that taxonomies, however apparently extraneous, are important to this text: they effect the imposition of order upon rampant disorder. It is presumably possible, though mercifully not necessary, to interpret the novel according to these titles.

Such games and allusions are important to the texture of *Lost Children Archive*. Luiselli's stylistic freedoms—roaming from the adult narrator's highly realistic (and, one suspects, often autobiographical) reflections to the child's frankly implausible fairy tale adventure, to the dark myth-like storytelling of the *Elegies*—form a patchwork designed simultaneously to reflect and reinterpret our current reality.

The mother's narrative voice, in its varying registers, sounds as natural as is possible. Her thoughts meander between history and the present day ("Searching online about the children's crisis, I find a *New York Times* article from a couple of years back, titled 'Children at the Border.' . . . No one thinks of those children as consequences of a historical war that goes back decades"); personal reminiscences ("And then the boy turned ten. We took him out to a good restaurant, gave him presents (no toys). I got him a Polaroid camera and several boxes of film, both black and white and color"); and literary and artistic analysis (of figures as varied as Walt Whitman, Susan Sontag, and Emmet Gowin). She recalls demonstrating outside an immigration detention center on Varick Street in New York, in the company of a priest named Father Juan Carlos. She remembers her mother leaving the family to join a Mexican guerrilla movement when she herself was ten years old (something that actually happened in Luiselli's life). She tells us about a remarkable (and real) educator named Stephen Haff, whose one-room schoolhouse in Brooklyn, Still Waters in a Storm, teaches underprivileged kids to translate Cervantes and instructs them in Latin.

The first half of the novel reads less like fiction than like a record of time spent in a café with a particularly interesting friend—one whose observations are alternately delightful and trenchant, unexpected and familiar; one whose presumption of her interlocutor's intelligence and erudition is both flattering and quickening. One passage, on our contemporary relationship to time, while not original (these thoughts have been articulated in the past), seems especially true today:

I'm not sure, though, what "for later" means anymore. Something changed in the world. Not too long ago, it changed, and we know it. We don't know how to explain it yet, but I think we all can feel it, somewhere deep in our gut or in our brain circuits. We feel time differently. No one has quite been able to capture what is happening or say why. Perhaps it's just that we sense an absence of future, because the present has become too overwhelming, so the future has become unimaginable. And without future, time feels like only an accumulation. . . . Perhaps if we found a new way to document it, we might begin to understand this new way we experience space and time.

It seems logical to infer from this astute observation that Luiselli's novel itself endeavors to find a new way to "document" the present. In a digression of impressive creative frankness, Luiselli's character muses on the perils of modern storytelling:

Political concern: How can a radio documentary be useful in helping more undocumented children find asylum? Aesthetic problem: On the other hand, why should a sound piece, or any other form of storytelling, for that matter, be a means to a specific end? I should know, by now, that instrumentalism, applied to any art form, is a way of guaranteeing really shitty results: light pedagogic material, moralistic young-adult novels, boring art in general. Professional hesitance: But then again, isn't art for art's sake so often an absolutely ridiculous display of intellectual arrogance? Ethical concern: And why would I even think that I can or should make art with someone else's suffering? Pragmatic concern: Shouldn't I simply document, like the serious journalist I was when I first started working in radio and sound production? Realistic concern: Maybe it is better to keep the children's stories as far away from the media as possible, anyway, because the more attention a potentially controversial issue receives in the media, the more susceptible it is to becoming politicized, and in these times, a politicized issue is no longer a matter that urgently calls for committed debate in the public arena but rather a bargaining chip that parties use frivolously in order to move their own agendas forward. Constant concerns: Cultural appropriation, pissing all over someone else's toilet seat, who am I to tell this story, micromanaging identity politics, heavy-handedness, am I too angry, am I mentally colonized by Western-Saxon-white categories, what's the correct use of personal pronouns, go light on the adjectives, and oh, who gives a fuck how very whimsical phrasal verbs are?

These reflections suggest how hampered Luiselli may have felt in approaching her intense and demanding factual material. Serious and highly literary, passionately politically engaged, unwilling to rely on forms that feel to her out of date and insufficient, she is, at the same time, constrained by an awareness of critiques that might be leveled against her fiction. For her fellow artists, the imposing reach of this project—both to acknowledge and somehow to assimilate all of these questions—is invigorating and absorbing. It is also risky. As she endeavors to marry fact-like fiction (the cross-country journey of a Luiselli-like storyteller in the company of her family) with fairy-tale-like fiction (the child's adventure story, complete with implausible happy ending), with dark myth (the *Elegies*), with a strong political intention that nevertheless aims to avoid propaganda, all the while spinning formal complexity upon formal complexity, there is ultimately a sense that the center cannot hold.

Art is an act of transformation: the passage of material through an imaginative crucible, and the creation of something new. That something new must have its own integrity, must be greater than the sum of its parts. Camus's explorations of the absurd in *The Stranger* and *The Myth of Sisyphus* measure the distinction between a novelistic embodiment of human experience and an essayistic distillation of thought. Many elements of *Lost Children Archive* are extraordinary, and yet the ultimate act of transformation has not occurred. One might of course contend that, in this ghastly time, such a transformation is no longer possible; but Luiselli's decision to write a novel at all surely affirms otherwise.

PART THREE

Criticism: Images

ALICE NEEL

Freedom's just another name for nothing left to lose: when Janis Joplin made this assertion famous, it was novel, perhaps, to the general population, but not to artists. The need to live an unencumbered life—to embrace a genuinely bohemian and precarious existence—was, for artists of the twentieth century, *a priori*: the starting point without which great work was considered impossible.

This *Weltanschauung* was formed in reaction to the fierce conventionality and constraint of the Victorian era; to the rise of the stolid middle classes and their opposite, the promulgation of Marxist ideals. It was enriched and emboldened by an insistence on artistic rigor—whether from the mid–nineteenth-century devotees of art for art's sake or from their modernist descendants—that saw an artist's vocation as pure and absolute, not unlike a religious calling. (As recently as 1990 when I was enrolled in an MFA program for fiction, we were inculcated with the familiar saw that an aspiring artist should allow in his or her life nothing that needed to be fed, watered, or walked. We joked about whether a plant was allowable.)

To choose the path of art may not have required a necessary vow of poverty; but it was widely understood that freedom frequently entailed financial want, and that it was a deliberate rejection of bourgeois tenets. As the French writer André Sieg-fried suggested, *"Un bourgeois c'est quelqu'un qui a des reserves"*—a bourgeois is someone who has reserves. A bohemian, in logical contrast, is someone who does not.

If, a hundred years ago as today, it was tough to be an artist, it was considerably more so for those without family resources, and harder still for women in that category. In literature, the twenti-eth century is marked by impoverished women who, free though they may have been in an artistic sense, were hampered in their work by the constant struggle to survive. From the British writer Jean Rhys or the Australian Christina Stead (both roughly con-temporary with Alice Neel; and the latter, like Neel, affiliated with communism) to, more recently, Penelope Fitzgerald, there is no shortage of women who "did without" in order to pursue their art: did without fame, to be sure, but sometimes without heat, or food, or a bed to sleep in. Isolation and discomfiture were part of the job. As Jean Rhys recalled in her autobiography, "I would never be part of anything. I would never really belong anywhere . . . I am a stranger and I always will be, and after all I didn't really care." These women had difficult lives and suffered greatly; like Neel, they found refuge and, belatedly, triumph in their work.

WHEN ALICE NEEL was born, with the century, in January 1900, in a small Pennsylvania town, ideas about bohemianism were already widespread. From early on, she chafed at the parameters of her parents' modest and conventional existence. In wanting to become an artist, she sought not only to follow the striver's time-honored passage from the provinces to the big city, but to shake off what her biographer Phoebe Hoban termed her home's "very puritanical atmosphere."* In 1921, after working for several years, she enrolled at the Philadelphia School of Design for Women, where the influential realist painter Robert Henri had taught. While she was there, he published his important book *The Art Spirit* (1923), in which he writes, tellingly, "Many things that come into the world are not looked into. The individual says 'My crowd doesn't run that way.' I say, don't run with crowds." Neel herself seems to have absorbed this proposition, adding, "You know what it takes to be an artist? Hypersensitivity and the will of the devil. To never give up."

JUST A FEW years later, however, having fallen in love with and married her fellow student, the Cuban artist Carlos Enríquez, Neel would confront the particular challenge faced by women artists: maternity. The birth of her daughter Santillana in Havana in December 1926 not only complicated Neel's ability to make art, but destabilized her relationship with Enríquez. Unhappy in Cuba, Neel returned to the United States with Santillana, first to her parents' in Colwyn, Pennsylvania, and then to New York, with Enríquez. During this period, Neel painted a number of watercolors that, as Hoban observes, "express what seems to have been her own 'quiet desperation.'" Broke, ambitious, hungry, and perhaps practically hapless in the bargain, the couple struggled to care for their daughter, to work, and to eat. As if the Fates determined that the balance of motherhood and art

---

* Phoebe Hoban, *Alice Neel: The Art of Not Sitting Pretty* (New York: St. Martin's Press, 2010).

was simply impossible, the small family was dealt a fatal blow: Santillana contracted and succumbed to diphtheria—tragically, shortly before the advent of the first vaccine—just before her first birthday.

Neel and Enríquez's grief-stricken response was to conceive again. Their second daughter, Isabella Lillian Enríquez, called Isabetta, was born in November 1928. Within eighteen months (in May 1930), Enríquez returned to his family in Havana with Isabetta, leaving Neel behind. The couple did not reunite; and Neel would see her second daughter only a few more times in her life. Isabetta would eventually commit suicide, in middle age. Neel said, much later, "You see, I had always had this awful dichotomy. I loved Isabetta, of course I did. But I wanted to paint."

The result of Neel's "dichotomy" was a serious nervous breakdown, from which she recovered only a year and a half later. She attempted suicide more than once. In one of her poems of this period, she wrote: "Oh, I was full of theories / Of grand experiments / To live a normal woman's life / To have children—to be the painting and the painter . . . / I've lost my child my love my life and all the god damn / business / That makes life worth living."

Whether or not she is inclined to motherhood, any woman artist can identify with the acute paradox of wanting "to be the painting and the painter." If the artist is, as Jean Rhys put it, "a stranger," the outsider whose very alienation enables her to *see*, to record life, this position is utterly at odds with an "ordinary woman's" desire to *live*. This complication—having to choose whether to see or to be—is not unique to women artists, but is experienced differently by women precisely with regard to motherhood.

There is no more fully embodied role. When you're a mother, particularly of an infant or small child, you are neither dispensable nor replaceable. Nor do you want to be. But if you are, in the true twentieth century sense, an artist—if you are committed, as Neel was, with the will of the devil, with the pure commitment of a religious vocation—then you may be called upon to renounce your child. It's a perspective that goes against our accepted cultural beliefs—even now, when so little remains untouchable, motherhood is sacred—and yet the bohemian sets herself, precisely, against accepted belief. She doesn't run with crowds. The cost of this conflict was, in Neel's case, a significant piece of her sanity.

Once recovered, Neel returned to New York and joined the artistic community in Greenwich Village. There, she was part of the vital artists' community; she started showing her work in various exhibitions. Her portraits of Joe Gould and Christopher Lazar date from that period. She made friends both artistic and political and met John Rothschild, a wealthy admirer and sometime lover whose support would be crucial to Neel over many years. She joined the Communist Party in 1935; and signed on first with the Public Works of Art Project (in 1933) and the WPA's Federal Art Project (in 1935).

Throughout the Depression and the run-up to the Second World War, Neel recorded images of human struggle that are both intimate and painful: *Untitled (Bowery)* (1936); *Men from Bleeker Street* [sic] (1933); *Spanish Mother and Child* (1942); and *Mother with Children* (1943). Such unflinching but occasionally whimsical works—cartoons, almost—recall Goya's etchings: brutal, almost satirical, profoundly human in their portrayals of suffering. Her subjects in these images are precisely what Henri would have said was "not looked into": Neel saw it as her role to look. She might herself have uttered the words attributed to the German artist and activist Käthe Kollwitz (1867–1945), some of whose drawings resemble Neel's (both women painted haunting images of wasting children entitled *Poverty*): "It is my duty to voice the suffering of men, the never-ending sufferings heaped mountain-high."

But Neel's own sufferings, too, were never-ending. If the Harvard-educated Rothschild served as Neel's sugar daddy, her then-boyfriend was a considerably less salubrious—and more appropriately bohemian—figure: Kenneth Doolittle was a sailor and a veteran of the Spanish Civil War who shared Neel's political views; but he was also a drug addict with a propensity for jealousy. In December 1934, he destroyed around sixty of Neel's paintings and two hundred of her drawings and watercolors in their Greenwich Village apartment. As Jeremy Lewison explains, their absence gives us a very different sense of Neel's early work than we might otherwise have. Put in other terms, having sacrificed her children for her art, she was then forced to lose her art as well.

José Santiago Negrón was a handsome musician ten years Neel's junior—beautifully, even lushly, depicted in his dressing gown in *José* (1936). With him, she moved from the Village (and its artists) to relative isolation in Spanish Harlem; and by him, she became pregnant again, and again. In 1937, she had a stillbirth; and in 1939, her son Richard was born. (John Rothschild had offered her the money for an abortion, but according to Hoban she "used the money to buy a phonograph instead." As with her previous relationship, Negrón was not keen on fatherhood, and Neel swiftly found herself alone with an infant.

Sam Brody, a Communist and film critic, entered Neel's life soon thereafter, and their son Hartley was born in 1941. Brody's relationship with his young stepson Richard was violent and difficult. Neel's haunting painting *Alice and Richard* (1943) reveals her angst; but she did not leave Brody, and the two stayed together until the mid-1950s, when he left her. In the wake of their separation, Neel drew *Self Portrait (Skull)* (1958), a truly shocking vision that harkens back to the grief she expressed after losing her daughters.

Neel fared much better, mercifully, with her two sons, and raised them lovingly and with considerable ingenuity, ensuring their private education even while the household was sometimes on welfare. For many years during which Abstract Expressionism held sway, Neel's work was resolutely unfashionable, and her paintings found no outlets. The turning point came in the mid-sixties, after which she began to show again and finally garnered the acclaim that attends her reputation today. Fortunately for us, she never gave up, and apparently never doubted the urgency and merit of her artistic endeavor. Footage from an interview in the early seventies shows Neel's apartment stacked with unsold canvases, a veritable trove of portraits piled up in her narrow hallway.

During that long period in the wilderness, while the art world was obsessed with abstraction—with rendering the concrete world abstract—Neel's journey was in the opposite direction: her later portraits are about making the abstract concrete. By this I mean that Neel's project was to do with paint and ink what novelists attempt with words: to illuminate the interiority of individuals, to put their souls on paper. As Diana Loercher wrote in a review of one of Neel's shows in the *Christian Science Monitor* in 1973, "In an entirely contemporary manner she gives universal significance to the individual and realizes the portraitist's traditional ideal of the portrait as a mirror of the mind." Or again, Elizabeth Hess, in the *Village Voice*, of a posthumous show of Neel's portraits of children: "Her canvases are a psychoanalytic battle between artist and subject (or patient and therapist) demonstrating that Neel not only knew many of her subjects, but was emotionally entangled with them."

A substantial proportion of Neel's work was devoted to her family. In a letter from the mid-fifties to her close friend, the Communist writer Phillip Bonosky, she wrote, "At first one resists children, tries to keep on with one's life, etc, however as time goes on more and more one becomes that normal thing— 'a parent' and relates with it . . . I'm working like mad painting Richard Neel and Hartley Neel. I've done one painting of Neel— strong I think—I'm never sure."

Her drawings and paintings of her sons are remarkable, and differently so in different moments. From the fragile, bulb-headed, moon-eyed children of the early sketches (*Richard*, 1943; *Hartley*, 1943, *Richard and Hartley*, c. 1943) to the nuanced, stylized portrayals of Richard as a young adult, Neel is unafraid of their vulnerability and, at the same time, of their privacy. In the two ink portraits of Richard from the late fifties, he looks away from his mother, sidelong, as if willing himself out of the frame: in the first, his face is open, as if he's listening to someone, engaged; in the second, his hand raised behind his head, his expression is jaded and sardonic, almost disgusted, and the crease in his cheek has the aspect of a vicious scar.

But it's in her numerous and varied depictions of her daughter-in-law Ginny that Neel most clearly reveals her analyst's fierce probing: in the extraordinary acid-yellow and blue painting *Hartley and Ginny* (1970), Ginny with her black hair and piercing green gaze glowers at Neel, her arm draped possessively around a pensive Hartley (whose eyes are averted). Ginny appears both hostile and triumphant; but Neel has painted her dangling hand upon Hartley's shirt as limp, almost dead-looking, as if to suggest that

Ginny's power is less absolute than Ginny believes. The complex relations of a mother and her daughter-in-law are present in the painting for all to see, even though Neel herself isn't there.

We see a different woman in *Ginny* (1975), in which she now appears almost a supplicant, girlish and expectant in her blue and green running gear, perched upon a slight stool, tanned, delicate, and openmouthed, her long neck vulnerable. And again, a radically other incarnation just two years later, in the colored ink drawing *Ginny* (1977), in which she reclines, exhausted, upon cushions, her face haggard, her lips a red gash, and her forehead a prominent dome, a curiously circled void. She is posed so that her crotch is front and center, behind it the virulent red blot of her T-shirt; her spidery hand off to the side, her bony feet, all convey a profound exhaustion that seems somehow maternal. The phrase that comes to mind is, "That really took it out of me"—in all its possible implications.

In this last image, Ginny seems somehow both mother and artist/intellectual, with the white-space emphasis like light upon her brain, the inked attention to her vagina, and the bloody sea of red between them. She is, it's true, immobile, for the moment *épuisée*; but you'd be mistaken to think she is spent. Her shadowed eyes are wary, and alert; and that spidery hand could spring at any moment. It is, again, a portrayal of complex energy and emotion, distinct and utterly memorable.

IN HERSELF, IN spite of the artistic "theories" of her youth, and in spite of her terrible losses and suffering, Neel was eventually able to reconcile the great dichotomy of the woman artist, to bring together her capacity to *see* and her capacity to *live*, to be the painter and the painting at once. Her beloved children, paradoxically, along with their spouses and children, enabled that resolution. As subjects, they were the source of some of her finest paintings, and the complex emotions Neel evokes in her art are nothing less than the contradictions of life itself.

For other artists, as for this novelist, she is a powerful inspiration, in the resilience and commitment of her life and in the wisdom and frankness of her painting. She did many things wrong—she suffered and caused suffering—but she did nothing for the wrong reasons. Passionately and unwaveringly committed to her art from the earliest days, she learned also to balance that commitment with the passions that matter for life—not for material things, nor for worldly success (though she was glad to have it when finally it came), but for the people that she loved, and loved with all their flaws.

As she wrote in the *New York Times* in 1976, "As for people who want flattering paintings of themselves, even if I wanted to do them, I wouldn't know what flattery is. To me, as Keats said, beauty is truth, truth beauty. Altered noses always look much worse. I paint to try to reveal the struggle, tragedy and joy of life."

MARLENE DUMAS

Since I was a child, I've wondered what it's like for someone else to read the same book as me, or to look at the same art-work, or to listen to the same music. When I experience art, I'm arrested, inspired, moved by particular details that strike me as significant: the emotion of a brief melody in a longer piece, or the expression of a dog at the foot of the portrait's subject, or an evocative description or illuminating metaphor ("Or, as the snail, whose tender horns being hit, / Shrinks backward in his shelly cave with pain / . . . So, at his bloody view her eyes are fled / Into the deep dark cabins of her head"). These are the moments in a work of art that open, like windows, to touch me. Or, to use another analogy, they are the threads that tie experiences and visions far from mine to my own life: they render something distant immediate and recognizable.

But the threads that perform this magic differ from person to person. Each encounter with an artwork imparts a differ-ent valence, a nuanced exhilaration, unique to the individual viewer. As Vladimir Nabokov wrote of literature, a novel or story involves the writer and the reader climbing the mountain from opposite sides to meet at the top: the particular imagination of any audience member is engaged in the creation—or the re-creation—of a work of art.

We've been taught, historically, that artworks have a fixed "meaning." Of course, over the past century artists have exploded this notion, granting primacy to subjectivity and interiority; but instruction has been slow to follow suit. And indeed, the wide-openness of Picasso or Joyce has been serially succeeded by visions more or less open. Literature, certainly, has largely seen a return to a realm of signifying consensus: some version of recognizable human realism is the norm. The visual arts offer far less directed experiences of "reading"; but even here, especially when approaching the figurative, the impulse toward potentially reductive analysis recurs.

The French psychoanalytic feminists of the 1970s and 1980s (Julia Kristeva, Luce Irigaray) argued that openness of vision and multiplicity of experience are affiliated with the feminine. *Jouissance* encompasses the idea that just as the multiple orgasm is a privilege of women's bodies, so, too, the (potentially disruptive) apprehension of multiple textual revelations, a nonlinear experience not directed to a single climax, is an expression of feminine experience. In the creation—as opposed to the consumption—of art, versions of artistic openness (which may occur in the work of artists of any gender) are, by this reading, "feminine," and work against traditional narrative or visual structures of meaning that both presume and imply a unitary self on a singular trajectory.

Marlene Dumas came of age at the height of these theoretical discussions and has surely absorbed their import, both because of where she was—at the Ateliers '63 art school in Haarlem—and because of when she was there—in the late 1970s—whether or not she was reading Kristeva, Irigaray, and Hélène Cixous. Transgressive, exuberant (and often funny) multiplicity is unquestionably central to Dumas's work: in conversation she speaks repeatedly of "openness," of seeking a fluidity both in her artistic process and in the images she seeks to create. Emphatically a figurative painter, Dumas is driven by gesture and serendipity alike, and by the confluence of diverse inspirations: if a viewer or reader experiences a work as a series of connecting threads, Dumas as an artist—in a manner recognizable to me, as a fiction writer—finds subject and form in a similar way. An artist's business is something like a magpie's, or indeed, like composting: you throw a bunch of different things onto the heap and hope something new will grow.

This is quite different from taking an existing story or image and producing one particular vision of it, which was the role of much classical art. Nor is it a straightforward representation of what is. Rather, it is an act of transformation. When Dumas has painted (from photographic sources) familiar icons— contemporary myths, if you will, like Amy Winehouse, or Osama bin Laden, or Marilyn Monroe—she has forced us to see them anew: dead Marilyn, rather than the sexy pinup; Osama as soft-eyed introvert, rather than ruthless terrorist. Similarly with her unforgettable giant babies, or with what is perhaps her most famous image, *The Painter* (1994), a portrait of her then-small daughter Helena, naked, glowering, with paint that resembles blood on her hands: in each instance, Dumas overturns visual expectations, marrying the known and the unknowable to create something novel.

In Dumas's 2018 exhibition at David Zwirner Gallery in New York, *Myths & Mortals*, inspirations are multiple, even in a single painting. She speaks freely about this, deconstructing or tracing different spurs involved in the evolution of particular works. She operates in a realm of myths, in a Jungian sense, where these are "revealed eternal 'truths' about mankind's psychic existence—about the reality of the psyche."[*] Her touchstones are as often autobiographical (her daughter Helena; conversations with Jan, her partner, or with friends; her own memories) as they are artistic (dialogue with the work of fellow artists, or with that of her predecessors; conversation with classical or ancient artistic forms), political (the inversion of norms; the exploration of current debates, such as the #MeToo movement), or cultural (the depiction of icons whose influence in popular culture, whether positive or negative, is abiding—from Barbie and Naomi Campbell to Nelson Mandela).

Then, too, challenges inherent in the execution play an important role: the shape of the canvas; the need to balance a composition; the constraints of a mass media image used as her model (often a photograph cut from a magazine or book); the serendipitous flow of the paint or ink upon the canvas, directed but unconstrained by Dumas.

Of a sweet ink wash of a dove, she explains:

> Drawing a dove means "competing" with Picasso's doves. Speed is essential. I had a date with Helena; we were going to go somewhere. I was sitting there, trying to do these

---

[*] Donald Kalsched and Alan Jones, *Myth and Psyche: The Evolution of Consciousness*, exhibition text, Hofstra University Museum, Hempstead, New York, 1986; www.cgjungny.org/d/d_mythpsyche.html (accessed November 16, 2018).

drawings; I heard her approaching and I still had no dove—
I had all these kitschy doves. Each time, the dove would
look like a budgie or some other stupid bird. And then I did
this [she points to the image of the dove]; the ink ran. This
was all done in one go. Afterwards, to make it look more
like a dove, I drew in the little face. So it's actually two
movements. That's conscious—I used to do it a lot in my old
collages, where a work starts with being all gesture, then
later you return to it and you just make a slight change, and
suddenly it looks like a flower, or it looks like something
which, without that addition, it would not.*

The fruit of many discarded attempts, this dove is but one in
a series of thirty-three ink-wash illustrations of Shakespeare's
rich and sensual early poem *Venus and Adonis* (based on the story
found in Ovid's poem *Metamorphoses*), commissioned on the
occasion of its translation into Dutch by the Moroccan-Dutch
author Hafid Bouazza. These gorgeous images form the core of
Myths & Mortals; indeed, the rest of the exhibition was more or
less conceived around them.

Dumas explains that she accepted Bouazza's invitation
because, "How can I say no to one of the most erotic narrative
poems?" But she was at the time in the middle of a challenging and consuming project, the altarpiece for the Annenkirche
in Dresden ("I found it extremely difficult. The poor congrega-

---

* All quotes by Marlene Dumas are from a conversation with the author,
August 5, 2018.

tion, I thought, they'll have to look at these works hanging there forever"), and she had, waiting after that project's completion, a commission for the Munch Museum in Oslo, an exploration of the ways her work is in conversation with Edvard Munch's.

When Bouazza contacted her, he hoped that she might "honor the story with two or three drawings"; when she agreed, she had no idea that she would embark on a series of such magnitude. But "with Shakespeare, the sexuality and the violence are always very close together, and emotions change all the time," and thus Dumas found that two or three images would not suffice.

As a child growing up in South Africa's Western Cape, knowing she wanted to be an artist but uncertain of how to do so, Dumas had imagined being an illustrator; so in a sense the *Venus and Adonis* project bore an echo of childhood. Bouazza shared with her his large collection of illustrated books, including *Alice's Adventures in Wonderland* and *A Thousand and One Nights*, but also other fairy and horror tales; she revisited, too, the illustrations of Dante Gabriel Rossetti and those of Édouard Manet for Edgar Allan Poe's "The Raven."

In some instances, Dumas was directly inspired by Shakespeare's language, by the words themselves:

> I didn't do all the drawings directly next to the text, but this one [gestures to the snail] was where Shakespeare expresses how Venus feels seeing the "murdered" body of Adonis for the first time. Her eyes are compared to the snail, "whose tender horns being hit shrinks backward in his shelly cave with pain"—here, I immediately physically understood what he meant. I first read the poem quite quickly, to get the overall feel, but had to reread it many times after for more

clarity. Hafid reminded me that a poem, just like a painting, needs more than just a swift glance to reveal itself.

This snail was the first work she produced in the series. It appears in Shakespeare's poem as a metaphor, and for Dumas, that linguistic turn proved exactly the sort of thread that could connect her viscerally to the text: Venus, in her grief, became present to Dumas in a new way. With the clarity of rereading came a new understanding of the myth itself: "In the beginning—because there are so many old paintings where Adonis is portrayed as much older, or they look as though they're the same age—I didn't quite realize just how young he was, that he almost didn't even have a beard yet. Really, when he says 'I'm so green and young,' *he means it*. Whereas she's been sleeping with Mars and others—she is an experienced woman."

How to portray Venus, in particular, proved a challenge:

> The most difficult was to choose what type of woman to use. The man was easier somehow—I left him as a Mediterranean type; I didn't try to change him much. But with the woman's image I had a lot of problems. I did not just want a sort of pinup blonde; but . . . then what was she like in that [Shakespearean] time? I hoped, through the fusion of different images (models), that one can then identify with all types of women.

Dumas remains keen that her diverse depictions of Venus not be seen as literal, but rather as an exploration of the openness of archetype. The relationship between Venus and Adonis is mythic rather than realistic, a myth that proves particularly resonant and unsettling in this cultural moment. (She also concedes that "with the animals I had less anxiety," which may be why she began with the delicate snail, the whimsical dove, the owl in flight, the knowing swan, and the vital, Rabelaisian wild boar, whose tusked snout erupts forward in one image as though he might leap from the page, and who, in another, glances sidelong, seeming almost to chortle in animal glee.)

In hewing, for the first time, to a literary text, Dumas returned to Munch's *Alpha and Omega*, an Adam and Eve–like fable that he wrote and illustrated, and with which *Myths & Mortals* is in conversation.

Dumas had long been familiar with Munch's tale:

> Long before I did anything with any of this, I always especially liked Munch's description of Omega: "Omega's eyes would change; on ordinary days they were pale-blue, but when she looked at her lovers, they became black with flecks of carmine, and occasionally she covered her mouth with a flower."
>
> It's similar to the Shakespeare [poem], but in a different way: it goes wrong, but it's very erotic, it's an erotic poem . . . It's not just that there's this terrible woman and she devours the man. It's very sensual: she likes the smell of the flowers and her favorite pastime is kissing. There is humor. There is tragedy, but it's quite gentle also. It's drawn very sweetly. There are so many elements in it.

This multiplicity is, of course, intrinsic to Dumas's oeuvre, as it is to Shakespeare's poem. It is not inadvertent that her images of Venus and Adonis that appear most erotic actually depict strife or injury: when Venus hovers over a recumbent Adonis, apparently on the verge of a passionate embrace, she hovers in fact over his dying corpse (*Venus with body of Adonis*; but also *The embrace*). When she appears to remonstrate with him, she in fact laments his death (*Venus curses Death*). When we see her most beautifully "in bliss," she is not in the throes of love's consummation, but alone. Even the apparent simplicity of a couple and their love story—of Alpha and Omega, or of Venus and Adonis—is false, as Dumas notes:

> This story is full of eroticism, but *she does not get him*. The boar gets him. And you know, this close friend who died recently, I said to him, "Marcel, I realize I'm talking about the couple all the time, but it's not only a couple, there's a third person, because the boar gets him, she doesn't. And with Alpha and Omega, all the animals come. So actually there are three." And he said, "But in every couple there's at least a third person. *At least* a third person."

This "third person," like the unknown import or the unexpected turn—the shadow truth—is always present, even when invisible. In Dumas's artistic world, certainty is a falsehood. Humor is essential. So, too, is a capacity to encompass darkness and ugliness. Apparent opposites are often perilously close; emotional poles coexist, in palimpsest. Death and pleasure are here intertwined, agony and ecstasy.

Just as the paintings move between emotional poles, so, too, they vary widely in scale. If the small, delicate illustrations for *Venus and Adonis* are at the heart of *Myths & Mortals*, an imposing series of full-length portraits, each over nine and a half feet tall, comprise the exhibition's spine. These seven magnificent paintings take on, among others, questions of agency, Eros, fertility, and isolation. As hung in the gallery, at Dumas's direction, *Spring* was the first monumental painting on display: a vibrantly painted woman—her blond curls reminiscent of Dumas's own; her age indeterminate, but not necessarily young; her underpants pulled down across her thighs, her firmly planted bare legs red—upending a bottle onto her crotch and rubbing herself with her free hand. Her stance is fierce, her pelvis thrust forward; her face is in comparative shadow. The bottle is clear, suggesting that it may contain water or vodka, or anything else, indeed. Beneath her glows a citron ground: perhaps an illuminated stage, or a painted floor, it seems above all an abstraction, an apt and intense assertion of emotion.

Dumas explains that this painting, its title both signifying rebirth and evoking the rush of liquid dripping down between the figure's legs, was inspired by a photograph from Haiti:

> It's a voodoo ritual, and it's vodka and peppers that she's using. I made it more suggestive, more like water, keeping that open. I believe you need to be a bit in love with what you do: you have to believe it's worth doing. I remember when painting this, I was really enjoying being alive. And I thought: Yes, "Rage, rage against the dying of the light."[*] Women especially like this work.

---

[*] From Dylan Thomas's poem "Do not go gentle into that good night," first published in 1951 in the journal *Botteghe Oscure*; see Dylan Thomas, *Collected Poems 1934–1952* (London: J. M. Dent & Sons, 1952), p. 116.

She laughs as she says this; but there is serious import in this portrait of a not-young woman so powerfully sexual and utterly independent in her pleasure. "When I chose this image, it was for the way she stood. It's fantastic that she stands like this, and so dynamic." Dumas is, if you will, creating a new myth for women: a myth in which woman is a sexual subject—the opposite of an object, responsible, autonomous, and assertive. This piece is, moreover, engaged in conversation with *Venus and Adonis*: when you're past forty, Dumas explains (she is now in her mid-sixties), and you encounter someone younger and attractive, you experience "the awkwardness of liking someone but not really knowing what type of role or relationship [it may be]." Being Venus, indeed, is as awkward as being Adonis.

The uncertainties of attraction are compelling in their many configurations. Each first kiss is born of risk. Awkwardness is inherent in Eros; indeed, awkwardness itself can be erotic. In *Awkward*, Dumas conveys this truth with thrilling tenderness. The canvas depicts a young couple in profile, holding each other by the arms, her foot sweetly riding on top of his. Between them stretches a sharply defined line of pale light that extends the length of their bodies, interrupted only by their arms. They themselves are blue; behind their backs pulse glimpses of red, as though their lust has not yet seeped into the space between them. They are decidedly awkward; they hover on the cusp of love; they are at once mortal and immortal. It is impossible not to recall Keats's "Ode on a Grecian Urn": "What men or gods are these? What maidens loth? / . . . Bold Lover, never, never canst thou kiss, / Though winning near the goal yet, do not grieve; / She cannot fade, though thou hast not thy bliss, / For ever wilt thou love, and she be fair!"

Dumas didn't have Keats specifically in mind, but she might as well have. She shows me an image of a Greek vase in a Dutch newspaper (from almost twenty years ago) that influenced *Awkward*. "I used to think it was a man and a woman, but it is a man and a young boy. . . . It doesn't really matter what sex you are: it's about two people, trying to touch one another." The figures took form out of the painting process itself. The awkwardness arose organically. The incipient lovers are, as a friend of Dumas's observed, "playing footsie"; they're holding hands; the rest is yet to come. As Keats writes, "More happy love! more happy, happy love! / For ever warm and still to be enjoy'd, / For ever panting, and for ever young."

The affect of two more of the tall paintings, *Bride* and *Birth*, emanates in each case from a different emotional realm. In discussing the first work, Dumas explains, "The veiled women in white always fascinated me. The bride eventually evolved into a mummified Egyptian. She's extremely gothic." This work, Dumas adds, emerged as a conversation in her imagination with the illustrations in Bouazza's book collection. "I come from a modernist background. As a child you illustrate, or you play with narrative; but as a painter you want your works to have as little narrative as possible." The *Venus and Adonis* project, she implies, freed her from certain long-standing tacit artistic constraints and enabled new types of cross-pollination in her work.

Birth, as magnificent and arresting an image as *Spring*, depicts a naked female figure, vastly pregnant, her hands raised on either side of her head. In preparation for this painting, Dumas looked at many goddesses, including Inanna, the Sumerian goddess that anticipated Aphrodite/Venus, worshipped as a deity of love, sex, fertility, and war, among other attributes. Inanna is often depicted with her hands in this pose. In the early Christian tradition, this gesture is seen also in the *orante*, a female figure in meditative prayer, evoking a state of peace with the universe. It is an ancient pose, replete with spiritual resonances, made only the more forceful by the unborn child at the painting's center. The fact that the woman's face is unreadable—is this defiance? is it alarm? resignation? or simply quietude?—is apt. Surely for an archetype, an immortal, openness is key: each mother will experience the imminent birth of her child differently; contained within that experience will be a gamut of emotions. Dumas allows here for the *jouissance* of maternity, many things at once.

Although substantial, the painting *Amends* does not have the full-length-portrait shape of the seven tall works. It is shorter and wider, for a reason: Dumas worked with a long-held photograph of a Greek boyfriend of hers from the 1970s, making a link with his history and her renewed interest in Greek mythology. The overdetermined nature of this image appealed: Dumas's Greek could be seen as her Adonis (although he was much older than she, rather than the inverse); he was a part of her personal mythology. He is also, in this depiction, a male figure standing passive and naked in front of an audience, at risk of objectification in the way of women in art since time immemorial. His wide-spread arms; his open, oversized, thickly outlined hands; the title of the painting—all of these suggest that he offers himself as a sort of recompense. And yet his beautiful face is solemn but dignified, as if he doesn't even see the audience within the canvas: instead, he looks straight out to the viewer. Like the pregnant figure in *Birth*, he has an otherworldliness: his expression can be read in a variety of ways.

Amends, like each of Dumas's paintings, has evolved out of a particular combination of autobiography, politics, culture, and the demands of the medium:

> To fit the stretched-out arms, I needed a different size canvas, because I wanted that gesture. But then his legs became too short, and it wasn't quite right. The contrast between his light body and the dark heads of the audience in front of him solved that. I wanted the body to be very open, almost sketch-like, with the soft pale blue background like that [she gestures], and then the bolder dark heads, *doof, doof* [she makes a painting gesture], and the face I changed several times because I found it difficult to decide on what type of expression he should have. . . . What a struggle to get it simple!

For the viewer, each experience of these works will similarly entail a particular combination of our own autobiography, political and cultural history, along with perhaps the mood or moment in which we stand before the painting. Part of Dumas's genius is always already to have understood this fact, and to approach her artistic process with this knowledge. Whatever the words one uses to articulate the result—"openness," "multiplicity," "*jouissance*"—the effect is the same: these are paintings that encourage each viewer to push further into the specificity of their encounter. This is no realm of abstraction; nor is it one of finite and directed significance. Dumas's subjects are at once myths and mortals, simultaneously familiar and strange. Awkwardness, the angle of a lover's foot, the protrusion of a nipple, the curve of a swan's neck, the roil of tongues—by these visceral specificities each of us will be tied to Dumas's world and her work. She offers, in these paintings, a multitude of possible threads.

Dumas says of Shakespeare's raw and gutting poem, "The more I read it, in the end it seemed very clear"; similarly, from the monumental ferocity of *Spring* or *Birth* to the tender intimacy of *The snail* or *The flower* in the *Venus and Adonis* series, each work speaks clearly, and distinctly, to each of us. Connection—whether in love or in art—entails risk; risk entails awkwardness. And it is through vulnerabilities that, as humans, we speak most profoundly, from the heart.

SALLY MANN

What makes a person herself? And what, if that person is an artist, makes her the particular artist that she has become? These questions are surely essential and also, on some level, unanswerable. That doesn't mean we shouldn't ask them. Sally Mann—whose fierce and glorious images have made her among the most acclaimed photographers of our time—was prompted to consider them by an invitation to give the Massey Lectures at Harvard University in 2011. The result is *Hold Still*, a memoir at once intimate and reserved.

Mann titles the prologue of her book "The Meuse," which is neither a typo for *muse* nor a reference to the river in France. Rather, she explains: "When an animal, a rabbit, say, beds down in a protecting fencerow, the weight and warmth of his curled body leaves a mirroring mark upon the ground. . . . This body-formed evidence of hare has a name, an obsolete but beautiful word: *meuse*." She is writing about the contents of the boxes in her attic, the traces, left by her parents and their forebears, from which she will attempt to reconstruct their selves; but she might as well be writing about her approach to memoir as a whole. Mann's family is her book's central focus. It is by them, by her home, and by her art—by all she loves most—that she is formed.

Hold Still covers a lot of ground. In Mann's richly compelling and evocative narrative (who knew that she could as easily have been a writer as a photographer?), she chronicles, among other things, the histories of her Bostonian mother's and Texan father's families; the sad fate, too, of her husband's parents in Connecticut; the story of her African American nanny and housekeeper, Gee-Gee, and of Mann's ongoing engagement with questions of race and the legacy of slavery in the South; the significance of motherhood; and the centrality of photography in her life, its processes, its themes, its subjects, and its effects.

She is everywhere in this account; and yet she is nowhere. Yes, the book offers us photographs of Mann at various ages, and many photographs taken by her, too, both famous ones and others not seen before (the interspersing of images in the text is one of its many pleasures). Yes, her voice and perspective shape each sentence. But this memoir is notably neither confessional nor self-regarding: Mann, ever the photographer, stays largely behind her lens, turning her "intensely seeing eye" on the people and the natural world around her. As with the rabbit's *meuse*, we will know Mann by the outline that she leaves, by what touches her and how.

In truth, it's the way we best know one another, since our life stories are so often distorted, whether willfully or inadvertently—we're all unreliable narrators. But in looking backward, or outward, and revealing what matters to us most, we expose ourselves most intimately. When this act of seeing is put under artistic pressure, it becomes, as Auden wrote of poetry, "a way of happening, a mouth." Mann's memoir enacts for us what it entails to live as an artist, and particularly as a woman artist—an artist who is a mother, wife, and member of her community.

When Mann started out, she photographed the Virginia landscape around her that she loves profoundly. Eventually, she took as her subjects her children in that landscape. In 1985, "I began, as I often do, with a promising near miss, using the 8 x 10 view camera to photograph [my daughter] Virginia's birth." Over the subsequent years, in what seems near-idyllic isolation on the family farm, Mann worked intensively and meticulously to create lasting images; in many of them, her children are naked. She remarks, "In the pictures of my children I celebrated the maternal passion their bodies inspired in me—how could I not?" and adds, "I never thought of them as being sexual; I thought of them as being simply, miraculously, and sensuously beautiful."

These photographs were published in 1992 in a collection titled *Immediate Family*. They reignited and complicated the era's intense and often vitriolic discussion of artists' freedom of expression, and Mann came under attack from feminists like the writer Mary Gordon, as well as from the Christian right.

It was an unexpected nightmare: "I was blindsided by the controversy, protected, I thought, by my relative obscurity and geographic isolation, and was initially unprepared to respond to it in any cogent way," she recalls. Now, years later, in *Hold Still*, Mann offers us a principled and beautifully articulated stance. For Mann, ethical and philosophical questions are as important as aesthetic ones. She tackles, unabashedly, the fundamental issue of an artist's authority, her license to make art, and says, "To be able to take my pictures I have to look, all the time, at the people and places I care about . . . with both warm ardor and cool appraisal . . . in that ardent heart there must also be a splinter of ice." Inevitably, "exploitation lies at the root of every great portrait, and all of us know it. Even the simplest picture of another person is ethically complex."

Mann is too thoughtful to provide simple answers. She asserts that "if transgression is at the very heart of photographic portraiture, then the ideal outcome—beauty, communion, honesty, and empathy—mitigates the offense." And, quite aside from any ambition to attain laudable ideals, she asserts the importance of artistic freedom, and the irrelevance of the artist's character to the quality of the art itself: "Do we deny the power of *For Whom the Bell Tolls* because its author was unspeakably cruel to his wives? . . . If we only revere works made by those with whom we'd happily have our granny share a train compartment, we will have a paucity of art."

Mann knows all too well that the value of her work lies in itself, not in the admiration of the world, and that the calling of art is precisely to turn the "intensely seeing eye" on life's inadmissible truths. Mann is not the kind of artist for whom *épater le bourgeois* is a rallying cry, but if shock is the result of her images then so be it. The work—much of it spectacular and profound, all of it hard-won—takes precedence.

Mann's logic—the artist's logic of centuries' standing—is to many of us *a priori*: as Simone Weil wrote, "love is not consolation, it is light," and for the serious artist, art is a pursuit of truth, however challenging. Currently, these fundamental assumptions are in some quarters in question—I'm reminded of a distinction made by Maxim Gorky, an apologist for Stalin, in his rebuke of Vasily Grossman's then-unpublished first novel: "We know that there are two truths and that, in our world, it is the vile and dirty truth of the past that quantitatively preponderates . . . it is a truth we must struggle against and mercilessly extirpate."

Mann would be shocked, as Vassily Grossman was shocked, at the idea of distorting or turning away from the truth before her, out of expedience or a desire to console. She has said in an interview that "unless you photograph what you love, you are not going to make good art"; and that, moreover, "it's always been my philosophy to make art out of the everyday, the ordinary." In service to her truth, Sally Mann became best known for the controversy surrounding the photographs of her children. Each artist must calibrate the balance between her privacy and that of her loved ones, and the need to explore domestic or intimate material for her art. The poet Sharon Olds for many years insisted formally on privacy, though her poems were in fact grounded in autobiography: in a 2008 *Guardian* interview, she said: "What I'm nervous about is making explicit and part of the record connections between poems and actual people." This willed distinction—behaving "as if," which is in literature commonplace in differing degrees (think of the number of autobiographical novels)—is not possible for a photographer like Mann: the mediation of language allows for slippage, or potential slippage, in a way that photography does not. An intimate photographic record—of a child, a partner, a parent—is manifestly that, and its artistic intimacy—its force—arises in part from that fact. Sally Mann is frank about this reality, and about the need for this particular form of courage to expand the art form itself.

In a particularly tender digression, she explains that she has always taken photographs of her husband and continues to do so as they age, in spite of his "affliction of a late-onset muscular dystrophy." "I called this project Proud Flesh," she writes: "While working on these pictures, I joined the thinly populated group of women who have looked unflinchingly at men, and who frequently have been punished for doing so. . . . The act of looking appraisingly at a man . . . is a brazen venture for a woman; for a male photographer, these acts are commonplace, even expected."

Death, too, is an abiding preoccupation—one inherited from her father, just as she believes her mother's Welsh heritage gave her "*hiraeth*," meaning "'distance pain' . . . the pain of loving *a place*." Such passions illuminate Mann's work as much as they do her spirit, and *Hold Still* is replete with them. Throughout, family remains the key.

The frisson of notoriety surrounding the photographs in *Immediate Family* may be what motivates the broader public to turn to Mann's memoir. If so, readers will be wonderfully surprised by the swaths of tabloid-worthy family history (her maternal grandparents might have been on *The Real Housewives of Boston* in their day; her husband's parents' tragic fate is pure true crime); distressed by her current family's near-tragedies (the agony of her son's being hit by a car; the terror of an armed fugitive at large on their property); and consoled by the stable, clear-eyed, open, and somewhat eccentric personage whose *meuse* we ultimately discern.

For all these reasons, *Hold Still* is an unforgettable memoir. But it's more than that: For any artist or aspiring artist, it is an inspiration and a reminder of what matters. In writing about her friendship with Cy Twombly, who lived near the Manns in Virginia, she observes: "Choosing to work outside the art world's urban centers, as both he and I have done, is difficult, at least it certainly has been for me. More than any artist I know, Cy managed this classical remove, embracing James Joyce's artistic intent, summed up in three words at the end of *A Portrait of the Artist as a Young Man*: 'silence, exile, cunning.'"

For this reader, the abiding and precious gift of this book is precisely this: Mann's highly personal exploration of her passion, and her perseverance. She makes clear that she works, loves her work, and loves her life with equal and unflagging intensity. She is never not seeing the world, never not learning. All of it—including the hardest times—is grist for the artist's mill.

A HOME FROM HOME:
BOSTON'S MUSEUM OF FINE ARTS

I first came to Boston as a teenager, enrolled in a boarding school in the southern suburbs once attended by the young T. S. Eliot. The school was founded in 1798—which, in American terms, is old. For me, Boston was the stuff of novels: after a childhood largely spent in Sydney and Toronto, in what seemed to me a sort of Commonwealth periphery, I was headed, at last, for a city about which memorable stories had been told and great poems written.

It was also a city in which extraordinary paintings had been collected. I loved the fact that so much of Boston's cultural identity had been confected by eccentric hybrids and expatriates, by odd, thoughtful people who lived between America and Europe—Whistler (born in Lowell, Massachusetts, he was happy when mistaken in Europe for a Russian), Sargent (born in Europe to American parents, he consolidated his Boston connections only later in life), Henry James (who, in spite of his British naturalization, is buried in the Cambridge Cemetery, half a mile from my house), Edith Wharton ("I was a failure in Boston . . . because they thought I was too fashionable to be intelligent, and a failure in New York because they were afraid I was too intelligent to be fashionable"). With a French father, a Canadian mother, and the only American passport in the family, I was often anxious about not being American enough: all these artists were reassuring to me. Most of the United States has little interest in Europe, but that seemed not to be the case in Boston—not if you judged it by its art.

As a schoolgirl, I went rarely to the Museum of Fine Arts: the café was expensive, the gift shop didn't sell anything we wanted. We gravitated to the pavements of Harvard Square and Newbury Street, opting for the museum only in winter, to get out of the cold.

But somehow those adolescent visits impressed upon me a proprietorial sense about the place, an almost familial pride. When I returned twenty years later to live here with my husband and young children, I came back to the MFA as if to the embrace of extended family: there were my old friends, John Singleton Copley's *Watson and the Shark*, Thomas Sully's *The Torn Hat*, Sargent's *The Daughters of Edward Darley Boit*. They became my children's friends, too. We joined the museum so as to visit for half an hour without guilt, and went briefly and often.

The children found their favorites, and have them still. My daughter Livia, at about six, tried to copy a Frank W. Benson painting of three kids in a boat. Her version hangs in her bedroom, and she thinks of the original as her own. My son Lucian likes Whistler's *Nocturne in Blue and Silver: The Lagoon, Venice.* We all like Childe Hassam's *Boston Common at Twilight.* With its grimed snow and sulfurous dusk, it evokes exactly our own winter evenings, erasing the 130 years between then and now.

THE MUSEUM FIRST opened its doors about a decade before that work was painted, on Independence Day 1876; it moved to its current quarters in 1909. There have been multiple expansions since, including the glassy new Art of the Americas wing designed by Norman Foster, which opened in 2010. These big bright spaces sit surprisingly well around the original 1909 Beaux Arts building, but the quiet core remains my favourite— sepulchral in the way of museums of my childhood, largely unwindowed, with broad corridors and staircases, hushed and echoey like a library, where every footfall speaks.

Rearranged in the new wing, some of our favorites are hard to find. *Watson and the Shark* used to be visible from miles away, illuminated at the end of a long corridor, but can now only be seen from much closer up, and seems a little cramped. More dismayingly, Sully's *The Torn Hat*—that boy who was like a cousin to Livia and Lucian—is no longer on display at all. After a brief and unfortunate spell behind glass in a mocked-up nineteenth-century sitting room, it has returned to the mysterious vaults where, I'm told, 95 percent of the museum's holdings mutter in darkness. An early nineteenth-century American portrait of a long-nosed chap with what looked like a sock on his head has vanished, too; though others, like Sargent's Boit sisters, have fared well and are now beautifully shown.

Still, it's a relief to return to our family's old haunts—to the damask-lined Koch Gallery with the European masters or to the Impressionist gallery—and find things where we expect them to be. One unchanged corner which I always visit, hoping to find it empty, is the little vaulted room containing the twelfth century Spanish frescoes *Christ in Majesty with Symbols of the Four Evangelists*, taken from a small chapel in the Spanish Pyrenees. Mysterious and solemn but full of delight (who is that dancing fellow in blue pleats, apparently raising a curtain, stage right?), these frescoes afford an opportunity for contemplation, a moment of retreat.

Even more than these figures with their beautiful Byzantine eyes, I come to this space to visit the Italian sculpture of the Virgin and Child, of the same vintage. Many renditions of the Christ child make me smile (how oddly proportioned He can be, and what funny colors!), but this one brings me near to tears. He and his mother have oddly long heads, it's true, and in this way are stylized and foreign; but the folds of her dress, the precision of their limbs, the intensity of their embrace, the insistence of his small hand at the back of her neck, the yearning stretch of his face toward her cheek, his slight frown—I feel I know them, and their intense emotion. Theirs is at once the longing of every small child for its mother's body, and at the same time, strangely, discomfitingly, this Christ has about him something almost adult. The passion of their familial intimacy is recognizable across almost a millennium; this is the most human Christ I have ever seen.

In a completely different manner, Van Dyck's Princess Mary is totally present, too. She's one of the few genuinely old paintings that my kids, it seems, can really see. The daughter of Charles I of England, Mary is captured around the time of her betrothal to William of Orange; and is fittingly satined and bejeweled. Her sleeves look like they weigh a ton. But what's wonderful about young Mary—aside from the shimmer of her fabrics and the precision of their ornamentation, or the light folding of her childishly plump hands over her stomach—is the luminous rendition of her face and its familiar expression. My husband says, each time he sees her, "Oh, there's Amy!" because she so thoroughly resembles a former colleague of his.

Mary is wary—as she should be, standing stiffly for this great Flemish portraitist, about to be married off at the tender age of nine. She'd be widowed at nineteen, shortly after the execution of her father at the hands of Oliver Cromwell. And she'd be dead herself by twenty-nine. She looks as though she has some sense that her road will not be easy, and that all the luxurious garments in the world cannot protect her.

This Princess Mary came to America in the 1920s, sold by the Earl of Normanton and bought by Alvan Tufts Fuller, a wealthy car dealer who became governor of Massachusetts and lived to the ripe age of eighty. If she could only have married him instead.

MY KIDS LOVE the Impressionist gallery best, as I did when I was young—the acid-bright Van Goghs, the hazy purple and blue Monets, the bright flower-filled Renoirs. Even as a teenager, my daughter retained a frank affection for Degas's sculpture of the little fourteen-year-old dancer, her chin up and her hands behind her back, her tulle skirt rather grubby but her satin hair ribbon brand-new. Livia would stand beside the glass case and mimic the girl's pose. Even though she'd given up ballet years before, she did it pretty well.

My own favorite Degas is the *Ballet Dancer with Arms Crossed*, an unfinished work bought at his posthumous studio sale in 1919. With her folded arms and averted gaze, she appears thoughtful, or near-tearful, possibly even sulky—it's hard to tell, just as it might be in life. Her face is largely in shadow, though her orangey lipstick glows; and her décolleté is an almost bruised gray, which, along with the black ribbon around her neck, imparts an atmosphere of darkness against the half-painted scarlet background. Her form is harshly outlined in black (how big and clumsy her right hand looks, when she is so generally graceful!); her skirt is pure white; and then, around her, the thin application of red paint allows the raw canvas to show through, balancing the white

skirt with white patches on the left of the painting. Degas abandoned it in about 1872, but she remained for over forty-five years
in his studio: there's a strange intimacy in seeing this girl, whom
the famously difficult painter could neither approve of nor relin-
quish, standing in her sad defiance on the wall.

Times have changed, and she no longer appears unfinished.
A little blurred, off-color, but intensely alive, she anticipates the
contemporary work of, say, Marlene Dumas. Her presence, no less
intense than Princess Mary's, is more emotional and interior, a
presence that insists upon the filter of the artist's eye. As Edmond
de Goncourt wrote after visiting Degas's studio, "Of all the men I
have seen engaged in depicting modern life, he is the one who has
most successfully rendered the inner nature of that life."

Which brings me back to Sargent. Everyone at our house has
his or her particular favorite: mine is *The Daughters of Edward
Darley Boit*. John Singer Sargent (1856–1925) was a portraitist of
extraordinary facility. Claimed by Auguste Rodin as the "Van
Dyck of our times," he had the gift, like Van Dyck with Princess
Mary, of capturing surfaces so precisely that their interior is
evoked. For many years a society painter, he was both adored and
disdained for the elegance and sensuousness of his work.

There's a celebration of loveliness and ease that cumulatively
can seem superficial, insufficient, a rich man's delight in velvet, brocade, and Italian gardens, all of it underwritten by the
wealthy and aristocratic patrons whose commissions for so many
years occupied Sargent's time. But the jewel in the MFA's collection of his paintings is an antidote to this glossy illusory perfection, and proof that he was capable of darkness and complexity.
The Daughters of Edward Darley Boit was painted in Paris in 1882,
when the artist was in his mid-twenties. The Boits were Ameri-

can friends of Sargent's, originally from Boston but living in luxury in the 8th arrondissement. The four girls—from left to right, Mary Louisa, Florence, Jane, and Julia—were painted in the foyer of their apartment, their white pinafores glistening in the gloom. The MFA's Erica Hirshler tells us that Sargent was influenced by Velázquez's *Las Meninas*, which he'd studied at the Prado in Madrid. But the painting is far from traditional: only one of its subjects, four-year-old Julia, looks directly at the viewer, her legs stuck out before her and her doll upon her lap. For these girls, growing older appears to be a matter of retreat. Mary Louisa, the next in age, stands to the left of the painting, staring into the middle distance, her hands behind her back. Her frock is a warm old rose, the brushwork of her pinafore thick and brilliant, slashes of extra white upon her waistband: she is still very much in the light. But the two elder sisters, Florence and Jane, in black dresses beneath their pinafores, have stepped back into the corridor, and Florence has largely turned her back to us, leaning against one of the enormous Japanese vases that command as much attention as the girls. Florence's eye is on Jane, who has something lost about her, her stance and expression more tentative, more expectant, than her sisters'.

Only little Julia engages with the viewer, and only grown-up Florence engages with one of her sisters. The other two are abstracted, even isolated. As with Degas's dancer, their thoughts remain opaque, even as we can be certain that they're thinking.

Sargent, more than twenty years Degas's junior, was ultimately the less adventurous painter. In his later years, rather like Edith Wharton, he came to be seen as old hat, obsolete, the fusty representative of a lost world. But even today, there's something about this painting—the four sisters, none of whom would marry, and one of whom would struggle with mental illness—that is profoundly moving, and intimately familiar.

Those girls, like Princess Mary, enjoyed the blessings of privilege and wealth, which cushioned but could not save them. Thanks to their peripatetic parents, they lived between cultures and countries, just as they stand in the painting in their apartment's dark foyer on their way to somewhere else. There are advantages to this liminal state, but how relieving, too, at the last, to have a home (not having had one, I wanted to make sure my children did); and how fitting a home the MFA is for these enigmatic Sargent girls, with one eye on the past and the other on the future.

My grandparents Gaston and Lucienne Messud, with their
friend Marcel Perraud. Istanbul, summer 1941.

Acknowledgments

M ost of these essays were published, albeit in different form, in magazines and newspapers. I am extremely grateful to those publications and to my editors for their faith and support. My particular thanks to David Lynn and the *Kenyon Review*; Chloe Schama and *Vogue*; Lucas Zwirner and Zwirner Books; Leon Wieseltier and the *New Republic*; Albert Mobilio and *Bookforum*; M Mark and *PEN America: A Journal for Writers and Readers*; Nadja Spiegelman and the *Paris Review Online*; Judith Gurewich and the Other Press; Catherine Taylor and Folio Press; Daniel Halpern and Ecco Press; Alida Becker and the *New York Times Book Review*; and Maggie Fergusson and *Intelligent Life* (now *1843 Magazine*). I am forever indebted to John Freeman (of *Granta*, *LitHub*, and *Freeman's*) for his generosity, kindness, and editorial acumen, and for laughing when I told him about our dogs. And my incalculable thanks to the late Bob Silvers, whose unforgettable voice is always in my ear, whose wisdom and attention to the text shaped my critical writing, and whose faith meant a great deal to me. I miss his presence in the world and am grateful to his colleagues, Lucy McKeon, Matt Seaton, and Eve Bowen among them, for the continued vitality of the *New York Review of Books*.

My thanks also to the extraordinary team at the Wylie Agency, with particular gratitude to Sarah Chalfant, Rebecca Nagel, and Luke Ingram; and to my brilliant editor, Jill Bialosky—with whom it is such a gift to work—and to everyone at Norton, especially Drew Weitman and Erin Lovett. My thanks also to my wonderful editor in the UK, Ursula Doyle, and to the team at Fleet/Little Brown, with special thanks to Charlie King and Zoe Hood.

My colleagues at Harvard University and, before that, at Hunter College CUNY have been precious interlocutors in literary conversation, as have several dear friends who generously read some of these pieces along the way, among them Shefali Malhoutra, Mary Bing, Mark Gevisser, and Ira Sachs. Thanks also to Michael Ravitch and Itamar Kubovy for invaluable conversations in person and on the page. And in Cambridge, to Homi Bhabha, Melissa Franklin, Susanna Kaysen, John Daniels, Sheila Gallagher, and Neel Mukherjee.

As these essays make clear, my family is at the heart of it all: my gratitude and love, as always, to dear JW, to Livia and Lucian, and to my amazing sister, Elizabeth. She and I are the only ones left, now, of the family that was; the spirits of our parents and grandparents live on in their words.

Index of Publications

Earlier versions of the essays listed below were previously published, as indicated.

"Then," *Kenyon Review*, 2004

"Nostalgia," *Vogue*, 2018

"The Road to Damascus," *Granta*, 2012

"Mother's Knee," first published in Virago's 40th Anniversary book.

"Kant's Little Prussian Head and Other Reasons Why I Write," *Lit Hub*, 2015

"Our Dogs," *Freeman's*, 2016

"How to Be a Better Woman in the Twenty-First Century," *PEN America: A Journal for Writers and Readers*, 2014

"Teenage Girls," *Vogue*, 2017

"The Time for Art Is Now," *Paris Review Daily*, 2018

"Camus and Algeria: The Moral Question," *New York Review of Books*, 2013

"A New *L'Étranger*," *New York Review of Books*, 2014

"The Brother of the Stranger: Kamel Daoud," *New York Review of Books*, 2015

"Kazuo Ishiguro," introduction to *Never Let Me Go* (London: Folio Society Edition, 2012)

"Jane Bowles," introduction to *Two Serious Ladies* (New York: Ecco Press, 2014)

"Italo Svevo," *New Republic*, 2002

"Teju Cole," review of *Open City*, *New York Review of Books*, 2011

"Magda Szabó," review of *The Door*, *New York Times Book Review*, 2015

"Rachel Cusk," review of *Transit*, *New York Review of Books*, 2017

"Saul Friedländer," introduction to *When Memory Comes* (New York: Other Press, 2016)

"Yasmine El Rashidi," review of *Chronicle of a Last Summer: A Novel of Egypt*, *New York Review of Books*, 2016

"Valeria Luiselli," review of *Lost Children Archive*, *New York Review of Books*, 2019

"Alice Neel," catalogue essay for *Alice Neel: Drawings and Watercolors, 1927–1978* (New York: Zwirner, 2015)

"Marlene Dumas," catalogue essay for *Myths & Mortals: Works by Marlene Dumas* (New York: Zwirner, 2019)

"Sally Mann," originally published as "Fierce Attachments" in *Bookforum*, June/July/August 2015.

"A Home from Home: Boston's Museum of Fine Arts," *1843 Magazine*, 2014